THE SHOCK OF
THE ANTHROPOCENE

THE SHOCK OF THE ANTHROPOCENE

The Earth, History and Us

Christophe Bonneuil
and Jean-Baptiste Fressoz

Translated by David Fernbach

VERSO
London • New York

This book has been published with the help of the project
with reference code HAR2013-40760-R of the Ministry
of Economy and Competitiveness (Spain)

First published by Verso 2016
Translation © David Fernbach 2016

1 3 5 7 9 10 8 6 4 2

Verso
UK: 6 Meard Street, London W1F 0EG
US: 20 Jay Street, Suite 1010, Brooklyn, NY 11201
www.versobooks.com

Verso is the imprint of New Left Books

ISBN-13: 978-1-78478-079-1 (PB)
eISBN-13: 978-1-78478-081-4 (US)
eISBN-13: 978-1-78478-082-1 (UK)

British Library Cataloguing in Publication Data
A catalogue record for this book is available from the British Library

Library of Congress Cataloging-in-Publication Data
A catalog record for this book is available from the Library of Congress

Typeset in Minion by Hewer Text UK Ltd, Edinburgh, Scotland
Printed in the US by Maple Press

to Maia, Cecilia, Esteban, Pierre and
all other marbled newts

To Zam and all her chthonian regenerative forces

Contents

Acknowledgements

Our thanks to François Jarrige, Séverine Nikel, Clara Breteau, Alice Leroy, Josette Fressoz, Cecilia Berthaud and Rebecca Berthaut for their close readings of all or part of the manuscript, to David Fernbach, our translator, and Seb Budgen from Verso Books, to all our colleagues in the environmental sciences and humanities with whom we have had the pleasure of discussing the Anthropocene, and to the students of the seminar 'Une histoire de l'Anthropocène' held for the last four years at the École des hautes études en sciences sociales.

Preface

What exactly has been happening on Earth in the last quarter of a millennium?

The Anthropocene.

Anthropo-what?

We already live in the Anthropocene, so let us get used to this ugly word and the reality that it names. It is our epoch and our condition. This geological epoch is the product of the last few hundred years of our history. The Anthropocene is the sign of our power, but also of our impotence. It is an Earth whose atmosphere has been damaged by the 1,500 billion tonnes of carbon dioxide we have spilled by burning coal and other fossil fuels. It is the impoverishment and artificializing of Earth's living tissue, permeated by a host of new synthetic chemical molecules that will even affect our descendants. It is a warmer world with a higher risk of catastrophes, a reduced ice cover, higher sea-levels and a climate out of control.

The Anthropocene label, proposed in the 2000s by specialists in Earth system sciences, is an essential tool for understanding what is happening to us. This is not just an environmental crisis, but a geological revolution of human origin.

We should not act as astonished ingénues who suddenly discover they are transforming the planet: the entrepreneurs of the industrial revolution who brought us into the Anthropocene actively willed this new epoch and shaped it. Saint-Simon, the herald of what was already called 'industrialism', maintained in the 1820s that:

The object of industry is the exploitation of the globe, that is to say, the appropriation of its products for the needs of man; and by accomplishing this task, it modifies the globe and transforms it, gradually changing the conditions of its existence. Man hence participates, unwittingly as it were, in the successive manifestations of the divinity, and thus continues the work of creation. From this point of view, Industry becomes religion.[1]

His pessimistic counterpart, Eugène Huzar, predicted in 1857:

In one or two hundred years, criss-crossed by railways and steamships, covered with factories and workshops, the world will emit billions of cubic metres of carbonic acid and carbon oxide, and, since the forests will have been destroyed, these hundreds of billions of carbonic acid and carbon oxide may indeed disturb the harmony of the world.[2]

The present book sets out to comprehend this new epoch through the narratives that can be made of it. It calls for new environmental humanities to rethink our visions of the world and our ways of inhabiting the Earth together. Scientists have built up data and models that already situate us beyond the point of no return to the Holocene, on the timetable of geological epochs. They have produced figures and curves that depict humanity as a major geological force. But what narratives can make sense of these dramatic curves?

This is by no means a theoretical question, as each account of 'How did we get here?' makes assumptions through which we frame 'What to do now?'

There is already an official narrative of the Anthropocene: 'we', the human species, unconsciously destroyed nature to the point of hijacking the Earth system into a new geological epoch. In the late twentieth century, a handful of Earth system scientists finally opened our eyes. So now we know; now we are aware of the global consequences of human action.

1 *Doctrine de Saint-Simon*, vol. 2, Paris: Aux Bureaux de l'Organisateur, 1830, 219.
2 Eugène Huzar, *L'Arbre de la science*, Paris: Dentu, 1857, 106.

This story of awakening is a fable. The opposition between a blind past and a clear-sighted present, besides being historically false, depoliticizes the long history of the Anthropocene. It serves above all to credit our own excellence. Its reassuring side is demobilizing. In the twenty years that it has prevailed, there has been a great deal of congratulation, while the Earth has become ever more set on a path of ecological unbalance.

In its managerial variant, the moral of the official account consists in giving the engineers of the Earth system the keys to 'Spaceship Earth'; in its philosophical and incantatory variant, it consists in calling first and foremost for a revolution in morality and thought, which alone will allow the conclusion of an armistice between humans and non-humans, and reconciliation of all of us with the Earth.

To see the Anthropocene as an event rather than a thing means taking history seriously and learning to work with the natural sciences, without becoming mere chroniclers of a natural history of interactions between the human species and the Earth system. It also means noting that it is not enough to measure in order to understand, and that we cannot count on the accumulation of scientific data to carry out the necessary revolutions or involutions. It means deconstructing the official account in its managerial and non-conflictual variants, and forging new narratives for the Anthropocene and thus new imaginaries. Rethinking the past to open up the future.

Is the Anthropocene the age of man? Perhaps, but what does it mean for us, humans, to have the future of a planet in our hands? While welcoming the work of scientists and philosophers with open arms, we seek to comprehend the Anthropocene as historians, since, if ecological unbalance is now greater than ever before, this is not the first time that humans have asked themselves what they are doing to the planet. To forget past reflections and understandings, struggles and defeats, illusions and mistakes, would mean losing an experience that is precious for the present challenges.

We have passed the exit gate from the Holocene. We have reached a threshold. Realization of this must revolutionize the views of the world that became dominant with the rise of industrial capitalism based on fossil fuel. What historical narratives can we offer of the last quarter of a millennium, able to help us change our world-views and inhabit the Anthropocene more lucidly, respectfully and equitably? Such is the object of this book.

The first part presents the scientific dimensions of the Anthropocene (Chapter 1) along with its major implications for our views of the world, and for the human and social sciences (Chapter 2). The second part discusses the problems of the 'geocratic' account of the Anthropocene that is currently dominant. This depicts the Earth as a system seen from nowhere (Chapter 3), and history as a contest between the human species as a whole and the planet, with societies as ignorant and passive masses who can only be guided by scientists and saved by green technologies (Chapter 4). We shall show that an account of this kind naturalizes and depoliticizes our geohistory more than enables us to understand it. The third part sets out to trace different historical threads from the eighteenth century to today: a political history of energy and CO_2 (Chapter 5, Thermocene), a history of the determining role of the military in the Anthropocene (Chapter 6, Thanatocene), a history of the making of the consumer society (Chapter 7, Phagocene), a history of environmental grammars, knowledge and warnings (Chapter 8, Phronocene), a history of the intellectual constructions that made it possible to ignore and marginalize these warnings and deny planetary limits and boundaries (Chapter 9, Agnotocene), an attempt at a joint history of capitalism and the Anthropocene (Chapter 10, Capitalocene), and finally, a history of socioecological struggles and challenges to the damages of industrialism (Chapter 11, Polemocene).

PART ONE: WHAT'S IN A WORD?

CHAPTER 1

Welcome to the Anthropocene

In February 2000, a conference of the International Geosphere-Biosphere Programme held in Cuernavaca, Mexico, hosted a heated discussion about the age and intensity of human impacts on the planet. Paul Crutzen, an atmospheric chemist and Nobel Prize winner for his work on the ozone layer, stood up and exclaimed: 'No! We're no longer in the Holocene but in the Anthropocene!' This was the birth of a new word, and above all of a new geological epoch. Two years later, in an article in the scientific periodical *Nature*, Crutzen developed his assertion further: the stratigraphic scale had to be supplemented by a new age, to signal that mankind had become a force of telluric amplitude. After the Pleistocene, which opened the Quaternary 2.5 million years back, and the Holocene, which began 11,500 years ago, 'It seems appropriate to assign the term "Anthropocene" to the present, in many ways human-dominated, geological epoch.'[1]

The Nobel laureate proposed a starting date for this new era of 1784, the year that James Watt patented the steam engine, symbolic of the start of the industrial revolution and the 'carbonification' of our atmosphere by the burning of coal extracted from the lithosphere.

From the ancient Greek words *anthropos* meaning 'human being' and *kainos* meaning 'recent, new', the Anthropocene is then

---

1   Paul J. Crutzen, 'Geology of Mankind', *Nature*, 415, 3 January 2002: 23.

the new epoch of humans, the age of man. The Anthropocene is characterized by the fact that 'the human imprint on the global environment has now become so large and active that it rivals some of the great forces of Nature in its impact on the functioning of the Earth system'.[2] This is not the first time scientists have attested to or foreseen such human power over the fate of the planet, whether to celebrate it or as a cause for concern. As recently as 1778, in his *Epochs of Nature* volume of *Histoire naturelle générale et particulière*, Buffon explained that 'the entire face of the Earth today bears the imprint of human power'. This imprint would be particularly exerted on climate. By judiciously modifying its environment, humanity would be able to 'modify the influences of the climate it inhabits, and set the temperature to the level that suits it best'.[3] Following him, the Italian geologist Antonio Stoppani defined man in 1873 as a 'new telluric power', and in the 1920s Vladimir I. Vernadsky, who introduced the concept of the biosphere, emphasized the growing human effect on the globe's biogeochemical cycles.[4]

Nor was this the first time that scientists succumbed to anthropocentrism in making humanity a geological marker: the start of the Quaternary, in fact, was fixed to coincide with the appearance of the genus *Homo* 2.5 million years ago in Africa (*Homo habilis*), and the Holocene or 'recent epoch' was proposed by the geologist Charles Lyell on the basis of the end of the last glaciation but also on the then-believed coincident emergence of humans. The idea of adding the Holocene to the geologic time clock was put forward by Charles Lyell in 1833, but accepted only in 1885. Geologists, accustomed to working on the scale of the Earth's 4.5-billion-year history, have no reason to hurry in making our entry into the Anthropocene official. Besides, if the history of our planet is reduced to a day of

---

2   Will Steffen et al., 'The Anthropocene: Conceptual and Historical Perspectives', *Philosophical Transactions of the Royal Society* A, 369:1938, 2011: 842.

3   Georges-Louis Leclerc de Buffon, *Histoire naturelle générale et particulière*, Supplement 5: *Des époques de la nature*, Paris: Imprimerie royale, 1778, 237.

4   Steffen et al., 'The Anthropocene: Conceptual and Historical Perspectives'.

twenty-four hours, *Homo habilis* appeared only in the final minute, the Holocene began in the last quarter of a second, and the industrial revolution only in the two last thousandths of a second. With the Pleistocene counting in millions of years, and the Holocene in thousands, Crutzen's boldness in proclaiming a new Anthropocene dating back no more than a couple of centuries is readily understandable. His proposal will very likely continue to be debated for a while to come. At the 34th congress of the International Union of Geological Sciences, held in Brisbane in 2012, it was decided to establish a task group that would submit its report in 2016.

While awaiting official validation by stratigraphers, however, the Anthropocene concept has already become a rallying point for geologists, ecologists, climate and Earth system specialists, historians, philosophers, social scientists, ordinary citizens and ecological movements, as a way of conceiving this age in which humanity has become a major geological force.

What humans are doing to the Earth

What are the arguments put forward? What imprints do humans make on the planet, albeit in a differentiated way that we shall explore below? For atmospheric chemists such as Paul Crutzen, or climatologists such as the Australian Will Steffen and the Frenchman Claude Lorius, the weapon that put an end to the Holocene is to be found in the air: 'The air trapped in ice is an abrupt indication that the hand of man, by inventing the steam engine, upset the world machine at the same time.'[5] Fingers point to the greenhouse gases emitted by human activity. In relation to 1750, as a result of these emissions, the atmosphere has been 'enriched' in methane (CH_4) to the tune of 150 per cent, nitrous oxide (N_2O) by 63 per cent and carbon dioxide (CO_2) by 43 per cent. As far as the last of these is concerned, its concentration has risen from 280 parts per million (ppm) on the eve of the industrial

---

5   Claude Lorius and Laurent Carpentier, *Voyage dans l'Anthropocène. Cette nouvelle ère dont nous sommes les héros*, Arles: Actes Sud, 2010, 11.

revolution to 400 ppm in 2013, a level unmatched for 3 million years. New ingredients have also entered the atmosphere since 1945: fluoride gases such as the CFCs and HCFCs particularly emitted by our refrigerators and air conditioners.

All these are 'greenhouse' gases inasmuch as they retain the heat that the Earth, warmed by the Sun, emits into space. And the accumulation of these gases in the atmosphere has not taken long to raise the planet's temperature. Since the mid nineteenth century, the thermometer has already risen by 0.8°C, and the scenarios of the UN Intergovernmental Panel on Climate Change (IPCC) foresee, depending on the political response they find, a total rise by the end of the present century of between 1.2°C and 6°C. A rise of 2°C in relation to the pre-industrial level, considered by the majority of climatologists as a danger threshold, will be very hard not to breach given the current lack of international political will, and, if the present tendency is not radically modified, climate experts predict a rise of 3.7°C to 4.5°C by 2100, with a whole train of meteorological disturbances and human miseries in its wake. The IPCC's latest report even envisions a rise of 8°C to 12°C by 2300, given a 'business as usual' scenario. The Andean ice cover in Peru has disappeared in twenty-five years, and the polar ice has been melting in the last few years much faster than experts had expected. While the climatologists of the 1980s and '90s conceived the relationship between concentration of greenhouse gases and climate change in a more or less global and linear fashion, systemic approaches and recent advances in modelling show that a small variation in the globe's average temperature can lead to sudden and disorderly changes.

The generalized degradation of Earth's living tissue (the biosphere) is the second element attesting to our swing into the Anthropocene. The collapse of biodiversity is bound up with the general movement of simplification (by anthropization through agriculture and urbanization), fragmentation and destruction of the globe's ecosystems, but it is also accelerated by climate change. An article published in *Nature* in June 2012 indicates that, even in an optimistic scenario, by the end of the twenty-first century, climate conditions on between 12 and 39 per cent of the Earth's surface will be such as present living organisms have never before faced.[6] On top of those extinctions directly caused by climate change, there is the damage to sea life caused by the acidification of the oceans (up 26 per cent in relation to the pre-industrial period), since these absorb a quarter of our CO_2 emissions.[7] In the last few decades, the rate of extinction of species has been from 100 to 1,000 times greater than the geological norm: biologists speak of a 'sixth extinction' since the appearance of life on Earth.[8] Since the Convention on Biological Diversity of 1992, the pace of extinction has in no way slowed down, for lack of action on the main forces of degradation, and it is estimated that the 100,000 currently protected areas in the world will save at best 5 per cent of all species. Three-quarters of the world's fishing zones are at maximum production or over-exploited. The mass of humans (32 per cent), along with that of their domestic animals (65 per cent), now makes up 97 per cent of the total biomass of land vertebrates, leaving only 3 per cent for the remaining 30,000 land-dwelling vertebrate species.[9] At the current rate, 20 per cent of the planet's species will have disappeared by 2030,[10] but many essential 'services' provided to humanity by the biosphere – pollination, carbon capture, protection from erosion, regulation of water quality and quantity, etc. – have already been greatly reduced.

As well as climate change and the collapse of biodiversity, scientists also note other major transformations that attest to our entry into the Anthropocene. These include in particular the biogeochemical cycles of water, nitrogen and phosphate, each as important as that of carbon, which have also come under human control in the course of the last

6   Anthony D. Barnosky et al., 'Approaching a State Shift in Earth's Biosphere', *Nature*, 485, 7 June 2012: 52–8.

7   For a recent study of this, see World Meteorological Organization, 'Record Greenhouse Gas Levels Impact Atmosphere and Oceans', Press Release No. 1002, 9 September 2014, wmo.int.

8   Stuart L. Pimm et al., 'The Biodiversity of Species and Their Rates of Extinction, Distribution, and Protection', *Science*, 344:6187, 30 May 2014, sciencemag.org.

9   Vaclav Smil, *The Earth's Biosphere: Evolution, Dynamics, and Change*, Cambridge, MA: MIT Press, 2002, 284.

10   Edward O. Wilson, *The Future of Life*, London: Vintage, 2003, 102.

two centuries. The modification of the continental water cycle is massive, with the draining of half the planet's wetlands and the construction of 45,000 dams with heights of more than fifteen metres, together retaining 6,500 cubic kilometres of water, some 15 per cent of the total flow of the world's rivers.[11] These transformations have substantially modified the processes of erosion and sedimentation, without however freeing the greater part of humanity from water insecurity.

The nitrogen cycle has been radically transformed with industrialization (the burning of fossil fuel releasing nitrous oxides) and the Haber-Bosch process (1913) that converts atmospheric nitrogen into nitrogen suitable for fertilizer. These two phenomena represent nitrogen flows twice as great as the 'natural' flow through the biosphere, basically bound up with biological fixing by bacterial symbiosis.[12] The nitric oxide released by fertilizers accentuates the greenhouse effect, and excess urea and nitrates enter water-tables, rivers and estuaries, causing eutrophication and hypoxia.

The global phosphorous cycle also bears the mark of human domination, with an anthropic flow eight times greater than the natural one. Some 20 million tonnes of phosphorous are extracted each year from phosphate mines in the lithosphere, chiefly to be used for fertilizer. It is estimated that 9 million of these 20 million tonnes end up in the oceans.[13] Scientists have shown that an increase in phosphate level of only 20 per cent in relation to the underlying natural flow was in the geological past one of the causes for the collapse of the oxygen level in the oceans, leading to the massive extinction of aquatic life.

Scientists and geographers have also attempted to estimate the extent to which terrestrial ecosystems have been turned into the

---

11   Christer Nilsson et al., 'Fragmentation and Flow Regulation of the World's Large River Systems', *Science*, 308, 15 April 2005: 405–6.

12   Johan Rockström et al., 'A Safe Operating Space for Humanity', *Nature*, 461, 24 September 2009: 472–5; James N. Galloway et al., 'Transformation of the Nitrogen Cycle: Recent Trends, Questions, and Potential Solutions', *Science*, 320:5878, 2008: 889–92.

13   Ibid.

artificial ones of pasture, crop-land and cities. It turns out that the human species, having increased from a population of 900 million in 1800 to 7 billion in 2012, takes nearly a third of the production of continental biomass for its own needs (in terms of food, clothing, housing and many less vital things),[14] and consumes each year one and a half times what the planet can annually produce on a sustainable basis. This means that 'we' – meaning above all the 500 million most well-off inhabitants of the globe – are not only consuming the fruits of the tree on which we sit but also sawing through its branches.[15]

The Anthropocene is characterized by an unprecedented upsurge in energy mobilization: first with coal, then with hydrocarbons and uranium, which increased energy consumption by a factor of forty between 1800 and 2000.[16] This leap in energy has served to transform the planet with multiplied power, to plough up, urbanize and domesticate ecosystems. Pasture, crop-land and cities, which represented 5 per cent of the Earth's land area in 1750 and 12 per cent in 1900, today cover close to a third. Including partially anthropized biomes, it is estimated today that 84 per cent of the ice-free land surface of the planet is under direct human influence.[17] Ninety per cent of photosynthesis on Earth occurs in 'anthropogenic biomes', that is, ecological ensembles modified by human beings. As the geographer Erle Ellis concludes, the new model of the biosphere 'moves us away from an outdated view of the world as "natural systems with humans disturbing them" and towards "human systems with natural ecosystems embedded within them"'.[18]

14   Helmut Haberl et al., 'Quantifying and Mapping the Human Appropriation of Net Primary Production in Earth's Terrestrial Ecosystems', *Proceedings of the National Academy of Science, USA*, 104, 2007: 12,942–7; Rockström et al., 'A Safe Operating Space for Humanity'.

15   Global Footprint Network, footprintnetwork.org.

16   Steffen et al., 'The Anthropocene: Conceptual and Historical Perspectives'.

17   Erle C. Ellis, 'Anthropogenic Transformation of the Terrestrial Biosphere', *Philosophical Transactions of the Royal Society A*, 369:1938, 2011: 1,010–35.

18   Erle Ellis and Navin Ramankutty, 'Anthropogenic Biomes', in *The Encyclopedia of Earth*, eoearth.org.

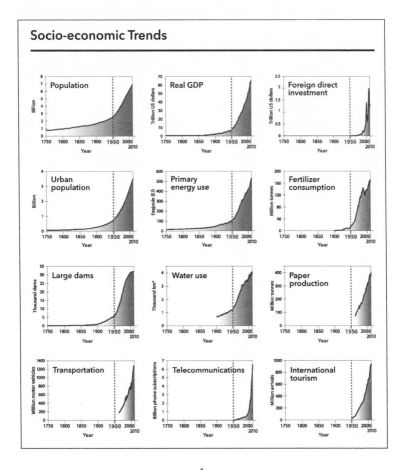

1a

Figure 1 (1a and 1b on facing page): *Dashboard display of the Anthropocene*
For these twenty-four parameters of the Earth system, a take-off can be observed
around 1800, and a 'Great Acceleration' after 1945.[19]

19   Details on the source data for all figures are to be found as part of the Illustration Credits.

Earth System Trends

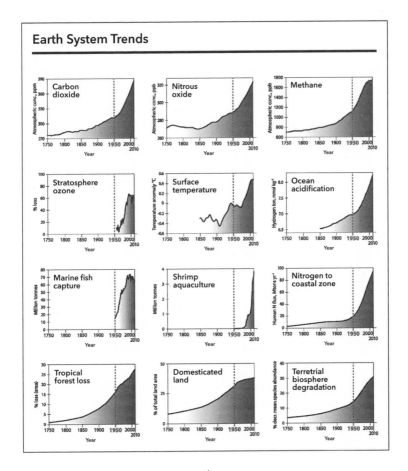

1b

Figure 1 gives a dashboard display of the Anthropocene, showing the evolution of twenty-four parameters of the Earth system since 1750. For the nine most important of these, a team of scientists from the Resilience Centre in Stockholm studied possible tipping points affecting biodiversity (the risk of collapse of certain 'services' that nature performs for us, such as pollination), air and atmosphere pollution, the intensification of biogeochemical cycles and the anthropization of land. They then set for each of these nine parameters a limit not to be crossed. For four of these, however, the limit (danger threshold of a sudden tipping of the Earth system into a catastrophic state) has already been approached (or passed): nitrogen cycle, greenhouse gas emissions, extinction of biodiversity and phosphate cycle.[20]

In order to agree to inscribe the Anthropocene in the series of geological epochs, however, stratigraphers are not content with models or predictions. What they need is something solid – sediment, a stratigraphic division that can be seen and measured here and now. Three arguments can be given here in support of the Anthropocene.

First of all, the level of atmospheric carbon dioxide has not been equalled for 4 million years (Pliocene), and future warming will lead the Earth to states unknown for 15 million years. The extinction of biodiversity is taking place with a suddenness matched only by five other episodes in the entire 4.5 billion years of life on Earth. The last extinction, which did away with the dinosaurs among others, goes back 65 million years and has left stratigraphic markers of the clearest kind. These phenomena, therefore, have the dual property of being caused by humans and being of a scale rarely noted in the geological past.

Secondly, the anthropic changes in the composition of the atmosphere have left traces even in the Antarctic ice cores. Extinctions and modified distributions of species (explosive invasions in the last few centuries, migrations bound up with climate change or the anthropization of biomes) cannot fail to leave fossil traces in the sediments. The transformations of lake-side and coastal fauna and flora caused by the human forcing of nitrogen and phosphorus cycles have also left a specific mark. As for the biomass of the 7 billion humans and their domestic animals, this makes up the predominant share of the overall

---

20   Anthony D. Barnosky, 'Approaching a State Shift in Earth's Biosphere'; Will Steffen et al., 'Planetary Boundaries: Guiding Human Development on a Changing Planet', *Science*, 347:6223, 13 February 2015.

biomass of terrestrial vertebrates, which will certainly appear remarkable to future palaeontologists.[21] Finally, the stratigraphic indication left by urbanization, dams, industrial production (the world automobile stock has reached 1,000 billion tonnes)[22] and mining and agricultural activity is notable and unique in the history of the Earth. It has even been recently shown that global warming, by modifying the volumes of glaciers, has an effect on volcanic and tectonic activity.[23]

Finally, entirely new substances deposited in the planet's ecosystems over the last 150 years (synthetic organic chemistry, hydrocarbons, plastics, some of which form a new type of rock,[24] endocrine disturbants, pesticides, radionuclides dispersed by nuclear tests, fluoride gases) constitute a typical signature of the Anthropocene in the sediments and fossils in the course of formation.

In a few million years from now, therefore, it is probable that geologists (if this profession typical of the Anthropocene survives), examining the rock deposits left by our epoch, will detect a transition as sudden as certain past somersaults in the Earth's billion-year history, such as the famous transition between the Cretaceous and the Tertiary 65 million years ago, when a meteor that hit what is now Central America led to the disappearance of three-quarters of the planet's species, including the dinosaurs. Yet today's geologists do not possess the strictly stratigraphic proof carved in the rock that they generally seek. Nonetheless, even if stratigraphers leave until later its validation in the official series of geological epochs, the Anthropocene thesis remains more robust in its wider geological definition, in terms of the sciences of the Earth system, than those of stratigraphy alone. This interdisciplinary field views the Earth as a complex system, from its core up to the high atmosphere, with subsystems (atmosphere, biosphere, hydrosphere, pedosphere, etc.) that are pervaded and connected by constant flows of matter and energy, in immense

---

21   Smil, *The Earth's Biosphere*, 186, 283–4.

22   Ibid., 269.

23   Bill McGuire, *Waking the Giant: How a Changing Climate Triggers Earthquakes, Tsunamis, and Volcanoes*, Oxford: Oxford University Press, 2012.

24   Patricia L. Korkoran, 'An Anthropogenic Marker Horizon in the Future Rock Record', *GSA Today*, 24:6, June 2014: 4–8.

feedback loops. In this perspective, as Jan Zalasiewicz, head of the Anthropocene Working Group of the International Commission on Stratigraphy explains, 'The Anthropocene is not about being able to detect human influence in stratigraphy, but reflects a change in the Earth system.'[25]

When did the Anthropocene begin?

If it is not the end of the world, it is certainly the end of an epoch: that of the Holocene, in which we have been living for the last 11,500 years. But at what time by the geological clock was the crime committed? Do we have to incriminate *Homo sapiens*, who appeared in Africa 200,000 years ago and went on to colonize Eurasia, the Americas and the Pacific islands? Did this species not bring about the disappearance of the megafauna (reptiles, birds and giant marsupials, the sabre-toothed tiger, the American lion, the European mammoth) by fire and hunting, everywhere that it settled? These transformations have left traces detected by geologists and archaeologists. Or should we locate the beginning of the Anthropocene just a few thousand years after that of the Holocene, as proposed by William Ruddiman, paleoclimatologist at the University of Virginia? Ruddiman argues that some 5,000 years ago humans had already emitted sufficient greenhouse gases – by deforestation, rice cultivation and stock-raising – to modify the Earth's climatic trajectory. These emissions and the warming they produced delayed the moment of entry into a new glacial episode. So, according to this controversial hypothesis, human action would already have contributed from the Neolithic age (as Buffon boasted in 1778!) to make the Holocene the longest interval of climate stability for 400,000 years (Figure 2). It was even this stabilization of the climate by human action in the Neolithic age that permitted the development of civilizations.

The problem with Ruddiman's thesis is that by focusing on the (slow) rise in CO_2 and methane emissions, on the deforestation and

---

25   Jan Zalasiewicz, response to Adrian J. Ivakhiv's 'Against the Anthropocene' blog post, *Immanence*, 7 July 2014, blog.uvm.edu.

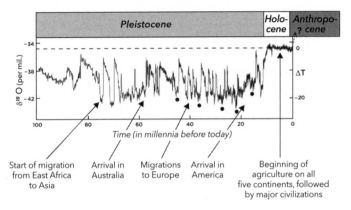

Figure 2: *Temperature and human history over 100,000 years.*
Note the remarkable stability of climate during the Holocene.

agricultural practices of the Neolithic age, it does not take into account the changes of scale brought about by the industrial revolution. For Erle Ellis, who at one time supported this argument before rejecting it, it is only since the nineteenth century that humans have transformed the majority of biomes on the planet.[26]

At the end of the day, Ruddiman's evidence does not contradict that of an Anthropocene beginning with the industrial revolution. After having stabilized the Holocene climate in the Neolithic age (if this hypothesis is confirmed), since the nineteenth century humanity has started to bring the Earth out of the Holocene, entering an Anthropocene marked by sudden swings.

The British geographers Simon Lewis and Mark Maslin have recently proposed starting the Anthropocene with the European conquest of America. This major historical event, so fateful for the Amerindian people and foundational for a capitalist world-economy, did indeed leave its mark in our planet's geology. The unification of the flora and fauna of the Old and New Worlds caused an upheaval in the agricultural, botanical and zoological map of the globe, newly mingling in a biological globalization forms of life separated 200 million years earlier with the break-up of Pangaea and

---

26   Ellis, 'Anthropogenic Transformation of the Terrestrial Biosphere'.

the opening of the Atlantic Ocean. The demographic collapse of the Amerindian population (from between 54 and 61 million in 1492 to just 6 million in 1650, following the wars of conquest, infectious diseases brought by the Europeans, and forced labour) also had the effect of an urban and agricultural retreat and the reforestation of more than 60 million hectares of the American continent, which, by capturing CO_2, reduced the carbon concentration in the atmosphere from around 279 to 272 ppm between the start of the sixteenth century and 1610.[27] But if this low tide of atmospheric carbon is an ominous stratigraphic marker of one of the most terrible events in human history, the variation does not lie outside the general Holocene range of 260 to 284 ppm.

It was around 1809, under the effect of emissions caused by the growing use of coal, that the concentration of CO_2 reached the Holocene maximum (284 ppm), going on to reach 290 ppm by the mid nineteenth century. This time the break was of geological amplitude and not simply historical: the terrestrial atmosphere emerged from the Holocene in the early nineteenth century, and it was with the power of fossil fuels that human activities so profoundly transformed the Earth system's biology and geology (Figure 1), thus supporting Paul Crutzen's proposal of beginning the Anthropocene with the industrial revolution.

Other authors, such as the geologist Jan Zalasiewicz, chair of the Anthropocene Working Group, see unambiguous traces of a change of geological epoch in the mid twentieth century. The new radionuclides emitted into the atmosphere from 16 July 1945, when the first atom bomb was exploded in the Nevada desert, the novelty of petrochemical products and the sudden expansion in the use of synthetic nitrate fertilisers, all present very clear stratigraphic signals. The exponential acceleration of human impacts since the Second World War reinforces this hypothesis. The advantage of having the Anthropocene start at this time is that the type of proof sought by stratigraphers can be adduced right away (for example,

---

27   Simon L. Lewis and Mark A. Maslin, 'Defining the Anthropocene', *Nature*, 519, 12 March 2015: 171–80, nature.com.

the presence even at the poles of radioactive isotopes non-existent in nature).[28]

Other members of the community of Earth system scientists, as well as that of the human and social sciences, stand by Paul Crutzen's initial proposal to begin the Anthropocene at the end of the eighteenth century. For if 1945 presents an appropriate stratigraphic signal and indicates a destructive intensification of the Anthropocene, this belated date masks deeper causes and processes, and obscures the major rupture, both environmental and civilizational, of the entry into thermo-industrial society based on fossil fuels. In the present book, while discussing the importance of the conquest of America (Chapter 10) and the 'Great Acceleration' after 1945, our focus will be on the last quarter of a millennium.

Let us sum up. Succeeding the Holocene, a period of 11,500 years marked by a rare climatic stability (apart from the 'little ice ages', significant only on the scale of human history), a period of blossoming agriculture, cities and civilizations, the swing into the Anthropocene represents a new age of the Earth. As Paul Crutzen and Will Steffen have emphasized, under the sway of human action, 'The Earth currently operates in a state without previous analogy.'[29]

The advances in Earth system sciences presented in this chapter offer a new and fundamental regard on the Earth as a complex and fragile system, non-linear and ultimately highly unpredictable. By demonstrating the telescoping of the short timescale of human action and the long timescale of the Earth, these sciences have also opened a new field of investigation that is absolutely fundamental, at the intersection of the natural sciences and the humanities.

Contrary to the end of the Cretaceous period, or Lars von Trier's film *Melancholia*, the Anthropocene shock is not the result of a foreign

---

28   Jan Zalasiewicz et al., 'When Did the Anthropocene Begin? A Mid-Twentieth Century Boundary Level Is Stratigraphically Optimal', *Quaternary International*, 2015 (early online edition available at ib.berkeley.edu/labs/barnosky).

29   Paul Crutzen and Will Steffen, 'How Long Have We Been in the Anthropocene Era?' *Climatic Change*, 61, 2003: 251–7, 253.

body that strikes the Earth from outside and derails its geological trajectory. It is our own model of development, our own industrial modernity, which, having claimed to free itself from the limits of the planet, is striking Earth like a boomerang.

CHAPTER 2

Thinking with Gaia: Towards Environmental Humanities

The Anthropocene is an event, a point of bifurcation in the history of the Earth, life and humans. It overturns our representations of the world. According to the philosopher Bruno Latour, it is 'the most decisive philosophical, religious, anthropological and, as we shall see, political concept yet produced as an alternative to the very notions of "Modern" and "modernity".[1] Continuing the systemic ecology which forty years ago framed human activities in an analysis of the functioning of ecosystems and the biosphere, the Anthropocene idea abolishes the break between nature and culture, between human history and the history of life and Earth.

From Buffon to Lyell and Darwin, biology and geology extended terrestrial time to hundreds of millions of years, creating a context that was seemingly external, almost immobile and indifferent to human tribulations. In parallel with this, the bourgeois and industrial Enlightenment emphasized the value of man, the modern subject, as autonomous agent acting consciously on his history and settling social conflicts by dominating nature. We shall see how this break between nature and society was constructed in the nineteenth century, and the part played in it by the emerging human and social sciences. We shall

---

1 Bruno Latour, *Facing Gaia: Six Lectures on the Political Theology of Nature*, Gifford Lectures, 2013, 77, bruno-latour.fr (accessed 22 June 2013, link since suppressed).

go on to see how this forceful, even violent, return of the history of the Earth into world history creates a new human condition and requires us to reintegrate nature and the Earth system at the heart of our understanding of history, our conception of freedom and our practice of democracy.

Rethinking the environmental crisis: an end to 'sustainable development'

By offering a reading of the ecological impacts of our model of development over two and a half centuries and on a planetary scale, the concept of the Anthropocene profoundly shifts our understanding of the contemporary 'ecological crisis'.

A few decades ago, the 'environment' was still understood as that which surrounds us, the place where humans went to extract resources, deposit waste, or even that in certain places was to be left virgin. Economists spoke of environmental degradations as 'externalities'. In the forms of natural parks, ecosystems and environment, subsequently that of 'sustainable development', nature was recognized until relatively recently as essential but separate from us. It hardly seemed to present a serious limit to growth, a watchword intoned in chorus by business leaders, orthodox economists and policy-makers.

The concept of Anthropocene challenges this separation and the promise to perpetuate our economic system by modifying it at the margin. In place of 'environment', there is now the Earth system. While triumphant industrial modernity had promised to prise us away from nature, its cycles and its limits, placing us in a world of boundless progress, the Earth and its limits are today making a comeback. We are facing 'the intrusion of Gaia', in the words of Isabelle Stengers – Gaia being the Greek goddess of the Earth.[2] The global and profound biogeochemical processes that we have disturbed are forcing their way into the centre of the political stage and of our everyday lives. Instead of 'masters and possessors of nature', we find

---

2 Isabelle Stengers, *Au Temps des catastrophes*, Paris: Les Empêcheurs de penser en rond/La Découverte, 2009.

ourselves each day a bit more entangled in the immense feedback loops of the Earth system. There can be no more talk of a linear and inexorable progress that used to silence those who challenge the market-based, industrial and consumerist order by accusing them of seeking to return us to a bygone age; from now on, the future of the Earth and all its creatures is at stake. And this uncertain becoming, strewn with tipping points, scarcely resembles the radiant future promised by the ideologists' progress of the last two centuries, whether liberal, social democratic or Marxist.

As for the word 'crisis', does it not maintain a deceptive optimism? It leads us to believe, in fact, that we are simply faced with a perilous turning-point of modernity, a brief trial with an imminent outcome, or even an opportunity. The term 'crisis' denotes a transitory state, while the Anthropocene is a point of no return. It indicates a geological bifurcation with no foreseeable return to the normality of the Holocene.

The warning given by the Anthropocene concept, and the recent advances in the sciences of the Earth system, thus go much further than an anthropocentric view of the 'environmental crisis', no matter how alarming. The problem is not only that our environment is being degraded, nor that 'resources' (another category that postulates an external and static character to the Earth and its beings and processes) are being exhausted, increasing social inequalities and thus threatening the planet with major geopolitical disturbances. The double reality that the Anthropocene presents is that, on the one hand, the Earth has seen other epochs in the last 4.5 billion years, and life will continue in one form or another with or without humans. But the new states that we are launching the Earth into will bring with them a disorder, penury and violence that will render it less readily habitable by humans. Even if the human species manages to reduce its ecological footprint drastically and invent a more sober civilization, we will not have settled accounts with Gaia. The Earth would take at least centuries if not hundreds of thousands of years to get back to the climatic and geobiological regime of the Holocene. The traces of our urban, industrial, consumerist, chemical and nuclear age will remain for thousands or even millions of years in the geological archives of the planet.

The new sciences of the Earth system also give us a non-linear view of the past and future of our planet. We are no longer in a reassuring model in which x hectares of forests converted into fields leads to the disappearance of n per cent of species, causes y per cent extra greenhouse gas and generates z°C increase in global temperature. In both geological history and their own modelling of the future, scientists have detected climatic tipping points and sudden-collapse thresholds of ecosystems. Thus, noting that for the last 400,000 years the Earth has swung between a cold glacial state and a warm interglacial state, they suspect the existence of a tipping point (around +2°C or +3°C?) beyond which the Earth system will undergo a change of attractor and tend towards a new stable state that is decidedly warmer (some +5°C or even +10°C or more – no climatologist can predict), such as existed some tens of millions of years ago, long before the appearance of the human species, and lasted for millions of years. Well beyond the linear predictions of the International Panel on Climate Change's first reports, this would be a real leap into the unknown. Living in the Anthropocene, therefore, means inhabiting the non-linear and highly unpredictable world of the Earth system's (or Earth history's) responses to our disturbances. For the Earth is 'perhaps a mother, but an irritable and touchy one', as Isabelle Stengers reminds us in tracing a mythological portrait of Gaia.[3]

The Anthropocene thus cancels the peaceful and reassuring project of sustainable development. This concept derived from the notion of 'maximal sustainable yield' conceived by (ecological) fishery science in the 1950s, which itself came from the notion of 'sustainable (*nachhaltig*) management' developed by German forestry science in the eighteenth century (see Chapter 9). Today it fosters illusions that are belied by the advent of the Anthropocene.

First of all, it supports belief in the possibility of perpetuating economic growth by means of a bit more 'conservation' of the environment. Publications from the early 1970s on the impossibility of indefinite growth on a finite planet (the *Limits to Growth* report of the Club of Rome in 1972, Nicholas Georgescu-Roegen's thesis on entropy

---

3   Ibid., 53.

and degrowth, etc.) were carefully swept under the carpet by the new watchword of 'sustainable development'. While these writings proposed an economy in the service of society and within the biophysical limits of the planet, the discourse of sustainable development that arose in the 1980s claimed that three well-identified poles could be mutually negotiated: the economic, the social and the environmental. Instead of a concentric view in which the economy is within the social, itself framed by a thousand feedback loops within the biosphere and the Earth system, the environment became a new column in the bookkeeping of big corporations, which gave themselves new sustainable development divisions. The project of the 'green economy', born within international institutions in recent years, accentuates this development, with the celebrated 'ecosystem services' now being the object of markets: the biosphere, the hydrosphere and the atmosphere appear as mere subsystems of the financial and commodity sphere (see Chapter 9).

The mechanical theory of maximum sustainable yield was refuted in 1973 by the ecologist Crawford S. Holling, who saw it as a reductionist and linear view that was responsible for the sudden collapse of certain ecosystems such as fishery resources. For him, 'The well-being of the world is not adequately described by concentrating on equilibria and conditions near them ... [The] effort to provide a maximum sustained yield from a fish population ... may paradoxically increase the chances of extinctions.'[4] Accordingly, before cofounding the Resilience Alliance in 1999, Holling had proposed already in 1973 the concept of 'ecological resilience' as the capacity of an ecosystem to maintain certain of its features despite and through sudden changes of state.

This systemic and complex view of our planet breaks with the posture of control by scientists and engineers imbued with certainty and able to standardize environmental conditions. We enter a world of limits, which is also marked by a greater visibility of the limits of scientific knowledge. Faced with the highly unpredictable character

---

4   Crawford S. Holling, 'Resilience and Stability of Ecological Systems', *Annual Review of Ecology and Systematics*, 4, 1973: 2.

of ecosystems and the Earth, the uncertainties are structural, and it is no longer a matter of believing that a simple compromise can be found between exploitation and conservation. What can help us to inhabit the Anthropocene collectively, therefore, is not, as Holling already said, 'the presumption of a sufficient knowledge, but the recognition of our ignorance.'[5] Far from the glorious advent of an 'age of man', the Anthropocene thus rather attests to our striking impotence.[6]

A geopolitical event

Besides being a geological event, the Anthropocene is at the same time a political event. In the IPCC's hypothesis (by no means the most pessimistic) of an increase in average temperature of 3.7°C by 2100, the Earth will be warmer than it has ever been for 15 million years. As for the extinction of biodiversity, this is already proceeding at a speed unmatched for 65 million years. This means that human societies will have to face up in the coming decades to changes of state in the Earth system to which the genus *Homo*, which appeared only two and a half million years ago, has never experienced, and to which therefore it is neither biologically adapted nor culturally prepared. The Anthropocene thus opens a new situation for humanity, a new human condition.

If the climatic stability of the last 10,000 years of the Holocene made possible the rise of cultures and civilizations on five continents, the end of this epoch and the entry into a new one will not be a smooth and steady process for human societies. Global warming means that people will die and countries disappear. The food situation already faces an uncertain future: the climate change of the last few decades has caused a shortfall of 4 to 5 per cent in world wheat and maize production in relation to 1980.[7]

---

5   Ibid., 21.

6   We owe the idea of 'powerful impotence' to Michel Lepesant.

7   David B. Lobell et al., 'Climate Trends and Global Crop Production since 1980', *Science*, 333, 2011: 616–20.

At the present time, 20 to 30 million people each year migrate in the wake of natural disaster, and the UN envisages 50 million environmental migrants a year by 2030, due in particular to changes linked to climate disturbance. Already today, therefore, there are 'victims of the Anthropocene',[8] and there will be more in the future. As Harald Welzer suggests, with constraints on both resources and climate, the Anthropocene promises to be violent. The geopolitics of the present century may prove more full of conflict, more barbaric, than the twentieth century. The question in the twenty-first century will be how to inhabit the Earth less frightfully.[9]

What levels of climate change and sea-level rise are acceptable? Which Pacific islands are condemned to disappear? How many other species besides our own will we allow to survive? At what point will the acidification of the oceans and the spilling of toxic substances be declared intolerable? If scientists can cast light on these questions, the answers are political decisions. In the time of the Anthropocene, the entire functioning of the Earth becomes a matter of human political choices. For example, knowing that the warming of recent decades has been limited by urban and industrial emissions of sulphur dioxide (an aerosol reflecting solar radiation), particularly in Asia,[10] the international community finds itself facing the dilemma of reducing SO_2 emissions by anti-pollution measures, at the risk of increasing global warming, or instead limiting these measures or even conducting projects of geoengineering that consist in massively spraying SO_2 into the atmosphere so as to limit this warming, at the cost of millions of premature deaths from respiratory diseases caused by this gas.

---

8   François Gemenne, 'The Anthropocene and Its Victims', in Clive Hamilton, François Gemenne and Christophe Bonneuil (eds), *The Anthropocene and the Global Environmental Crisis: Rethinking Modernity in a New Epoch*, London: Routledge, 2015.

9   Harald Welzer, *Les Guerres du climat. Pourquoi on tue au XXIe siècle*, Paris: Gallimard, 2009.

10   Robert K. Kaufmann et al., 'Reconciling Anthropogenic Climate Change with Observed Temperature, 1998–2008', *PNAS* 108:29, 19 July 2011: 11,790–3; see also 'Anthropogenic Global Cooling', blog post, *Open Mind*, 23 August 2010, tamino.wordpress.com.

The slogan of the Rio+20 conference was 'The future we want'. It thus expresses, not without an ambivalence that concedes to Promethean optimism, the fact that the planet will become what humans make of it, more or less voluntarily and more or less democratically. The Anthropocene is thus a political issue as well as a category in Earth sciences. We cannot be content with invoking demographic growth (the population increase of 2.4 times between 1950 and 2000) or world GDP (which multiplied by seven in the same half century) as explanations of the increasing human sway over the Earth (Chapter 4). In the same way, the emission of one kilogram of carbon dioxide or methane does not fulfil the same function for all human beings. For some people it is a question of survival, in the form of the available ration of rice, while for others it is simply increasing a consumption of meat (cattle, like rice fields, are great emitters of methane) that is already excessive from a medical point of view, monopolizing half of the planet's cereal crop-land for cattle feed and generating 18 per cent of greenhouse gas emissions, or more than the entire transport sector.[11]

We are therefore not in the peaceful and infra-political problematic of a reconciliation of humans with nature: the Anthropocene is political inasmuch as it requires arbitrating between various conflicting human forcings on the planet, between the footprints of different human groups (classes, nations), between different technological and industrial options, or between different ways of life and consumption. The Anthropocene has therefore to be given a political charge in order to overcome the contradictions and limits of a model of modernity that has spread globally over the last two centuries, and to explore the paths of a rapid and equitably divided reduction of the ecological footprint.

---

11 UN Food and Agriculture Organization, *Livestock's Long Shadow: Environmental Issues and Options*, Rome: 2006, fao.org.

The great temporal and ontological divide between nature and society

Whereas the Biblical account, like many other non-Western origin myths, made it possible for a long time to view human history as closely linked to that of the Earth, and Buffon proposed in his *Epochs of Nature* a great fresco tracing the common destiny of Earth and mankind, these two domains became increasingly separated in the course of the nineteenth century, as the prehuman history of the Earth became longer. Two major texts from the early 1830s, by the geologist Charles Lyell and the historian Jules Michelet, attest to this great discordance. In Michelet's universal history of humanity:

> Along with the world there began a war that will end together with the world and not before: that of *man against nature*, of spirit against matter, liberty against fatality. History is nothing else than the account of this interminable struggle . . . the gradual triumph of freedom . . . What is bound to encourage us in this endless struggle is that, by and large, the one side does not change, while the other changes and becomes stronger. Nature remains the same, whereas every day man gains some advantage over her. The Alps have not grown taller, while we have driven a road across the Simplon pass; the waves and winds are no less capricious, but the steamship breaks the waves heedless of the caprice of wind and sea. Follow the migrations of the human race from east to west, along the route of the sun and the magnetic currents of the globe: observe it on this long journey from Asia to Europe, from India to France, and you will see at each point the fatal power of nature diminish, and the influence of race and climate become less tyrannical.[12]

Continuing Michelet's vision, the great historian of the Renaissance, Burckhardt, depicted the modern conception of history as 'the break with nature caused by the awakening of consciousness'.[13]

---

12   Jules Michelet, *Introduction à l'histoire universelle*, Paris: Hachette, 1831, 5–7; our emphasis.

13   Cited by Dipesh Chakrabarty, 'The Climate of History: Four Theses',

In symmetry with this 'history against nature', nature dismissed to immobility, at least on the human timescale, Lyell inaugurated with his *Principles of Geology* a view of the Earth's geological history as indifferent to human action. An intelligent observer arriving on our planet and assessing the role of human action, he explained:

> would soon perceive that no one of the fixed and constant laws of the animate or inanimate world was subverted by human agency, and that the modifications now introduced for the first time were the accompaniments of new and extraordinary circumstances, and those not of a *physical* but a *moral* nature . . . so that, whenever the power of the new agent was withheld, even for a brief period, a relapse would take place to the ancient state of things.[14]

The great discrepancy between a long history of the Earth, impassive to human action, and a history of the emancipation of the latter from any natural determinism, was based on a separation of timescales allowed by the gradual extension in the estimated age of the Earth. Buffon proposed a preliminary estimate of 77,000 years, which already broke with the Biblical canon. This was based on the cooling time of an initially very hot planet, extrapolating to the planet the cooling times of metal spheres as measured in his forge. With Lyell, we advance to a timescale of tens of millions of years. The geologist's uniformitarianism allowed very slow phenomena to have great effects. He accordingly opposed other theories, championed in particular by Georges Cuvier, known as 'catastrophist' because they minimized the Earth's timescale and had to explain geological formations by the existence in the past of abrupt phenomena that had ceased to play a role since the appearance of man.[15] The history of the Earth that Lyell proposed was one of slow

Critical Inquiry, 35:2, 2009: 197–222. We take up in this section Chakrabarty's key thesis, according to which the Anthropocene shatters the temporal disjunction between human history and natural history.

14   Charles Lyell, *Principles of Geology*, vol. 1, London: John Murray, 1830, 164.

15   On Lyell and uniformitarianism, see Martin Rudwick, *Worlds before Adam: The Reconstruction of Geohistory in the Age of Reform*, Chicago: University

and regular forces on which man had no hold, in relation to which 'the modifications in the system of which man is the instrument, do not, perhaps, constitute so great a deviation from previous analogy as we usually imagine'.[16] In 1862, the physicist William Thomson (the future Lord Kelvin) gave an age of 400 million years for the Earth (the present estimate is 4.5 billion).[17]

The Lamarckian theory of evolution, for its part, and following it that of Darwin, extended the time frame of the history of life, with the appearance of man from a simian ancestor being only a belated episode in this.

In the nineteenth century, the natural sciences also stripped away the telos from both life and the Earth, while the human and social sciences became teleologically progressive. The former removed from life and Earth their sensitivity to human action, while the latter declared their autonomy by assiduously detaching the explanation of human and social phenomena from natural causes. History applied to the study of 'human affairs' the methods of the natural sciences: the quest for archival traces as evidence, after the model of fossil traces; the accumulation and comparison of 'series'; and, in the twentieth century, the 'immobile history', as Fernand Braudel put it, of structural, economic and social evolutions. But within this common paradigm of process and history, forming the cultural matrix of the industrial nineteenth century, a division of fields of authority occurred: the history of the Earth and life was the province of natural scientists, and the history of 'progress in human affairs'[18] that of historians and social sciences – a division that still casts a shadow today. As we shall see, this great temporal and ontological divide broke with the conception of connections between climate, environment and society that had prevailed in the late eighteenth century (Chapter 8) and formed a cultural precondition for the swing into the Anthropocene, by constructing a great

of Chicago Press, 2008, 297–315.

16   Lyell, *Principles of Geology*, 161.

17   Martin Rudwick, *Bursting the Limits of Time: The Reconstruction of Geohistory in the Age of Revolution*, Chicago: University of Chicago Press, 2005.

18   John Dalberg-Acton (Lord Acton) (1896), quoted by E. H. Carr, *What Is History?*, Harmondsworth: Penguin, 1965, 111.

external nature, slow, immense and undaunted, and thereby making invisible the limits of the planet (Chapter 9) and the unequal socio-economic relations of nascent fossil capitalism (Chapter 10).

Profiting from this open discordance between the time of nature and the time of man, liberal economists such as Jean-Baptiste Say, considering that the exhaustion of natural resources was a matter for a distant future beyond the grasp of economic rationality, broke with Malthus and proclaimed a nature placed outside of economic thought as a free gift: 'We leave the study of natural wealth to the scholars who deal with natural things.'[19] 'Natural wealth is inexhaustible . . . Unable to be either multiplied or exhausted, it is not the object of economic science.'[20]

This divide between the natural and the human sciences was further accentuated between 1850 and 1960. Climatology became the science of an external, global climate, conceived as an averaging out of thermometric data over a very large scale, and no longer as the science of places and topographies, the basis for reflection on the human making of climate and the climatic making of societies.[21] In a related fashion, public health and its revolutionizing by Louis Pasteur and Robert Koch focused medical attention on microorganisms, thus marginalizing the earlier neo-Hippocratic medical paradigm which viewed the body as shaped by a far wider number of elements in the environment such as light, temperature, climate, wind, odour and 'miasmas'.[22] After 1900, the new science of genetics promoted a 'modern conception of heredity' centred on the isolated gene, which ruled out the idea (which only recently came back with epigenetics) of a heredity co-determined by

19   Jean-Baptiste Say, *Cours d'économie politique*, Paris: Garnier-Flammarion, 1996, 98.

20   Jean-Baptiste Say, *Cours complet d'économie politique pratique*, vol. 1, Brussels: Meline, 1832, 83.

21   Jean-Baptiste Fressoz and Fabien Locher, 'Modernity's Frail Climate: A Climate History of Environmental Reflexivity', *Critical Inquiry*, 38, Spring 2012: 579–98.

22   Jean-Baptiste Fressoz, 'Circonvenir les circumfusa. La chimie, l'hygiénisme et la libéralisation des choses environnantes (1750–1850)', *Revue d'Histoire Moderne et Contemporaine*, 56:4, 2009: 39–76.

the influence of the environment.[23] With the exception of geography, almost all the social sciences defined their object in a way that assiduously removed it from nature: thus social and cultural anthropology separated off from physical anthropology, and Émile Durkheim excluded climatic parameters from the pertinent causes of suicide, the nascent sociology making a watertight division between society and the natural environment.[24] In this respect, Durkheim followed Comte, who with his *Course of Positive Philosophy* had founded sociology as a 'genuine science of social development' that obeyed the specific laws of the 'general progression of humanity' rather than environmental influences.[25] For Comte, in fact, Montesquieu in *The Spirit of the Laws* had exaggerated the influence of 'local physical causes' such as climate on the social and political organization:

> The true political influence of climate is misconceived, and usually much exaggerated, through the common error of analysing a mere modification before the main action is fully understood . . . This error was inevitable under Montesquieu's necessary ignorance of the great social laws . . . Montesquieu did not even perceive . . . that local physical causes, very powerful in the early days of civilization, lose their force in proportion as human development admits of their being neutralized.[26]

Likewise, in the age of empires, an 'environmental orientalism' reserved the 'external' influences of the environment on human history to discourses on 'less advanced' societies, as a counterpoise to an industrial society moved above all by an 'internal' logic of

---

23   Christophe Bonneuil, 'Pure Lines as Industrial Simulacra: A Cultural History of Genetics from Darwin to Johannsen', in Christina Brandt, Staffan Müller-Wille and Hans-Jörg Rheinberger (eds), *Exploring Heredity,* Cambridge, MA: MIT Press, 2015.

24   Émile Durkheim, *Suicide* (1897). See also Chapter 3, 'Suicide and Cosmic Factors'. One of the first analysts of this 'social only' paradigm was Serge Moscovici, *Essai sur l'histoire humaine de la nature*, Paris: Flammarion, 1968.

25   *The Positive Philosophy of Auguste Comte*, New York: Calvin Blanchard, 1858, 440ff.

26   Ibid., 443.

progress.[27] Soon after, Freud separated the adult individual from the world, decreeing that the cosmic feeling of 'being in correlation with the surrounding world' – Romain Rolland's 'oceanic feeling' – was no more than a childish illusion.[28] He thus separated out a psychic interiority that the analyst could study in abstraction from its vast ecological context.[29]

Beyond the great separation

On one side, therefore, were the natural sciences with their non-human objects, their concept of objectivity and their modern certainties; on the other, humanities and social sciences became 'a-natural'[30] by conferring on 'society' a self-sufficient totality, free from natural determination (despite the observations of Marx, Sergei Podolinsky, Patrick Geddes and many others on socio-ecological metabolisms; see Chapter 8). The natural sciences postulated a physical continuity between humans and other entities that obscured the social production and social relations of nature, while the field of human sciences was defined by a meta-physical discontinuity postulated between humans and everything else, hence obscuring the natural production and relations of social order by what Peter Sloterdijk has called a 'backstage ontology'.

The Anthropocene, as the reunion of human (historical) time and Earth (geological) time, between human agency and non-human agency, gives the lie to this – temporal, ontological, epistemological and institutional – great divide between nature and society that widened in the nineteenth and twentieth centuries. The new geo-historical epoch signals the irruption of the Earth (its temporality, its

27   Fressoz and Locher, 'Modernity's Frail Climate'.

28   Sigmund Freud, *Civilization and Its Discontents*, Standard Edition, vol. 21, London: Hogarth Press, 1961, 64–5.

29   Restoration of this connection is the task of today's 'ecopsychology'. See Andy Fisher, *Radical Ecopsychology*, Albany, NY: SUNY Press, 2013.

30   We gratefully borrow this critique of 'anaturalism' from a book in preparation by Frédéric Neyrat, *Enquête sur la part inconstructible de la Terre*.

limits, its systemic dynamics) into what sought to be a history, an economy and a society emancipating themselves from natural constraints. It signals the return of the *Earth* into a *world* that Western industrial modernity on the whole represented to itself as above the earthly foundation. If our future involves a geological swing of the Earth into a new state, we can no longer believe in a humanity making its own history by itself. This nature that Michelet saw as the static scene of our exploits has clearly entered the game in the most powerful and dynamic manner possible. The Anthropocene thus requires the substitution of the 'ungrounded' humanities of industrial modernity by new environmental humanities that adventure beyond the great separation between environment and society.[31] Environmental history, natural anthropology, environmental law and ethics, human ecology, environmental sociology, political ecology, green political theory, ecological economics, etc., are among the new disciplines that have recently begun to renew the human and social sciences, in a dialogue with the sciences of nature. They sketch new environmental humanities that go beyond the two cultures' fissure and put an end to the jealous division of territories. In the Anthropocene, it is impossible to hide the fact that 'social' relations are full of biophysical processes, and that the various flows of matter and energy that run through the Earth system at different levels are polarized by socially structured human activities.

But how are we to conceive conjointly a society structured by nature and a nature structured by the social? In 1998, the ecologists Fikret Berkes and Carl Folke proposed the concept of 'socioecological systems'.[32] A whole field of research (continuing the work of Georgescu-Roegen and Howard T. Odum) has since established itself, to integrate the analysis of flows of matter and energy, and of 'socioecological

---

31   For the critique of this great separation, see Bruno Latour, *Politics of Nature: How to Bring the Sciences into Democracy*, Cambridge, MA: Harvard University Press, 1999.

32   Fikret Berkes and Carl Folke (eds), *Linking Social and Ecological Systems: Management Practices and Social Mechanisms for Building Resilience*, New York: Cambridge University Press, 1998.

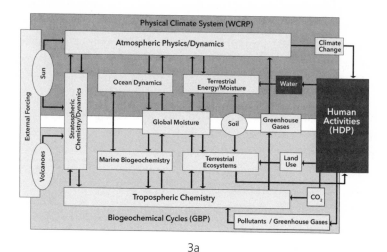

3a

3b   3c

Figure 3: *Standard representations of human activities in relation to the Earth system.*

metabolisms', into the social sciences.[33] These approaches conceive society and the compartments of the Earth system as two structures connected by exchanges of matter and energy. The diagrams in Figure 3 illustrate the theoretical frameworks employed by the main interdisciplinary projects that study socioecological systems.

In the first diagram (Figure 3a), 'human activities' comprise a homogeneous black box, while attention is focused on the 'natural compartment' of the Earth system. In the second (Figure 3b), commonly adopted by the 'socioecological systems' approach, we have two compartments connected by two paths: the impacts of human management of ecosystems and feedback from the latter. The third diagram (Figure 3c) adds to these two paths an intersection between the two compartments, that of ecosystem services and their use.

This type of representation errs by its excessive simplicity and the functionalism of its description of the social. First of all, the historical, material and cultural dynamics of human societies, their asymmetries and relations of domination, are obscured in a black box. Secondly, in all three diagrams, socio-natural metabolisms are reduced to a play of pressures and responses, whereas what is needed is an understanding of the energy and matter metabolisms operated in and by the social system that is as fine-grained as the analysis of biogeochemical flows in the Earth system. It is hard to grasp what is happening if the Anthropocene is represented by a box of 'human activities' that interacts with boxes for the atmosphere, biosphere, etc. We are rather dealing with an intricate network in which social and natural arrangements mutually reinforce each other: European consumer attitudes and the orangutans of Indonesia, markets and rainforests, social inequalities and endocrine disturbance, state powers and the chemical composition of the atmosphere, representations of the world and energy flows. And this 'socio-bio-geosphere' in its uncertain becoming

---

33   Not without a totalizing and demiurgic perspective of optimal planetary management. See Chapter 4 below, and Peter Baccini and Paul H. Brunner, *Metabolism of the Anthroposphere: Analysis, Evaluation, Design*, Cambridge, MA: MIT Press, 2012.

can only be understood in a dialogue of disciplines with varying levels of analysis, from the molecular level of environmental effects on our heredity through to the global level of flows of matter and capital organized by the WTO, by way of local scenes at industrial sites or socio-environmental mobilizations.

How then are we to overcome the dualism between nature and society that persists in the approaches supported by the three above diagrams, a relation that remains one of externality even if a connected one? First of all, as proposed by the interdisciplinary field of political ecology, we have to think of ecology and power relations together if we are to understand the formation of social and environmental inequalities.[34] We then have to envisage a double relation of internality:[35]

— *Natures pervaded by the social*, by the thousand and one sociotechnical interventions that are historically situated, and that are only dimly understood when placed in compartments connected by the ever-repeated 'pressure-response' pair. The nature of the Anthropocene is above all a 'second nature' fostered by powerful institutions (the great networks of capitalism, technological systems, military apparatuses, etc.), which does not rule out the alterity of nature nor the fact that the Earth is not just a social construct.

— *Societies pervaded by nature*, in which social relations and cultural norms are structured and rigidified by mechanisms that organize metabolisms of matter and energy, and that govern the social uses of nature. Far from surrounding the social, the environment traverses it, and the history of societies, cultures and socio-political regimes cannot ignore the flows of matter, energy and information that frame them.

---

34   Richard Peet, Paul Robbins and Michael Watts (eds), *Global Political Ecology*, London: Routledge, 2010.

35   This perspective is located at the junction of Earth system sciences, the philosophies of Whitehead and Deleuze, Bruno Latour and the 'co-productionist' studies of the sciences, and the ecologized Marxism of Jason Moore, who talks about 'society-in-nature' and 'nature-in-society'. See Jason Moore, *Capitalism in the Web of Life*, London: Verso, 2015.

In this perspective of a double-framing internality, each of the two former supposed 'compartments' must thus be studied by combining the approaches of the so-called social and so-called natural sciences, rather than by an interdisciplinarity of adjacency in which each would reign over its own compartment. The joint history of the Earth and of human societies then appears as the co-evolution of metabolic (material-energetic) regimes and social orders. In each period, a set of world-views and social relations supports sociotechnical arrangements that organize the metabolisms of a given society and world-system and alter the functioning of the Earth system. And reciprocally, the metabolisms thus constructed have also political agency; they make possible, robust and 'natural' a certain social order, a hierarchy between nations, a certain type of lifestyle and vision of the world.

Reintegrating nature into history

From the time of Michelet and Jacob Burckhardt, history has been above all the history of 'human affairs', those of men making history. It could scarcely interact with the history of nature, the timescales being quite different. After the Second World War, historians following Fernand Braudel[36] distinguished three temporalities: that of nature and climate, almost immobile and not affected by human action; the slow temporality of economic and social facts; and finally, the rapid temporality of events, vibrating to the rhythm of battles, diplomacy and political life. This separation of domains and time frames between nature and society, the legacy of industrial modernity, has had profound consequences for the writing of history. Many historians have related the history of scientific and technological mastery of nature. But until the emergence of environmental history, particularly in the United States in the late 1960s, it was rare indeed for historians to 'think like a mountain', in the expression of Aldo Leopold, i.e., to narrate history from the point of view of animals, ecosystems and other non-human entities. And until the

---

36   Fernand Braudel, *The Mediterranean and the Mediterranean World in the Age of Philip II* (2 vols), London: Fontana, 1966.

1960s, few historians addressed the alterations of the environment caused by human action and the effects these in turn had on societies.

Rather than an environmental history as had developed in the United States, what we had in France first of all was a 'history of the environment', a new object for history as defined by the Annales School. The quest for scientific authenticity, taken over from historical climatology, and the view of nature as an environment external to society, led Emmanuel Le Roy Ladurie to concern himself with climatic history as a 'history without men'. This was the basis out of which environmental history painfully emerged in France, its protagonists, unlike their American counterparts, maintaining a *cordon sanitaire* against the ecological mobilizations of the 1970s.[37]

As an exact opposite of this objectivist history of an environment 'without men', other French historians developed a cultural history concerned with environmental representations and sensibilities. Alongside a host of scholarly works on the feeling for nature or the representations of landscapes, Alain Corbin's *Le Miasme et la jonquille*, published in 1982, is a magisterial text emblematic of this cultural history. But by reading nature in terms of sensibilities and their historical situatedness, Corbin tended to relegate to the back burner the question of the very material effects of industrial activities on the bodies of workers, local residents and ecosystems.

Basically, the polarity between the objectivist perspectives of an environmental history impassive to human action and the constructivist ones of a cultural history of representations of the environment still reproduced the dividing lines between Lyell and Michelet. Taking the Anthropocene seriously as a historian means rejecting a duality that is unsatisfactory and departing from a Braudelian discordance of time frames that is no longer valid.[38] Thus it is well established today

---

37 See the very significant issue of *Annales* on the environment, 29:3, May–June 1974. On the 'delay' and specific characteristics of French environmental history, see Geneviève Massard-Guilbaud, 'De la "part du milieu" à l'histoire de l'environnement', *Le Mouvement social*, 200, July–September 2002, 64–72.

38 Chakrabarty, 'The Climate of History'.

that the little ice age, the cooling of the climate between 1450 and 1800 with a minimum in the period 1640–1730, was not simply a natural development experienced by human societies, but the product of a reciprocal interaction. If a cyclical reduction in solar activity was one factor involved, human action itself was another: the demographic collapse of the Amerindian population by some 50 million after 1492 led to an extension of forests and a fall in atmospheric CO_2, hence a reduction in the greenhouse effect.[39] The work of Earth system scientists on the Anthropocene question has thus challenged the externality of the climate in relation to human action even in the pre-industrial age. After the epoch of separate histories of nature and of human societies, only a shared history can do justice to the reality of the Anthropocene.

Several works of environmental history have sought to combine material readings framed by the 'hard' sciences (Alfred Crosby, John McNeill) with political and cultural readings, to integrate socionatural metabolisms and environmental mutations into a historical account. The notion of a 'second nature' shaped by capitalist dynamics, used by William Cronon in his key work *Nature's Metropolis*, Edmund Russell's 'evolutionary history' perspective of the interactions between human technology and the responses of living organisms, and the history of Western democracies revisited through the energy prism by Timothy Mitchell, are three stimulating examples taken from the field of environmental history that we shall draw on in the third part of this book.[40]

---

39   William F. Ruddiman, *Plows, Plague and Petroleum*, Princeton: Princeton University Press, 2005; Richard J. Nevle et al., 'Neotropical Human-Landscape Interactions, Fire, and Atmospheric CO_2 during European Conquest', *Holocene*, 21, 2011: 853–64; Robert A. Dull et al., 'The Columbian Encounter and the Little Ice Age: Abrupt Land Use Change, Fire, and Greenhouse Forcing', *Annals of the Association of American Geographers*, 100:4, 2010: 755–71; Simon L. Lewis and Mark A. Maslin, 'Defining the Anthropocene', *Nature*, 519, 12 March 2015: 171–80, nature.com.

40   William Cronon, *Nature's Metropolis: Chicago and the Great West*, New York: Norton, 1991; Edmund Russell, *Evolutionary History: Uniting History and Biology to Understand Life on Earth*, Cambridge: Cambridge University Press, 2011; Timothy Mitchell, *Carbon Democracy: Political Power in the Age of Oil*, London: Verso, 2013.

Rediscovering freedom in the age of attachments

The Anthropocene challenges certain distinctions that were formerly deemed fundamental to the modern West: human exceptionalism[41] and the ontological break between the human being as *subject* of entitlement and the *object* of nature. Environmental ethics therefore undertakes a basic rethinking of the foundations of the different moral rules that organize relations between humans and non-humans. A distinction is generally made between three major ethical proposals: anthropocentric (sustainably managing the Earth for man), biocentric (respecting the intrinsic right to existence of every being on Earth) and ecocentric ('thinking like Gaia', in the words of J. Baird Callicott, following on from Aldo Leopold). An entire field of philosophy (as well as law and political science) now explores the question of environmental law, or even the rights of nature (already sketched out in the constitution of Ecuador) and the Earth, and relations between nature and sovereignty.[42]

In the same way, the Anthropocene challenges the modern definition of freedom, long conceived in opposition to nature. John Stuart Mill related the freedom and autonomy of individuals to the achievement of 'a high degree of success in their struggle with Nature.'[43] A freedom understood in this way sets human emancipation against nature, against the Earth as a whole. This modern conception of freedom clearly comes up against global limits in a disturbing way. Benjamin Constant, in 'The Liberty of Ancients Compared with That of the Moderns', argued in 1819 that the situation of the citizens of his time, gathered in great national political

---

41   Riley E. Dunlap and William R. Catton, 'Struggling with Human Exemptionalism: The Rise, Decline and Revitalization of Environmental Sociology', *American Sociologist*, 25, 1994: 5–30.

42   Michel Serres, *The Natural Contract*, Ann Arbor, MI: University of Michigan Press, 1995; Gérard Mairet, *Nature et souveraineté*, Paris: Presses de Sciences Po, 2013.

43   John Stuart Mill, *Considerations on Representative Government* (1861), Rockville, MD: Serenity Publishers, 2008, 40.

spaces, could not underpin the same conception of liberty and sovereignty as that of the citizens of the civic democracies of antiquity.

Dominique Bourg and Kerry Whiteside have taken up this argument to maintain that today, in a time of global ecological disruptions of human origin, we need to invent a new ideal of emancipation different from that of the 'moderns'.[44] For Constant, liberty was synonymous with 'security in private enjoyments', those permitted by a government that limited itself to guaranteeing property and free exchange. For this liberal there was no question of limiting the propensity of individuals to produce, exchange, consume and even waste. If the early socialists opposed to this a different ideal of emancipation, one egalitarian and co-operative, so as to limit the struggle of all against all and the 'material degradation of the planet' as Charles Fourier expressed it (see Chapter 11), we have to acknowledge that the actual socialism of the twentieth century was not ecological, and that it is Constant's market-based, individualist and consumerist view of liberty that is culturally dominant on the planet as a whole.

As the Anthropocene pursues its course, we find ourselves facing these limits, along with a host of non-human beings and caught in the feedback loops and boomerang effects of Earth history striking back. What use is it then to conceive liberty, as did Bacon, Descartes, Michelet or Sartre, in terms of a tearing away from nature? What use is it to believe, with Luc Ferry, that man is a 'being of anti-nature', and profess this view of liberty as a 'glorification of uprootedness, or innovation'?[45] As soon as it is no longer possible to abstract from nature, we have to think *with* Gaia. One of the major tasks of contemporary philosophy is undoubtedly to rethink freedom in a different way than

---

44   Dominique Bourg and Kerry Whiteside, *Pour une démocratie écologique*, Paris: Seuil, 2010, 21–5.

45   Luc Ferry, *The New Ecological Order*, Chicago: Chicago University Press, 1995, 92. Jean-Claude Michéa responds that this uprootedness is 'simply the other name for liberal anthropology' and shows how the early socialists of the first half of the nineteenth century opposed this. See Jean-Claude Michéa, *Les Mystères de la gauche*, Paris: Climats, 2013.

this wrenching away from natural determinations, to explore what may be infinitely enriching and emancipatory in those attachments that link us with other beings on a finite Earth. What infinity remains in a finite world?

Rethinking democracy in a finite world

Freedom can only be conceived in the context of social arrangements and institutional constructions. But, as the historian Dipesh Chakrabarty observes, these political constructions are themselves put in question by the disturbances of the Anthropocene: 'the mansion of modern freedoms stands on an ever-expanding base of fossil-fuel use,'[46] which today are either growing scarce or disturbing the climate. How can the ideal of democracy be founded anew when the dream of material abundance is evaporating? How should politics be conceived in the age of the Anthropocene?

Faced with the rise of ecological movements, the first approach of political science was to take these as objects and investigate the relative novelty of their 'offer' in relation to other political paradigms. Other authors have used this situation to proclaim the 'end of modernity', or at least of the 'simple', non-reflexive modernity that environmental and health risks are putting in crisis.[47] Bruno Latour, for example, uses the pertinence of ecology today to argue against those modernizers who sharpen the arrow of time and who manufactured a 'before', when nature was supposed to have been less separated from society and society less detached from beliefs and ideologies. He proposes to 'ecologize' instead of modernize, and, in the wake of Michel Serres's *The Natural Contract*, bring nature into politics by a set of institutions (a 'parliament of things') so as to assess the place – irremediably uncertain and controversial – in our common world of a multitude of beings, none of which can any longer serve simply as 'means' for others.[48]

46   Chakrabarty, 'The Climate of History', 208.
47   We shall discuss the theses of Ulrich Beck, Bruno Latour and Anthony Giddens in Chapter 4.
48   Latour, *Politics of Nature*, and *An Inquiry into Modes of Existence: An Anthropology of the Moderns*, Cambridge, MA: Harvard University Press, 2013.

After this 'postmodern' phase, the aggravation of ecological disturbances indicated by scientists and the rise of the concept of Anthropocene have favoured a third wave of more materialist work on the foundations of democracy. Philosophers, political scientists and historians are shedding light on how deeply the political theories of the past were conditioned by particular eco-biogeochemical metabolisms – either explicitly (with Hobbes or Grotius, the state was justified by the scarcity of resources) or implicitly (in the Fordist compromise based on an unequal exchange with the Third World). Effective democracy is as dependent on material foundations as is liberty, foundations that were unequally assured in the past and seem unsustainable in the future, hence the importance of new political theories that integrate the material and energy metabolisms that are the basis for political representation, the state, security, citizenship, sovereignty, justice, etc. This new field of green political theory (Andrew Dobson, Robyn Eckersley, Luc Semal, etc.) is thus questioning the standard political theory – contractualist, anthropocentric and blind to the limits of the planet.[49] In this way it will be possible to discern the conditions in which the necessary de-carbonification of our societies, or even an overall energy reduction, could change our democracies. Recent texts have thus explored the rise of a post-growth activism and of territorial policy initiatives of energy sobriety. They show that, far from prefiguring a totalitarian regression, these 'catastrophist' initiatives (plans for local energy reduction, transition towns, etc.) can open new spaces for strong democracy, new participatory forecasting and policy-making, and new social inclusiveness.[50]

Questions of environmental justice also open up new and challenging fields for the social sciences. Can we speak of an ecological debt

---

49   Andrew Dobson et al., 'Andrew Dobson: Trajectories of Green Political Theory', *Natures Sciences Sociétés*, 22:2, April–June 2014: 132–41; Andrew Dobson, *Green Political Thought*, London: Routledge, 2007; Andrew Dobson and Robyn Eckersley (eds), *Political Theory and the Ecological Challenge*, Cambridge: Cambridge University Press, 2006.

50   Luc Semal, *Politiques catastrophistes. Pour une théorie politique environnementale*, Paris: PUF, 2015; also Agnès Sinaï (ed.), *Penser la décroissance. Politiques de l'Anthropocène*, Paris: Les Presses de Sciences Po, 2013.

owed by the rich countries? How do environmental regulations in these countries, along with globalization, relocate polluting activities to poor regions? How does this affect social groups in these regions differently? Can exposing another party to environmental nuisance and catastrophe be analysed as a form of violence?[51]

To understand what is happening to us with the Anthropocene requires the mobilization of all forms of knowledge. If the natural sciences are essential to understanding the intrinsic dynamics of the Earth and its inhabitants, conceiving the Anthropocene also requires new environmental humanities. For this strange species, the 'naked ape' that has plunged the Earth into the uncertain future of the Anthropocene is not simply a biological entity. It is also made up of social and ideological systems, institutions and imaginations, pervaded by power relations that govern an unequal distribution of the benefits and ravages of Gaia, of legitimacy in speaking *of* and *for* the planet, and of the possibilities of influencing technological and economic choices – starting with the ability to tell the Anthropocene and its history.

---

51   Rob Nixon, *Slow Violence and the Environmentalism of the Poor*, Cambridge, MA: Harvard University Press, 2011.

PART TWO: SPEAKING FOR THE EARTH, GUIDING HUMANITY: Deconstructing the Geocratic Grand Narrative of the Anthropocene

CHAPTER 3

Clio, the Earth and the Anthropocenologists

The scientists who invented the term 'Anthropocene' did not simply produce fundamental data on the state of our planet or advance a systemic and fruitful perspective on its uncertain future. They also proposed a history, a story seeking to respond to the question 'How did we get here?' In this way, they developed an authorized narrative of the Earth, its past and its future shared with the human species, a narrative that makes the management of the Earth system a new object of knowledge and government.

The concept of the Anthropocene continues a number of previous narratives, produced in the course of history, of the global environment, the Earth and its proper usage. The world's centres of government have long been the places where what balances or unbalances the planet has been spoken and demonstrated. They construct spheres in which the proper ways of handling it, tempering it or acclimatizing it are presented: from the greenhouses of the Jardin du Roi where Buffon wrote his *Epochs of Nature* to the projects of geoengineering promoted by Paul Crutzen, by way of the Crystal Palace of London's Great Exhibition of 1851, symbol of the commercial organization of the world,[1] or again the geodesic dome conceived by Buckminster Fuller – of the 'Spaceship Earth' metaphor – for the United States pavilion at

---

1   Peter Sloterdijk, *In the World Interior of Capital: Towards a Philosophical Theory of Globalization*, Cambridge: Polity, 2013, pp. 169–76.

the Montreal Universal Exhibition of 1967, presenting the first image of an 'Earthrise' seen from the Moon.[2]

The elites of the French colonial empire in the eighteenth century, such as Pierre Poivre and Georges-Louis Leclerc de Buffon, those of the British empire in the nineteenth century, such as the economist William Stanley Jevons and the forester Dietrich Brandis, those of the conquest of the American West, such as Gifford Pinchot, or of US hegemony in the 1950s, such as Henry Fairfield Osborn, all developed in their time knowledge and global environmental warnings that dovetailed into systems of world domination – while attempting to inflect these a little (see chapters 8 and 11). Far from being the hallmark of our present era, knowledge of the global environment has thus for a very long time been part of imperial cosmographies.

There is some reason to suspect, therefore, that the knowledge and discourse of the Anthropocene may itself form part, perhaps unknowingly, of a hegemonic system for representing the world as a totality to be governed. To analyse this new cosmography, we shall study those texts most often cited by the scientists, historians and philosophers who have introduced and discussed the notion of Anthropocene on the international stage.[3] For simplicity's sake, we shall refer to this

---

2   Sebastian Grevsmühl, *La Terre vue d'en haut. L'Invention de l'environnement global*, Paris: Seuil, 2014.

3   In particular, Paul Crutzen's article 'Geology of Mankind', *Nature*, 415, 3 January 2002: 23; that by the climatologist Will Steffen, together with Paul Crutzen and the historians Jacques Grinevald and John McNeill, 'The Anthropocene: Conceptual and Historical Perspectives', *Philosophical Transactions of the Royal Society A* 369:1938, 2011: 842–67; a programmatic article on the piloting of the planet, by Will Steffen and Paul Crutzen along with the geologist Jan Zalasiewicz, 'The Anthropocene: From Global Change to Planetary Stewardship', *Ambio*, 40, 2011: 739–71; and that of Johan Rockström, specialist in 'systems approaches' and director of the celebrated Resilience Centre in Stockholm. This body of work is enriched by some other articles, including those on 'planetary limits', published also by Rockström together with some thirty colleagues (including Steffen and Crutzen, but also the American climatologist James Hansen as well as Robert Costanza, the ecologist who calculated in 1997 the monetary value of the services rendered by the biosphere), 'A Safe Operating Space for Humanity', *Nature*, 24, September 2009: 472–5; or 'Planetary Boundaries: Exploring the Safe Operating Space for Humanity', *Ecology and Society*, 14:2, 2009: 1–33.

phalanx of renowned scholars who made the bold gesture of naming our epoch as 'anthropocenologists'.

Submitting these narratives to criticism does not mean denying the value of the investigations of these anthropocenologists. It is rather a matter of opening up the official narrative of the Anthropocene to discussion, so as to enable closer reflection on the particularities of our representations of the world. So that other voices *from* and *for* the Earth can be heard, coming from other cultures and other social groups; so that other explanations of 'how we got to this point' and other proposals for 'what is to be done' may also have their say. Otherwise the seductive Anthropocene concept may well become the official philosophy of a new technocratic and market-oriented geopower.

In order to make fruitful use of the advances in the Earth system sciences, we have to learn to distrust the grand narratives that come with the Anthropocene concept, to pass them through the sieve of criticism. This is the way in science, history and democracy.

A history of 'stages'

Anthropocenologists seem attracted to historical narration. What is more natural than to explain the human dynamic that has tipped the Earth into a new state? Since the Anthropocene is a new epoch, the question of knowing how we arrived here arises quite immediately, and science presents an account of 'the evolution of humans and our societies from hunter-gatherers to a global geophysical force'.[4] To tell the Odyssey of humans, still in the nineteenth century 'frail bent reeds . . . with their feet plunged unto death into the immemorial soil',[5] but who have today become beings 'equipotent to the Earth',[6] as Michel Serres puts it, anthropocenologists have

---

4   Will Steffen, Paul J. Crutzen and John R. McNeill, 'The Anthropocene: Are Humans Now Overwhelming the Great Forces of Nature?', *Ambio* 36:8, 2007: 614–21, 614.

5   Michel Serres, *The Natural Contract*, Ann Arbor: University of Michigan Press, 1995, 17.

6   Ibid., 110.

constructed a narrative, searched for founding events and causal chains, and marked out periods.

In 2000, Crutzen and Eugene Stoermer posited the invention of the steam engine in 1784 as the start of the Anthropocene.[7] They also mentioned scientific precursors of the Anthropocene concept, from Antonio Stoppani and George Perkins March in the nineteenth century to Vladimir Vernadsky.[8] Since then, articles proposing a historical narrative of the Anthropocene have proliferated, as well as interdisciplinary projects that bring together scientists and historians (such as the IHOPE project: Integrated History and Future of People on Earth).[9] Specialists in environmental history such as John McNeill and Libby Robin have likewise joined with scientists in elaborating a historical account of the interactions between the human species and the Earth system since the end of the eighteenth century.[10]

The narratives of the anthropocenologists propose three 'stages'. The first, from the beginnings of the industrial revolution to the Second World War, corresponds to the turn into the Anthropocene, with the thermo-industrial revolution raising the concentration of atmospheric carbon dioxide from 277 to 280 parts per million (ppm) in the eighteenth century to 311 by the mid twentieth century (as against between 260 and 285 ppm for the 11,500 years of the Holocene). The mobilization of coal formed hundreds of millions of years ago started in China and in Europe in the eleventh century but only acquired a massive

7   Paul Crutzen and Eugene F. Stoermer, 'The "Anthropocene"', *Global Change Newsletter*, 41, 2000: 17–18. The steam engine, however, did exist before James Watt's patent of 1784, being basically used to pump water in mines.

8   We know from Georges Canguilhem the aporiai of the quest for precursors, and will not deal with this question in the present book.

9   Robert Costanza, Lisa J. Graumlich and Will Steffen (eds), *Sustainability or Collapse? An Integrated History and Future of People on Earth*, Cambridge, MA: MIT Press, 2007. See also aimes.ucar.edu/ihope.

10   Steffen, Crutzen and McNeill, 'The Anthropocene: Are Humans Now Overwhelming the Great Forces of Nature?'; Libby Robin and Will Steffen, 'History for the Anthropocene?', *History Compass*, 5:5, 2007: 1,694–719; John R. McNeill, *Something New under the Sun: An Environmental History of the Twentieth-Century World*, New York: Norton, 2001; Steffen et al., 'The Anthropocene: Conceptual and Historical Perspectives'.

scale from 1750 on, with the increase from some 500 steam engines in the whole world to hundreds of thousands by 1900. This fossil energy supplanted renewable energies, making possible the development of rail transport and global trade, facilitating access to water, and from the early twentieth century the chemical synthesis of nitrogen fertilizers that considerably increased agricultural yields. The availability of this 'ready' energy leads anthropocenologists to conclude that a rise in energy consumption by a factor of forty between 1800 and 2000 made possible economic growth by a factor of fifty, demographic growth by a factor of six, and an anthropic artificialization of land that increased by a factor of between 2.5 and 3 in this same period.[11]

A second stage in the Anthropocene opened after the Second World War. Anthropocenologists have called this the 'Great Acceleration,'[12] succinctly adducing a number of causal factors: the collapse of European pre-industrial institutions, a new international economic system of free trade, the technologies that were developed in the Second World War and now applied to civilian economic growth, and the establishment of markets and growth as 'central societal values.'[13] But the new historical stage is demonstrated above all by statistics. Figure 1 in Chapter 1 gives a dashboard display of twenty-four charts, measuring a spectrum of 'human activity indicators' characteristic of the Great Acceleration, from the concentration of atmospheric carbon and methane through to the number of large dams, by way of nitrogen and phosphorous cycles and the measure of biodiversity. All these graphs attest to an exponential upsurge in human impacts since 1950.

The third stage in the Anthropocene is seen as beginning around the year 2000, marked by a number of turning-points. As with the beginnings of the first stage, it is again carbon that governs this periodization, since the anthropocenologists note that 'environmental problems aroused little attention during the Great Acceleration . . . the major emerging environmental problems were largely ignored,'[14] and it

---

11   Steffen et al., 'The Anthropocene: Conceptual and Historical Perspectives', 848.

12   Ibid., 849.

13   Ibid., 850.

14   Ibid., 850 and 853.

was not until 2001 that the international scientific community, in the third report of the Intergovernmental Panel on Climate Change (IPCC), asserted for the first time with certainty the chiefly human origin of the climate change under way. The third stage in the Anthropocene was thus that of a new 'growing awareness of human impact on the global environment', as expressed by the IPCC or the Earth Summit of 1992 in Rio de Janeiro, as well as the 'first attempts to construct systems of global governance to manage the relations of humanity with the Earth system'.[15]

It was also the development of environmental accounting on a planetary scale that spurred these authors to discern a third phase: the perspective of the exhaustion of hydrocarbons (with a peak in conventional oil reached in 2006, according to the International Energy Agency), a phosphorous peak equally close and threatening agricultural production, and the accelerating reduction in biodiversity. As well as the volume of human impacts, it is also their distribution structure that is changing in this third stage. In the first decade of the new century, China overtook the United States as the world's largest emitter of carbon dioxide, while India took third place from Russia, South Korea caught up with the United Kingdom, and both Indonesia and Brazil overtook Germany. The countries of the OECD, which in 1971 emitted 67 per cent of carbon dioxide, made up only 42 per cent of the total in 2009.[16] The globalization of the development model born in the West is now making the upper social strata of the countries of the South into major contributors to human telluric action.

The story that anthropocenologists tell in these three phases presents a co-evolution of human species and the Earth system over the last centuries. Environmental history, which has long been mainly focused on particular territories or objects (fire, urban pollution, forests, pesticides),[17] thus advances to a global outlook, at the crossroads of recent advances in world history and the sciences of the Earth system.

---

15   Ibid., 856.

16   OECD, 'Emissions of Carbon Dioxide', in *OECD Factbook 2011–2012: Economic, Environmental and Social Statistics*, oecd-ilibrary.org.

17   With few exceptions, such as the works of Alfred Crosby and John McNeill.

After acknowledging the merits of this global perspective of socio-ecological metabolisms in the last quarter of a millennium, we can now question the particular forms of historical explanation as a function of the numbers and curves that this mobilizes.

A history in curves

The anthropocenologists' modalities of argument were imported into history from the environmental sciences, just as, in the mid twentieth century, history sought to become a science by way of quantitative series borrowed from the science of economics. Under the influence of economists such as Walt W. Rostow, whose classic *The Stages of Economic Growth* was published in 1960, the writing of history in terms of stages on a linear and universal path was standard practice: 'the traditional society, [then] the preconditions for take-off, [then] take-off, [then] the drive to maturity and [finally] the age of high mass-consumption'.[18] These stages were accessible to historical knowledge thanks to methods of the triumphant economic and social history that made quantity the key to historical narrative.

Let us look again at this second stage, the Great Acceleration. Some writers even propose having the Anthropocene start from this point in time, arguing from the vertiginous rise of the curves shown above. They point to a 'post-1950 acceleration' of different exponential curves with human impact on the planet.[19] By definition, an exponential curve is characterized by an increasingly steep slope (velocity) but a constant growth rate: there is no sudden jump in the growth rate at the end of the curve. Let us take for example the (almost exponential) curve of CO_2 emissions from fossil fuels – coal, gas and oil – as shown in Figure 4.

On Figure 4a, which shows emissions from 1750 to 2006, we can see a vertical rise after 1950. But let us now look at Figure 4b. This shows

18   Walt W. Rostow, *The Stages of Economic Growth: A Non-Communist Manifesto*, Cambridge: Cambridge University Press, 1960, 4.

19   Will Steffen et al., 'The Trajectory of the Anthropocene: The Great Acceleration', *Anthropocene Review* 2:1, April 2015 (first published online 16 January 2015): 81–98.

the same data but stops at 1914 and presents a similar vertical rise – though this time after 1880. Should we conclude that a 'great acceleration' took place in the years 1870–1914, and seek its causes in the second industrial revolution, the expansion of European imperialism, and the remarkable commercial and financial globalization of this period (Chapter 10)? Conclusion: if the seriousness and change of scale of human impacts on the Earth system from 1945 is incontestable, the slope of a curve is not in itself sufficient to decide on the start of a historical or geological epoch and can certainly not take the place of causal historical explanation.

Today, the notion of 'stages' seems to many historians obsolete and excessively teleological. And yet it has returned with the anthropocenologists' grand narrative, like an inverted replica of economic history

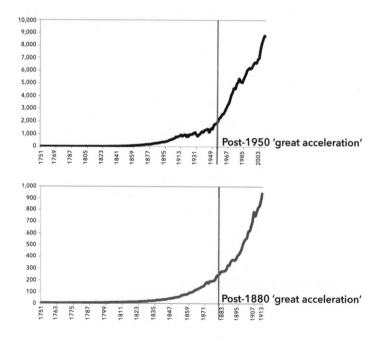

Figure 4: *Global carbon emissions from fossil fuels since 1751 (in millions of tons)*

à la Rostow. Just as the quantitative history of half a century ago, fascinated by the movement of technology and economics and challenging the primacy of politics, formed part of the productivist ideology of that time,[20] so the official narrative of the Anthropocene could well be part of the contemporary ideology of an ecological modernization and a 'green economy' that internalizes in markets and policies the value of the 'services' supplied by nature.

Indeed, quantifying nature is today big business, just as quantifying the economy had been after the Second World War. We should not be surprised, therefore, that the grand narrative of the anthropocenologists seeks truth by way of an accounting of the flows and stocks of nature. And it is no accident that one of their leading figures, the director of the IHOPE project, is Robert Costanza, a student of Howard T. Odum, the founder of the ecology of ecosystems. Costanza is a master in the accounting of nature. In 1997 he published a famous article in *Nature* that assessed the annual value of the services rendered by the biosphere at about $33 billion, or twice the world's GDP.[21] The notion of 'ecosystemic services' and the project of measuring their monetary value were inscribed in 2005 in the Millennium Ecosystem Assessment published by the UN. All values of nature, even those far upstream from production and including the most spiritual (renamed 'cultural services'), thus enter into an accounting logic. And the International Union for Conservation of Nature now presents nature as 'the largest company on Earth'.[22]

History as conceived by the anthropocenologists could thus be to contemporary green economics what economic and social history was to the Keynesian and productivist economics of the post-war

20 Jean-Baptiste Fressoz and François Jarrige, 'L'histoire et l'idéologie productiviste. Les récits de la révolution industrielle après 1945', in Céline Pessis, Sezin Topçu and Christophe Bonneuil (eds), *Une autre histoire des 'Trentes Glorieuses'. Modernisation, contestations et pollutions dans la France d'après-guerre*, Paris: La Découverte, 2013, 61–79.

21 Robert Costanza et al., 'The Value of the World's Ecosystem Services and Natural Capital', *Nature*, 387, 1997: 253–60, especially 254.

22 IUCN, 'Wildlife Crisis Worse than Economic Crisis – IUCN', news release, 2 July 2009, iucn.org.

period. Like the latter, it tells us a history governed by quantities, in this case biogeochemical and ecological ones. The principal marker that divides the Anthropocene into three stages is the concentration of carbon in the atmosphere, expressed in parts per million. This is followed in second place by other magnitudes such as global average temperature (an abstraction that does not correspond to any particular place), the percentages of the Earth's surface that are anthropized and the millions of tonnes of nitrogen and potassium that are in circulation. In each case, these quantities are related to the pre-industrial values as evidence of a leap into the Anthropocene and of limits that are dangerous to exceed.

This dominant history of the Anthropocene is written in the great book of global environmental accounting, with stocks being 'capital' and flows the 'impacts' or 'services' to be measured. In *Something New under the Sun*, the magnum opus on twentieth-century environmental history by the American historian John McNeill, the chapters are organized according to the various compartments of the Earth system: atmosphere, biosphere, hydrosphere, lithosphere.[23] This remarkable book of over 400 pages has only one page on the emergence of mass consumption and mass markets, five pages on international economic exchange and some twenty pages on political processes. The historical account of the environmental crisis that results from this is one of a more or less undifferentiated demographic, economic and technological growth, with no focus on the strategies of the actors involved, the choices that could have been made differently or the controversies and conflicts around these choices. We thus have a kind of global growth dynamic that serves as the motor of history and danger for the planet.

Systemization: the Earth as a great cybernetic machine?

Under such headings as 'Assessing Human Impacts on the Earth System' or 'Human-Nature Interactions', these historical narratives of a new type are full of concepts and methods that have been rather unfamiliar to historians until recently, such as 'non-linear systems',

23 McNeill, *Something New under the Sun*.

'multi-agent models', 'modelling', 'adaptive capacity', 'resilience' and 'socioecological systems'.[24] Such a story of the Anthropocene fits into a series of operations of systemization, which lead to conceiving the Earth as a 'complex system', a great self-regulating cybernetic machine (but one that human excesses could cause suddenly to deviate from its trajectory). It is important therefore to understand the historical genesis of this view, its contributions and its limitations.

The view of the Earth as a system lies at the source of modern geology. The term was used both by Charles Lyell and by James Hutton, his predecessor in the formulation of the uniformitarian theory. In his *Theory of the Earth* of 1788, Hutton presents the terrestrial system as 'a machine of a peculiar construction', with its components, mechanical principles and functions. But he goes on to add right away that the Earth can 'be also considered as an organized body', with 'a constitution in which the necessary decay of the machine is naturally repaired, in the exertion of those productive powers by which it had been formed'.[25] This tension between machine and organisms not only pervades all biological thinking, but also all thinking about the Earth.

After the Second World War, scientists sought to overcome this tension, to go beyond Cartesian analytic reductionism while preserving the ambition of control and engineering. This gave birth to the concepts of ecosystem and cybernetic machine, games theory and complex systems theory (or 'general system theory', in the title of the major book by the biologist and mathematician Ludwig von Bertalanffy, published in 1968).

James Lovelock, for his part, drew on this ambivalence between machine and organism in his famous 'Gaia hypothesis' of 1974.

---

24   See for example Marian Glaser et al. (eds), *Human-Nature Interactions in the Anthropocene*, London: Routledge, 2012.

25   James Hutton, *Theory of the Earth* (1788), 11 and 15. We are grateful to Pierre de Jouvancourt for drawing our attention to this author. See Pierre de Jouvancourt, 'Tenir à Gaïa. Une anthropologie politique de l'Anthropocène', master's thesis in philosophy, June 2013, University of Paris I; Christophe Bonneuil et Pierre de Jouvancourt, 'En finir avec l'épopée. Récit, géopouvoir et sujets de l'Anthropocène', in Émilie Hache (ed.), *De l'univers clos au monde infini*, Paris: Éditions Dehors, 2014, 57–105.

Having participated during the 1960s in a NASA project that aimed to identify criteria by which the possible presence of life on other planets could be detected, he asked what could explain such a long habitability of a planet by living beings as is found on Earth. Lovelock formulated the hypothesis that this habitability was also the product of the action of living beings themselves, acting to maintain conditions favourable to life.[26] The blue algae or 'cyanobacteria' that appeared more than 3 billion years ago actually changed the course of the Earth. As the first living creatures to practise photosynthesis, they fixed carbon from the atmosphere into sediment in the ocean depths and released oxygen into the air, making it possible for the animals that appeared later to breathe, and forming the ozone layer that protects the planet from highly mutagenic ultraviolet radiation. Without the action of algae and plants, the biogeochemical cycles that make it possible for various life forms to maintain themselves would not be the same. Hence the idea of Lovelock and Lynn Margulis that life, by acting on the various biogeochemical cycles, stabilizes the state of the Earth system, ensuring the continuous habitability of the planet. The Earth system sciences have in recent years confirmed the existence of feedback loops between the living world and the basic physico-chemical parameters of the Earth system, and recognized their intellectual debt to Lovelock.

If what is often associated with Lovelock is his image of a New Age sage, and the teleological tone of his theory, he was in reality a pure product of the scientific-military-industrial complex of the Cold War. After collaborating with NASA, he worked for the CIA during the Vietnam War on detecting human presence under forest cover. His post-democratic conception of planetary government, his apology for nuclear power and his systemic view of the planet as a self-regulated system are the legacy of a world-view born from the Second World War and the Cold War.

These global wars, in fact, promoted the emergence of new knowledge and world-views such as cybernetics, followed by

---

26 James Lovelock, *Gaia: A New Look at Life on Earth*, Oxford: Oxford University Press, 2001.

general systems theory, which claims to be applicable to all domains: every object of study from organisms to machines, cities to ecosystems, is broken down into discrete elements whose interactions and overall behaviour can then be analysed. Cybernetics, game theory and operational research became *the* privileged means for analysing situations, managing complex systems and rationalizing action, whether it was the Korean War, city planning, the management of health care or the whole Earth.[27] Simulations (computer models, war games or strategy games around the control of resources) thus played a determining role in the emergence of a new relationship to the Earth seen as a 'system'. The elites of the two post-war blocs conceived the planet as a 'closed world',[28] a unified theatre where the battle between the two super-powers was played out; a vast reserve of supplies of strategic resources to make possible a faster growth than the other bloc and ensure social peace; a 'gigantic laboratory'[29] with its thousands of nuclear explosions,[30] whose ecological and health effects were studied. Deriving from these 'closed world' views came the metaphor of

---

27   Amy Dahan and Dominique Pestre (eds), *Les Sciences pour la guerre, 1940–1960*, Paris: Éditions de l'EHESS, 2004; Peter Galison, 'The Ontology of the Enemy: Norbert Wiener and the Cybernetic Vision', *Critical Inquiry*, 21:1, 1994: 228–66; Robert Leonard, *Von Neumann, Morgenstern and the Creation of Game Theory: From Chess to Social Science 1900–1960*, Cambridge: Cambridge University Press, 2010; Geof Bowker, 'How to be Universal: Some Cybernetic Strategies, 1943–70', *Social Studies of Science*, 23:1, 1993: 117–27; Agatha C. Hughes and Thomas P. Hughes (eds), *Systems, Experts, and Computers: The Systems Approach in Management and Engineering, World War II and After*, Cambridge, MA: MIT Press, 2000.

28   The 'closed world' is the focus of the historian Paul N. Edwards, *The Closed World: Computers and the Politics of Discourse in Cold War America*, Cambridge, MA: MIT Press, 1997.

29   Georges Bernanos, 15 November 1945, quoted in Christophe Bonneuil, Céline Pessis and Sezin Topçu, 'Pour en finir avec les "Trentes Glorieuses". Vers une nouvelle histoire de la France des décennies d'après-guerre', in Pessis, Topçu and Bonneuil, *Une autre histoire des 'Trente Glorieuses'*, 19.

30   See the striking cartography of the 2,053 nuclear explosions between 1945 and 1998: 'A Time-Lapse Map of Every Nuclear Explosion Since 1945 – by Isao Hashimoto', YouTube video of Isao Hashimoto's 2003 multimedia artwork *1945–1998*, posted by 'aConcernedHuman', 24 October 2010, youtu.be/LLCF7vPanrY.

'Spaceship Earth'[31] that seen from the Moon suggests its finite and fragile character . . . not without giving a new sense of geo-technocratic power, the pleasure of imagining oneself piloting the whole system.

The Earth viewed from nowhere

The Anthropocene inherits a second element from the Cold War: a view of the Earth – and of our earthly issues – from above.[32] The V-2 missiles developed by Nazi technology were already used by the US Army in 1946 to measure solar radiation above the ozone layer and show the protective role this played.[33] Since the Cold War was global, the whole Earth became a strategic terrain to study. To guide ballistic missiles, a better knowledge of the atmosphere and geomagnetism was necessary. To cross and control the oceans, the oceanography of great depths had to be developed. To survey the movement of hostile subma-rines, it was necessary to know when and where they surfaced, and so to observe by satellite the polar ice caps and their seasonal changes.[34] According to the US Army in 1961, the 'environment in which the Army, Navy, Air Force and Marine Corps will operate covers the entire globe and extends from the depths of the ocean up to the far reaches of interplanetary space'.[35]

The scientific imaginary of the Anthropocene inherited ideologies, knowledge and technologies from the Cold War. Marshall McLuhan already proclaimed the end of Earth-nature and the emergence of a man-made Earth in a celebrated article of 1974:

---

31   The expression was coined by Kenneth Boulding in 1966.

32   The French term *vision déterrestrée* gets well to the point. It comes from Geneviève Azam, *Le Temps du monde fini. Vers l'après-capitalisme*, Paris: Les Liens qui libèrent, 2010. Heidegger already spoke in 1966 of an 'uprooting of man' by visualizations of Earth seen from space; see Benjamin Lazier, 'The Globalization of the World Picture', *American Historical Review*, 116:3, June 2011: 609.

33   Grevsmühl, *La Terre vue d'en haut*.

34   Ronald Doel, 'Quelle place pour les sciences de l'environnement physique dans l'histoire environnementale?', *Revue d'histoire moderne et contemporaine*, 56:4, 2009: 137–63.

35   Quoted in ibid., 158.

Sputnik created a new environment for the planet. For the first time the natural world was completely enclosed in a man-made container. At the moment that the Earth went inside this new artefact, Nature ended and Ecology was born. 'Ecological' thinking became inevitable as soon as the planet moved up into the status of a work of art.[36]

Hannah Arendt warned against this interpretation in 1958, opening her book *The Human Condition* with a reflection on the philosophical significance of Sputnik: man's alienation from 'an Earth who was the Mother of all living creatures under the sky',[37] from his original earthly cradle, detaching himself from it in order to look on it from above. She saw Sputnik as representing a modernist denial of the human condition, 'a rebellion against human existence as it has been given, a free gift from nowhere (secularly speaking), which he wishes to exchange, as it were, for something he has made himself'.[38]

These remarks of Arendt's could also apply to the Anthropocene: a humanity abolishing the Earth as natural alterity in order to occupy it entirely and transform it into a techno-nature, an Earth entirely permeated by human activity, as if only what *Homo faber* makes has any genuine value. Arendt denounced this 'instrumentalization of the whole world and the Earth, this limitless devaluation of everything given'.[39]

Since Sputnik, thousands of satellites have circled the Earth in ninety-minute orbits. Their electromagnetic waves now envelop the globe in a second atmosphere, a technosphere. The dense network of data gleaned from satellite observations, and the heavy computer infrastructure enabling this to be processed, are both part of the solution, by enabling us to know better the human impacts on the Earth, and part of the problem, the project of absolute domination of the planet that is one

---

36   Marshall McLuhan, 'At the Moment of Sputnik the Planet Became a Global Theater in Which There Are No Spectators but Only Actors', *Journal of Communication*, 24:1, 1974: 49.

37   Hannah Arendt, *The Human Condition*, Chicago: University of Chicago Press, 2013, 2.

38   Ibid., 2–3.

39   Ibid., 157.

of the causes of our further swing into the Anthropocene after 1945. This ambivalence was illustrated by the Apollo programme. On the one hand, it offered us the picture of the 'Blue Marble' (Figure 5), an iconic image for the Western environmental movement. On the other hand is the hubris of control: just after the 'conquest of the Moon' in July 1969, Werner von Braun – the Nazi inventor of the V-2 rocket, and subsequently father of the US space programme – announced to the press that 'from this marvellous observation platform we will be able to examine all the riches of the Earth: unknown oil wells, mines of copper and zinc'.[40] The Apollo missions also polluted the Moon by leaving behind plutonium-238 and caused the extinction of at least one species, the dusky seaside sparrow (*Ammodramus maritimus nigrescens*), killed by massive DDT spraying around NASA's space facility.[41]

Above all, the image of the Earth seen from space conveys a radically simplistic interpretation of the world.[42] It gives an intoxicating sense of total overview, global and dominating, rather than a sense of humble belonging. It crowns what Philippe Descola has called the 'naturalism' born in the West, by which we conceive other earthly creatures as sharing the same 'physicality' as we humans while having an interiority that is radically different from our own,[43] thus placing us at a vantage-point in relation to nature, a strategic external position from which the Earth system may be managed and piloted. This interpretation of our place on Earth from a spatial perspective thus extends a view of objectivity as the 'view from nowhere' born in the mid nineteenth century,[44] according to which true knowledge is that

---

40   See Eduardo Galeano, *Open Veins of Latin America*, London: Serpent's Tail, 2009, 134.

41   Fernando Elichirigoity, *Planet Management*, Evanston, IL: Northwestern University Press, 1999, 8. This bird species was endemic to the region of Florida that was set aside for space launches and sprayed with DDT.

42   Grevsmühl, *La Terre vue d'en haut*.

43   Philippe Descola, *Beyond Nature and Culture*, Chicago: Chicago University Press, 2013.

44   The notion of a 'view from nowhere' proposed by Thomas Nagel, and its history as a norm of scientificity in the nineteenth century, are analysed in Lorraine Daston, 'Objectivity and the Escape from Perspective', *Social Studies of Science*, 22:4, 1992: 597–618.

Figure 5: *The Earth seen from midway to the Moon, Apollo 17, 7 December 1972*

produced by abstraction from the system observed, so as to let nature speak for itself. In this view, it is only possible to understand and manage the planet's problems properly by looking at it from space, in a kind of 'de-Earthed' vision. This superior standpoint not only postulates that we have 'only one Earth' (the famous slogan of the Stockholm conference of 1972), but also that there is a superior knowledge of the planet's problems. It perpetuates a *naturalist* imaginary (which the anthropology of Philippe Descola has shown is only one of four main models for the relationship of humans to the world) and, still more, a 'de-Earthed' imaginary, the product of a techno-scientific culture that developed in parallel with the dynamics that have led us into the Anthropocene.

The dominant view of the Anthropocene hence encapsulates a long process of Weberian 'disenchantment', pre-eminence of 'instrumental rationality' (Adorno and Horkheimer) and negation of the world as given otherness (Arendt), a process that has made the moderns 'men without a world' (Déborah Danowski and Eduardo Viveiros de

Castro).[45] This imaginary is not neutral and dominates other imaginaries (such as those of indigenous communities and of other grassroots socio-environmental movements), which may themselves be the bearers of relevant perspectives and solutions in the face of our present ecological disarray.

---

45   Déborah Danowski and Eduardo Viveiros de Castro, 'L'arrêt de monde', in Hache, *De l'univers clos au monde infini*, 221–339.

CHAPTER 4

Who Is the Anthropos?

The official grand narrative of the Anthropocene presents not only a unique view of Earth, of which we should all have the same representation, 'from nowhere', but also a humanity seen as biological entity and geological agent. The grand narrative of the Anthropocene becomes that of 'the evolution of humans . . . from hunter-gatherers to a global geophysical force'.[1] The anthropocenologists then present themselves as guides for a 'humanity' deficient in knowledge, recommending it to 'reconnect with the biosphere'.[2] Let us decipher this view of *anthropos* and the implications it holds.

The odyssey of the species

'Humankind, our own species, has become so large and active that it now rivals some of the great forces of Nature in its impact on the functioning of the Earth system.'[3] This is the unchallengeable heart of the Anthropocene thesis. But it supports the idea of a totalization of the entirety of human actions into a single 'human activity' generating a single 'human footprint' on the Earth, an idea that

1   Will Steffen et al., 'The Anthropocene: Are Humans Now Overwhelming the Great Forces of Nature?', *Ambio*, 36:8, 2007: 614–21, 614.

2   Carl Folke and Lance Gunderson, 'Reconnecting to the Biosphere: A Social-Ecological Renaissance', *Ecology and Society*, 17:4, 2012: 55.

3   Will Steffen et al., 'The Anthropocene: Conceptual and Historical Perspectives', *Philosophical Transactions of the Royal Society A*, 369:1938, 2011: 842–67, 843.

deserves discussion. The key article on the Anthropocene and its history in *Philosophical Transactions* counts no less than ninety-nine occurrences of the adjective 'human' or the noun 'humanity'.[4] The anthropocenologists' dominant narrative of the Anthropocene presents an abstract humanity uniformly involved – and, it implies, uniformly to blame.

But viewing an undifferentiated *anthropos* as the cause of the Earth's new geological regime is scarcely sufficient. This explanation might be sufficient for polar bears or orangutans seeking to understand what species was disturbing their habitat.[5] And again, this would be orangutans and polar bears without much competence in 'humanology', unable to discern the 'dominant males' and asymmetries of power in the complex causal chain connecting the retreat of their habitat to human action. The human species' geological action is the product of cultural, social and historical processes.

The findings and approaches of decades of social sciences and humanities should not be overlooked in the name of ecological emergency and the interweaving of 'socio-ecosystems'. From the Marxist concept of class to the anthropology of Claude Lévi-Strauss, feminist and post-colonial studies, these works have attacked the old universalism of 'Man' and emphasized the equal dignity but also diversity of cultures, societies, social classes and sexual identities. And they have worked to make visible the mechanisms of domination by which certain of these collectives are destroyed, exploited or subjugated by others in asymmetrical social relations.

The advent of the Anthropocene concept turns the human and social sciences upside down, shaking their paradigms and categories.[6] Now it is the sciences of the Earth system, and no longer historians, who name the epoch in which we are living. And, as dizzying as it may

---

4   Ibid.

5   We have taken this joke from Andreas Malm and Alf Hornborg, 'The Geology of Mankind? A Critique of the Anthropocene Narrative', *Anthropocene Review*, published online 7 January 2014, anr.sagepub.com.

6   This is the contention of Dipesh Chakrabarty, 'Postcolonial Studies and the Challenge of Climate Change', *New Literary History*, 43:1, 2012: 1–18.

seem, scholars in the humanities need to rethink human action *also* on a geological scale of tens of thousands of years.

This dizziness has disarmed major thinkers in the human and social sciences, who, in their desire to contribute to the official narrative of the Anthropocene, have endorsed an all-inclusive view of humanity in which great socially indifferent causal factors such as demography, economic growth and the mobilization of fossil fuels are put forward as responsible for the unprecedented increase in the human footprint on the planet. In the end, however, these yield a rather poor explanatory grid. Thus, in an article of 2009 that drew great attention, Dipesh Chakrabarty, formerly a Marxist historian and a leading figure in subaltern studies, explained that the main critical categories he had previously applied to understand history had become obsolete in the time of the Anthropocene. He justified this great theoretical reversal as follows: 'A critique of capital is not sufficient for addressing questions relating to human history once the crisis of climate change has been acknowledged and the Anthropocene has begun to loom on the horizon of our present.'[7] In short, since capitalism has triggered a geological phenomenon far greater than itself, and one which will survive it, the critique of capitalism is no longer sufficient. Chakrabarty then gives the category of 'species' a major role in the historical narrative (fifty-one occurrences) and adopts the dominant phraseology of the anthropocenologists: 'Humans – thanks to our numbers, the burning of fossil fuel, and other related activities – have become a geological agent on the planet.'[8] This manner of envisaging causalities by placing humanity in the narrative as a universal agent, indifferently responsible, illustrates the abandoning of the grid of Marxist and postcolonial reading in favour of an undifferentiated humanity.

The dizziness of the human sciences in the face of the Anthropocene, the difficulty that they have in connecting socially differentiated historical phenomena with the evolution of the planet (with consequences

---

7 Dipesh Chakrabarty, 'The Climate of History: Four Theses', *Critical Inquiry*, 35; 2, 2009: 197–222, 212.

8 Ibid., 209.

for humans that are common yet differentiated), similarly emerges in the grandiose narratives of the environmental crisis. For major authors, either explicitly or implicitly, our ecological troubles are rooted in modernity itself. We find from their pens all the usual suspects in the great fresco of Western intellectual history: Greek science first of all, which conceived nature as an externality subject to laws independent of human intentions; then Christianity, which invented the singularity of man within a creation that was his to dominate; and finally the scientific revolution, which substituted for an organicist view of nature that of an inert mechanics which could be rationally modified.[9] The eschatological issue in the environmental crisis thus presses them to propose immense and majestic narratives, emphasizing a hypothetical 'great divide', a great separation between man and other beings.

Caught in the storm of Gaia, major sociologists and philosophers have decided to jettison from 'Spaceship Earth' the whole analytic, explanatory and critical arsenal of the human and social sciences. In a very influential essay, for example, Michel Serres deploys the geological metaphor of 'tectonic plates' visible 'from satellite': 'On Planet Earth, henceforth, action comes not so much . . . from the groups analysed by the *old social sciences* . . . no, the decisive actions are now, massively, those of enormous and dense tectonic plates of humanity'.[10] Whole books can now be written on the ecological crisis, on the politics of nature, on the Anthropocene and the situation of Gaia without so much as mentioning capitalism, war or the United States, even the name of one big corporation (one figure here, however: ninety corporations are responsible for 63 per cent of the cumulative emissions of carbon dioxide and methane between 1850 and today).[11]

---

9   Lynn White Jr., 'The Historical Roots of Our Ecological Crisis', *Science*, 155, 1967: 1,203–7; Carolyn Merchant, *The Death of Nature: Women, Ecology and the Scientific Revolution*, San Francisco: Harper, 1980; Philippe Descola, *Beyond Nature and Culture*, Chicago: Chicago University Press, 2013; Bruno Latour, *We Have Never Been Modern*, Cambridge, MA: Harvard University Press, 1991.

10   Michel Serres, *The Natural Contract*, Ann Arbor: University of Michigan Press, 1995, 16. Our emphasis.

11   Richard Heede, 'Tracing Anthropogenic Carbon Dioxide and Methane

A fruitful encounter between the Earth system sciences and the humanities would have to take into account social asymmetries and inequalities, exploring how these are mutually constructed – on different scales, including the global – with the distribution of flows of matter and energy through economic, political and technological mechanisms. This encounter has already taken place, for instance in dialogue between global history of the 'world-system' (in the wake of Immanuel Wallerstein's work) and the associated global ecological changes,[12] or again in the research field of political ecology.[13]

As a concept arising from Earth system sciences, it is natural that the Anthropocene should direct historical questioning according to their particular interests. For our anthropocenologists, the role of history consists in measuring the effect of human activities on the Earth system with a view to including them in the modelling, and, in return, testing the models in relation to past events. That is the specific perspective of the IHOPE project: Integrated History and Future of People on Earth.[14] The key terms here are biogeochemical cycles, integration (of data, systems, disciplines), complexity and non-linear systems. History might introduce a degree of unpredictability (how to model Hernán Cortés?), but in the end its results are fairly predictable: the Anthropocene is the product of a generalized increase in population, agriculture, industry, deforestation, mineral extraction and GDP.

Exaggerating a little, we could say that history for the anthropocenologists comes down in the end to a set of exponential graphs. The specificity of historical reasoning, the effort to construct an explanatory account, is eclipsed in favour of a descriptive and quantitative

---

Emissions to Fossil Fuel and Cement Producers, 1854–2010', *Climatic Change*, 122:1–2, 2014: 229–41.

12   Alf Hornborg, John R. McNeill and Joan Martínez Alier (eds), *Rethinking Environmental History: World-System History and Global Environmental Change*, New York: AltaMira Press, 2007; the writings of Kenneth Pomeranz, Mike Davis and Tim Mitchell also share this perspective.

13   See in particular Richard Peet, Paul Robbins and Michael Watts (eds), *Global Political Ecology*, London: Routledge, 2010.

14   Libby Robin and Will Steffen, 'History for the Anthropocene', *History Compass*, 5:5, 2007: 1,694–719.

view. But if the concordant upward curves are indeed chronological indexes, they are only explanatory at a secondary level. Environmental statistics simply measure the results of the historical phenomena that are the prime movers of the crisis. The less undifferentiated and more explanatory history of the Anthropocene that we propose in this book seeks to shift the focus of the study from the environments affected and the biogeochemical cycles disturbed onto the actors, institutions and decisions that have produced these effects.

The anthropocenologists' official narrative heralds the return of the human species into history. But what is this *anthropos*, the generic human being of the Anthropocene? Is it not eminently diverse, with extremely different responsibilities in the global ecological disturbance? An average American, for example, consumes thirty-two times more resources and energy than an average Kenyan. A new human being born on Earth will have a carbon footprint a thousand times greater if she is born into a rich family in a rich country, than into a poor family in a poor country.[15] Should the Yanomami Indians, who hunt, fish and garden in the Amazonian forest, working three hours a day with no fossil fuel (and whose gardens have a yield in energy terms nine times higher than the French farmers of the highly fertile Beauce),[16] feel responsible for the climate change of the Anthropocene? A recent report shows that the 1 per cent richest individuals on the planet monopolize 48 per cent of the world's wealth, while the poorer half of humanity have to make do with 1 per cent.[17] The eighty richest individuals in the world have a combined income higher than that of the 416 million poorest – each one

15   David Satterthwaite, 'The Implications of Population Growth and Urbanization for Climate Change', *Environment and Urbanization*, 21:2, 2009: 545–67. This study also shows how between 1980 and 2005 there was a negative correlation between greenhouse gas emissions and demographic growth.

16   Jacques Lizot, 'Économie primitive et subsistence. Essai sur le travail et l'alimentation chez les Yanomami', *LIBRE*, 4, 1978: 69–113. See also Geneviève Michon, 'Cultiver la forêt; sylva, ager ou hortus?', in Serge Bahuchet et al. (eds), *L'Homme et la forêt tropicale*, Châteaneuf-Grasses: Éditions de Bergier, 1999, 311–26. Our thanks to Thierry Sallantin for these references.

17   Credit Suisse, *Global Wealth Databook 2014*, Zurich: Credit Suisse Research Institute, 2014, credit-suisse.com.

earning more than a million times that of their fellow humans![18] This widening of inequalities is a major source of global ecological disarray, since the richest individuals set a standard of consumption that those below them seek to equal, and so on, as Thorstein Veblen already showed in 1899.[19] It follows from this, as has been recently demonstrated by economists, that policies of taxing the richest are beneficial to the environment.[20]

It would be better, indeed, to use Erik Swyngedouw's term 'Oliganthropocene', a geological epoch caused by a small fraction of humanity, rather than Anthropocene. The choice of this latter term, and the grand narrative that comes with it, actually uses the abstract category of 'human species' to mask the great differentiation of responsibilities and incidences between the classes, sexes and peoples of Gaia. This choice has its effects on the type of 'solutions' that are proposed for ecological problems, whether they are legitimated or not in the narrative of the anthropocenologists. The keynote article in *Philosophical Transactions* attests to this obscuring of asymmetries, which are mentioned only in passing in a delicate newspeak: 'Equity issues are often magnified in the Anthropocene.'[21]

We should be suspicious, therefore, of a grand narrative of the Anthropocene that presents interactions between the human species and the Earth system. This leads to historical explanations that are impoverished or erroneous, comforting the interests of a minority of the planet's population. On the contrary, the challenges of the Anthropocene demand a differentiated view of humanity, not just for the sake of historical truth, or to assess the responsibilities of the past, but also to pursue future policies that are more effective and more just; to construct a common world in which ordinary people

---

18   Hervé Kempf, *How the Rich Are Destroying the Earth*, White River Junction, VT: Chelsea Green Publishing, 2008.

19   Thorstein Veblen, *The Theory of the Leisure Class* (1899), Oxford: Oxford University Press, 2009.

20   Kempf, *Comment les riches détruisent la planète*.

21   Steffen et al., 'The Anthropocene: Conceptual and Historical Perspectives', 856.

will not be blamed for everything while the ecological crimes of the big corporations are left unpunished; in which the inhabitants of islands threatened by climate change will see their right to live on their territories recognized, without their weak numbers condemning them to statistical and political non-existence; a world in which the 30,000 people who still live as hunter-gatherers and are threatened with extinction by the year 2030 will continue to exist. The wealth of humanity and its capacity for future adaptation come from the diversity of its cultures, which are so many experiments in ways of worthily inhabiting the Earth.

'They knew not what they did': an account of the awakening of environmental consciousness

'Father, forgive them, for they know not what they do' are the words of Jesus on the cross as reported in the gospel of St Luke. Humans allowed the execution of the Saviour, but humanity is not irredeemably condemned as it could be in the Old Testament, once expelled from the Garden of Eden. Salvation is possible by conversion and faith.

Two centuries ago already, Charles Fourier used the rhetoric of revelation and pardon to foretell the 'material deterioration of the planet':

> This truth is more palpable for the moderns than for the ancients; the latter, still novices in the progress of society, may be pardoned for their illusions . . . but after the pictures that history has provided us with over 3,000 years . . . we have a superfluity of experience on the misdeeds of Civilization, and it is no longer permissible for upright men to deny that Civilization is the plague of humanity, that the present order of the globe is simply a material and social hell, and that reason should cease all other business to concern itself with seeking an escape from it.[22]

22   Charles Fourier, 'Détérioration matérielle de la planète', in René Schérer, *L'Écosophie de Charles Fourier. Deux textes inédits*, Paris: Economica, 2001, 81. This is a manuscript of 1820–21, published posthumously in *La Phalange* in 1847.

Two centuries after Fourier, the Anthropocene narrative works in a similar way: if the 'moderns' were at fault in disturbing the planet, they must be excused as they did not know what they were doing. They had neither science nor awareness of the global and geological character of their actions. The moderns only have to embrace the anthropocenic gospel to obtain remission of their sins and perhaps even salvation.

The grand narrative of the Anthropocene is thus the story of an awakening. There was a long moment of unawareness, from 1750 to the late twentieth century, followed by a sudden arousal. 'We are the first generation with the knowledge of how our activities influence the Earth system, and thus the first generation with the power and the responsibility to change our relationship with the planet',[23] the anthropocenologists maintain. 'Environmental problems received little attention during much of the Great Acceleration [after 1945]', and 'the emerging global environmental problems were largely ignored'.[24] In the same vein, James Lovelock asserted that 'by changing the environment we have *unknowingly* declared war on Gaia'.[25]

The media echo this cliché of an inadvertent environmental destruction and a quite recent awakening, the better to heroize those scientists who opened humanity's eyes. The newspaper *Libération* portrayed the glaciologist Claude Lorius in the following terms:

Now in the evening of his life, Claude Lorius knows that he was one of the scientists whose work enabled man to know what he is doing. And the question is not to pardon humanity for acting in the past without knowledge, but to act with this new knowledge that is inscribed in a new word . . . Anthropocene.[26]

---

23 Will Steffen et al., 'The Anthropocene: From Global Change to Planetary Stewardship', *Ambio*, 40, 2011: 739–61, 757.

24 Steffen et al., 'The Anthropocene: Conceptual and Historical Perspectives', 850 and 853.

25 James Lovelock, *The Revenge of Gaia*, London: Allen Lane, 2006, 13. Our emphasis.

26 Sylvestre Huet, 'Une ère conditionée', 22 January 2011, liberation.fr.

The *Economist* likewise evokes the coining of the new term in the first decade of the new century as 'one of those moments when a scientific discovery, as with Copernicus's understanding that the Earth moved around the Sun, could radically change our vision of things'.[27]

Major philosophers participate in this sublime concordance of contrition: in the past, we failed to recognize the global dimension of nature, we separated it from society, we reduced it to an external back-drop of human action. According to Michel Serres, it was only with the beginning of climate change in the late twentieth century that nature 'burst in on our culture, which had never formed anything but a local, vague, and cosmetic idea of them . . . What was once local – this river, that swamp – is now global: Planet Earth.'[28] In his commentary on an 1820 painting by Goya, with which Serres opens *The Natural Contract*, he maintains that at that time 'the world wasn't considered fragile',[29] while for Bruno Latour it is 'unwillingly' that humans have become geological agents.[30]

Whether scientists or philosophers, the anthropocenologists thus present subjects from the past who did not act deliberately, who were unaware – who once were blind but now can know. This accent on a radical break is a rhetorical feature of any prophetic discourse that seeks to win people to the idea of an advent. The narrative of the Anthropocene does not escape this.

But this binary narrative schema also derives from major social theories that oppose a non-reflexive moment of modernity (from the eighteenth to the twentieth century) to the emergence in the late twentieth century of a reflexivity on the side-effects of modernization such as health risks, major accidents and environmental crisis. This is the case with Anthony Giddens's thesis on 'reflexive modernity', Ulrich Beck's thesis on the 'risk society' heralding the end of a supposed

---

27   'The Geology of the Planet: Welcome to the Anthropocene', *Economist*, 26 May 2011.

28   Serres, *The Natural Contract*, 11.

29   Ibid., 3.

30   Bruno Latour, *Facing Gaia: Six Lectures on the Political Theology of Nature*, Gifford Lectures, 2013, 79, bruno-latour.fr (accessed 22 June 2013, link since suppressed).

innocence on the secondary effects of progress, or that of Michael Gibbons and his colleagues on a new 'mode 2' of production of knowledge, more open and reflexive.[31] It is also the perspective of the ecological modernization theory.[32]

We can include in this binary narrative the overly simple thesis according to which modernity has established a great separation between nature and society, a separation that allegedly prevented us from becoming aware of ecological issues, and that was only challenged quite recently. As if the thinkers of antiquity had not already established this division between nature and culture, whether to promote it or to question its value and limitations;[33] as if modernity, ever since the Renaissance, was not also constructed around knowledge that emphasized the belonging of human beings to the enveloping order of Nature.

Even from the subtle Bruno Latour, we find this 'great divide' narrative, only slightly modified. According to him, modernity lied to itself in believing it had cut itself off from nature, whereas in laboratories, the crucibles of this modernity, scientists enrolled non-human beings in combinations with humans, thus surreptitiously weaving new hybrid collectives despite claiming to separate nature and society, science and politics. Thus, for Latour, though 'we have never been modern' from the point of view of this break between nature and society, we can take account of this only now and thanks to his sociology of scientific practice, which makes it possible to solemnly close a falsely modern parenthesis of 300 years ... once again the alleged novelty of reflexivity![34]

---

31   Anthony Giddens, *The Consequences of Modernity*, Cambridge: Polity, 2013; Ulrich Beck, *Risk Society: Towards a New Modernity*, London: Sage, 1992; Ulrich Beck, Anthony Giddens and Scott Lash, *Reflexive Modernization: Politics, Tradition and Aesthetics in the Modern Social Order*, Cambridge: Polity, 1994; Michael Gibbons et al., *The New Production of Knowledge: The Dynamics of Science and Research in Contemporary Societies*, London: Sage, 1994.

32   Frederick H. Buttel, 'Ecological Modernization as Social Theory', *Geoforum*, 31:1, 2000: 57–65.

33   Stéphane Haber and Arnaud Macé (eds), *Anciens et modernes par-delà nature et société*, Besançon: Presses universitaires de Franche-Comté, 2012.

34   Jean-Baptiste Fressoz, 'The Lessons of Disasters: A Historical Critique of Postmodern Optimism', *Books and Ideas*, 27 May 2011, booksandideas.net.

The problem with all these grand narratives of awakening, revelation or arousal of consciousness is that they are historically wrong. The period between 1770 and 1830 was marked on the contrary by a very acute awareness of the interactions between nature and society (Chapter 8). Deforestation, for example, was conceived as the rupture of an organic link between woodland, human society and the global environment, and the use of coal was promoted as a way to restore forests. Neo-Hippocratic medicine explored interaction between the state of the organic body, that of the social body, and that of the environment. An organicist scientific thought conceived the Earth as a living being right to the mid nineteenth century. This attests to an intertwining of environments, bodies and societies. By proposing in 1821 that 'it is therefore the planet as a whole that is compromised [by deforestation and other environmental damages], and not just certain regions', Charles Fourier simply drew on a large number of scientific writings and warnings of his time.[35]

Yet it was in this very period that Western Europe plunged the world into the Anthropocene! Far from a narrative of blindness followed by awakening, we thus have a history of the marginalization of knowledge and alerts, a story of 'modern disinhibition'[36] that should be heeded (chapters 9 and 11). Our planet's entry into the Anthropocene did not follow a frenetic modernism ignorant of the environment but, on the contrary, decades of reflection and concern as to the human degradation of our Earth.

Likewise, the Great Acceleration of the Anthropocene after 1945 in no way went unperceived by the scientists or thinkers of the time (chapters 8 and 11). Well before the images of the Earth seen from the Moon, the atom bomb stood out as the event that unified the human condition and the Earth. The books *Road to Survival* by William Vogt and *Our Plundered Planet* by Henry Fairfield Osborn,[37] which together sold between 20 and 30 million copies, were organized respectively

---

35   Fourier, 'Détérioration matérielle de la planète', 117.

36   On the notion of 'modern disinhibition', see Jean-Baptiste Fressoz, *L'Apocalypse joyeuse. Une histoire du risque technologique,* Paris: Le Seuil, 2012.

37   Henry Fairfield Osborn Jr., *Our Plundered Planet,* Boston: Little, Brown, 1948; William Vogt, *Road to Survival,* New York: Sloane Associates, 1948.

around the inclusive categories of 'the planet' and 'the Earth', and launched a warning about the future of the global environment and its profound human repercussions. These authors already saw humanity as 'a geological force'.[38] Human action and natural cycles mutually determined one another in a 'total environment' of systemic character.[39] Following Svante Arrhenius, who explained the greenhouse effect in the late nineteenth century, the American scientists Roger Revelle and Hans Suess wrote in 1957:

> Human beings are now carrying out a large-scale geophysical experiment... Within a few centuries we are returning to the atmosphere and oceans the concentrated organic carbon stored in the sedimentary rocks over hundreds of millions of years. This experiment, if adequately documented, may yield a far-reaching insight into the processes determining weather and climate.[40]

It is either historical error or culpable ignorance, therefore, to maintain that 'we' entered the Anthropocene in the early nineteenth century, or with the Great Acceleration of the mid twentieth century, without awareness or knowledge of global ecological disturbances.

Why should we criticize the anthropocenologists, whether scientists or philosophers, for a grand narrative of this kind? After all, is this not needed to dismantle the opposing grand modernist narrative of progress? 'We have ... to counter a metaphysical machine with a bigger metaphysical machine!'[41] Does not the end (making humanity aware of the scale of ecological disarray) justify the means? Not as we see it.

First of all, because this fable, claiming to break with the worldview of the moderns that it incriminates, in the end actually

---

38   Osborn, *Our Plundered Planet*, 32 and 45.

39   Vogt, *Road to Survival*, 285.

40   Roger Revelle and Hans E. Suess, 'Carbon Dioxide Exchange between Atmosphere and Ocean and the Question of an Increase in Atmospheric CO_2 during the Past Decades', *Tellus*, 9, 1957: 18–27.

41   Bruno Latour, *An Inquiry into Modes of Existence: An Anthropology of the Moderns*, Cambridge, MA: Harvard University Press, 2013, 22.

reproduces it. It proceeds from the same regime of historicity that dominated the nineteenth century and a part of the twentieth, in which the past is assessed only as a backdrop, for the lessons it yields for the future, and in a representation of time as a one-directional acceleration.[42] It presents a 'modernization front',[43] leaving a blind past towards a future in which our knowledge will have become global and solid, eventually compelling us to take this into account in politics (but differently from before: with no 'great division', without an authoritarian Nature or blind certainties). The new teleology of ecological reflexivity and collective learning replaces the old teleology of progress. Such heralding of the end of modernization is in fact a new modernist fable.

Secondly, this narrative, 'forgetting' the environmental reflexivity of modern societies, tends to depoliticize the ecological issues of the past and thus obstructs understanding of present issues. Taken seriously, the Anthropocene and its continuing acceleration buries the dream of a society that has at last become reflexive. Who can still believe that if individuals, societies, states and corporations do not behave in an ecologically sustainable way, it is because the scientific knowledge to convince them is still too recent or not yet complete? Scholarly work in the human and social sciences shows how certain socio-economic and cultural processes are far more determining than the quantity of scientific information: such phenomena as lobbying, story-telling, rebound effect, technological coup, greenwashing, recuperation of criticism, complexification, banalization or a simulated taking into account.[44] There is a whole arsenal that makes it possible to ignore warnings and protests; it is important to see this at work in the past and propose a dynamic reading of it, one politically less naive than the grand narrative of an awakening of awareness (Chapter 11).

---

42   François Hartog, *Régimes d'historicité. Présentisme et experiences du temps*, Paris: Seuil, 2001.

43   The expression is Latour's, in *An Inquiry into Modes of Existence*.

44   Ingolfur Blühdorn, 'The Politics of Unsustainability: COP15, Post-Ecologism, and the Ecological Paradox', *Organization and Environment*, 24:1, March 2011: 34–53.

Rather than suppressing the environmental reflexivity of the past, we must understand how we entered the Anthropocene *despite* very consistent warnings, knowledge and opposition, and forge a new and more credible narrative of what has happened to us.

A grand narrative with scientists as its heroes

The assimilation of the environmental preoccupations and knowledge of the past to timid and incomplete 'precursors' leads to an exaggerated glorification of today's scientific knowledge. The grand narrative of the Anthropocene places *anthropos*, humanity, into two categories: on the one hand, the uninformed mass of the world population, who have become a geological agent without realizing it, and on the other, a small elite of scientists who reveal the dramatic and uncertain future of the planet. In the former, we have a non-reflexive group objectified by demography, biology and economics; in the latter, an idealist history made up of intellectual filiations, precursors and stubborn resistances:

> In the sixteenth century America was discovered. In the twenty-first century, it is not in the sense of an extension of space that other lands that are discovered, but rather in the sense of an intensification of our relationship to this Earth ... The Anthropocene and Gaia are two concepts developed by researchers in the exact sciences; extraordinarily more advanced for their time than the whole mass of intellectuals, politicians and artists interested only in the history of human beings.[45]

In this type of prophecy, the modernist fable that places specialists in the Earth system in the glorious filiation of the explorers of the sixteenth century (as if America had not been 'discovered' by the humans who crossed the Bering Strait more than 25,000 years ago,

---

45   Interview cited by Weronika Zarachowich, 'Gaia, la Terre mère, est-elle obligée d'aimer ses enfants?' *Télérama*, 3303, 4 May 2013, telerama.fr. This may well be more journalistic than the thought of Bruno Latour, but it is still significant in terms of the grand narrative.

by the Polynesians who brought back the sweet potato a thousand years before Christopher Columbus, and then by the Vikings around 1000 AD), scientists are represented as the ecological vanguard of the world. Not only do they appear as spokespeople for the Earth, but also as shepherds of a public opinion that is ignorant and help-less. In this dominant grand narrative of the Anthropocene, humans have been 'wandering in the desert', but can finally 'reach not the Promised Land but Earth itself, quite simply . . . the aptly named Gaia',[46] or again experience a new Renaissance by 'reconnecting with the biosphere'.[47]

This then is a prophetic narrative that places the scientists of the Earth system, with their new supporters in the human sciences, at the command post of a dishevelled planet and its errant humanity. A geo-government of scientists! By throwing overboard the categories of the 'old social sciences', bearing on asymmetries between human groups, do democratic political ideals also have to be cast adrift? What is left for a politics on the geological scale to which the Anthropocene summons us? What can we still do on the individual and collective scale given the massive scale of the Anthropocene? The risk is that the Anthropocene and its grandiose time frame anaesthetizes politics. Scientists would then hold a monopoly posi-tion both in defining what is happening to us and in prescribing what needs to be done.

This is how experts in global environment, in keynote articles that introduced the concept of Anthropocene in 2000 and 2002, imagine the rescue of humanity by science and engineering:

Mankind will remain a major geological force for many millennia, maybe millions of years, to come. To develop a world-wide accepted strategy leading to sustainability of ecosystems against human induced stresses will be one of the great future tasks of mankind, requiring intensive research efforts and wise application of the knowledge thus acquired . . . An exciting, but also difficult and daunting task lies ahead

---

46   Latour, *An Inquiry into Modes of Existence*, 23.
47   Folke and Gunderson, 'Reconnecting to the Biosphere', 55.

of the global research and engineering community to guide mankind towards global, sustainable, environmental management.[48]

A daunting task lies ahead for scientists and engineers to guide society towards environmentally sustainable management during the era of the Anthropocene. This will require appropriate human behaviour at all scales, and may well involve internationally accepted large-scale geo-engineering projects, for instance to 'optimize' climate.[49]

We see here how at the same time as the Anthropocene is announced, geoengineering (the set of technologies for manipulating climate on a global scale, by the emission of sulphurous aerosols into the atmosphere, iron into the oceans, reflective satellites around the Earth, etc.) is promoted, despite its uncertainties and dangers (hundreds of thousands of premature deaths to be imagined in the case of the 'solution' of sulphurous aerosols),[50] and despite the existence of a UN moratorium on such interventions. In the journal of the British Royal Society, four anthropocenologists precisely list the 'innovative approaches' that scientific technology can contribute as responses to ecological disarray. Not only do these include large-scale technological systems to pursue the observation of the planet and set scientifically the limits that humanity must not exceed, but also synthetic biology to create new artificial forms of biodiversity, adaptive management applying the rules of ecology to public action, and geoengineering to remake the climate.[51]

Does the irruption of nature into politics imply entrusting ourselves completely to scientists, or on the contrary a critique of technoscience and the abandonment of a posture of mastery of the Earth? The first option seems the only one possible in the

---

48   Paul J. Crutzen, 'Geology of Mankind', *Nature*, 415, 3 January 2002: 23.

49   Paul J. Crutzen and Eugene F. Stoermer, 'The "Anthropocene"', *Global Change Newsletter*, 41, 2000: 18.

50   For a discussion of the issues involved in geoengineering, see Clive Hamilton, *Earthmasters: The Dawn of the Age of Climate Engineering*, New Haven: Yale University Press, 2013.

51   Steffen et al., 'The Anthropocene: Conceptual and Historical Perspectives', 858.

Anthropocene's dominant grand narrative. If past innovations upset the planet, let's have the innovating approaches that contemporary technology presents. In the major scientific periodicals dealing with the Anthropocene, everything is presented as if the environmental knowledge and initiatives of civil society did not exist. Indigenous peoples struggling against the devastation of mining or oil exploitation on their lands, activists who build tree cabins in the path of bulldozers constructing pipelines and airports, antinuclear or neo-Luddite, anti-high-tech movements, collectives that experiment with less materialistic and 'simpler' ways of living, 'degrowth' practitioners or the 'transition towns' movement, all of these are absolutely invisible in the grand narrative. If we believe the anthropocenologist experts, serious solutions can only emerge from further technological innovation in the laboratory, rather than from alternative political experiment 'from below' in society as a whole! This is how Bruno Latour asks the sorcerer's apprentices to return to their laboratories to save humanity:

> We remember perhaps how, in the novel by Mary Shelley, Dr Victor Frankenstein accused himself of one sin – that of having been a sorcerer's apprentice – only to disguise another infinitely more serious, that of having been horrified by the sight of his creature, who had only become a monster because its author had abandoned it. Instead of crying: 'Victor, stop innovating, believing, growing and creating', it would seem more fruitful for him to have said, in the end: 'Dr Frankenstein, return to your laboratory and finally give a face to your unsuccessful attempt.' But how will we be able to return to our laboratories and revise every detail of our material existence?[52]

While criticizing the modernization project and viewing the Anthropocene as a refutation of modernity, Bruno Latour, together with the Breakthrough Institute's 'ecomodernists', urges us to 'love our monsters'. He reads Mary Shelley's *Frankenstein* not as a cautionary tale against technological hubris, but rather against irrational fears in

---

52   Bruno Latour, 'En attendant Gaïa', *Libération*, 29 June 2011.

the face of technology's side-effects. Dr Frankenstein failed not because he created a monster but because he fled in horror instead of repairing and improving him. 'The sin is not to wish to have dominion over nature', goes the story, 'but to believe that this dominion means emancipation and not attachment.'[53]

'They still don't know what to do': the 'public' seen by the Anthropocene experts

If humanity needs scientific shepherds and eco-Frankensteins, this is, according to the anthropocenologists, because traditional politicians have failed, while the public is insufficiently aware or trapped in a 'cognitive dissonance'. The whole world needs to be educated, enlightened by the luminaries of science:

> Up to now the concept of Anthropocene has been confined almost entirely to the research community. How will it be perceived by the public at large and by political or private sector leaders? . . . The notion, subsequently strengthened by further scientific research, that we are 'just' another ape and not a special creation 'above' the rest of nature shook the society of Darwin's time, and still causes tension and conflict in some parts of the world . . . The concept of Anthropocene, as it becomes more well known in the general public, could well drive a similar reaction to that which Darwin elicited . . . [T]he Anthropocene will be a very difficult concept for many people to accept.[54]

While the Earth system scientists compare themselves to Darwin, Latour compares Lovelock to Galileo and Pasteur.[55] Praise of this kind paints the picture of a science well above society, bringing revolutionary findings that shatter accepted beliefs. The anthropocenologists

---

53   Bruno Latour, 'Love Your Monsters', in Michael Shellenberger and Ted Nordhaus (eds), *Love Your Monsters: Post-Environmentalism and the Anthropocene*, San Francisco: Breakthrough Institute, 2011, 17–25, 24.

54   Steffen et al., 'The Anthropocene: Conceptual and Historical Perspectives', 860 and 862.

55   Ibid.

then turn to psychosociology to understand why the public resist the evidence of facts that show the gravity of global ecological unbalances. Diagnosis: the public suffer from cognitive dissonance, described half a century ago by psychology as a phenomenon of distancing between what one learns (in this case, for example, climate disturbance) and what one clings to (here, the continuance of a certain way of life): 'When facts that challenge a deeply held belief are presented, the believer clings even more strongly to his or her beliefs and may begin to proselytize fervently to others despite the mounting evidence that contradicts the belief.'[56]

After Galileo and Darwin, therefore, we are said to be in a new stage of history in which 'science' must turn upside down a 'system of belief' of society. Like the dogma of the virgin birth of Jesus, in which God saves the world without compromising himself with humans, it is from a distance, way above society, without a dialogue with socioecological movements or accepting its part and responsibility for the first two centuries of the Anthropocene, that science is presented as our saviour. In this logic, the right policy will be that which involves the 'advised application' of the neutral findings of science. Humanity will become ecologically sustainable when the scientific message has properly penetrated it and humanity has adopted its solutions.

Age of man, death of nature?

Announcing the advent of the Anthropocene makes it possible for certain anthropocenologists to proclaim the death of Nature with a capital 'N', nature seen as external to humans. We are said to be entering an anthropo-nature, a techno-nature, a post-nature (Latour) that is hybrid and dynamic, in which humans will at last recognize themselves as taking part: 'There is no ecosystem without humans and no humans who do not depend on the functioning of ecosystems.'[57]

The old nature no longer exists. The myth of the *wilderness*, external and virgin, is shattered. Natural parks and reserves are criticized on all

---

56   Ibid., 861–2.
57   Folke and Gunderson, 'Reconnecting to the Biosphere', 55.

sides for having excluded local populations: from now on nature has to be participative: 'No need to be a postmodernist in order to understand that the concept of Nature . . . has always been a human construction, forged for human purposes.'[58]

In fact, cybernetics and the cyborg science of the post-war era did not wait for Latour, Donna Haraway or Philippe Descola to celebrate the dissolution of the nature/culture boundary, since they precisely sought to optimize systems that connected humans and non-humans. Thus, as Catherine and Raphaël Larrère have shown, 'the thesis of the end of nature is that of its complete intelligibility . . . and of its complete mastery.'[59] In the sciences of conservation, the notion of the Anthropocene is accompanied by the diffusion of a doctrine accepting the inevitable character of certain modes of artificialization of nature, proclaiming that what matters is to preserve biodiversity as a function of the services it provides for humans rather than as a value in itself, or again presenting urban nature as having as much value as so-called 'wild' nature.

The dominant narrative of the anthropocenologists magnifies the irruption of human action as a telluric force. We have become 'equipotent to the Earth'.[60] The figure that is put forward is that of 'Man, gardener of the planet'. This new model of the biosphere moves us away from an outdated view of the world as 'natural ecosystems with humans disturbing them' and towards a vision of 'human systems with natural ecosystems embedded within them'.[61]

Thus, the sublime of catastrophe is succeeded by the giddiness of omnipotence. For Mark Lynas, 'Nature no longer runs the Earth. We do. It is our choice what happens here.'[62] After having briefly raised fear by imagining a planet out of control, a number of scientists and

---

58   Michelle Marvier, Robert Lalasz and Peter Kareiva, 'Conservation in the Anthropocene: Beyond Solitude and Fragility', *Breakthrough*, Winter 2012, thebreakthrough.org. See also Emma Maris, *Rambunctious Garden: Saving Nature in a Post-Wild World*, London: Bloomsbury, 2011.

59   Catherine and Raphaël Larrère, *Du bon usage de la nature*, Paris: Aubier, 1997, 9.

60   Serres, *The Natural Contract*, 110.

61   Erle Ellis and Navin Ramankutty, 'Anthropogenic Biomes', *The Encyclopedia of Earth*, 3 September 2013, eoearth.org.

62   Mark Lynas, *The God Species*, London: Fourth Estate, 2011, 8.

journalists have adopted the almost glorious story of the advent of humanity as pilot and engineer of the planet.[63]

What does it mean for us humans to have the future of the planet in our hands? A feeling of terror, very soon combined with a sense of power? After centuries of doing geo-bioengineering without knowing it, are we now in a position to make all our interactions with Gaia conscious, voluntary and scientifically calculated, to convert ourselves to a generalized ecological engineering? Whereas it should mean a call to humility, the Anthropocene is summoned in support of a planetary hubris. 'We've engineered every other environment we lived in, why not the planet?' asks Lowell Wood, an astrophysicist and champion of geoengineering.[64] We will be 'proud of the planet that we create', adds the geographer Erle Ellis, one of the first anthropocenologists and a member of the Breakthrough Institute, an eco-modernist think-tank that celebrates the death of nature and preaches a 'good anthropocene', one in which advanced technology will save the planet.[65]

To position humanity in this way as pilot means seeing the Earth as simply a cybernetic machine, rather than a dynamic becoming and a history. It also means, with the functional discourse of an anthropo-nature, denying nature and Gaia any alterity: even if we are part of it, and if nature must be brought within our collective politics, it is important to recognize this alterity, through a listening that is not instrumental and a respect for certain limits to human action. Fusion and omnipotence, these sentiments characteristic of early infancy, lie at the basis of such 'post-nature' discourse, participating in the dream of a total absorption of nature into the commercial technosphere of contemporary capitalism (Chapter 9).[66]

---

63   For an example of technophile and cornucopian vulgarization of the Anthropocene, see Christian Schwägerl, *The Anthropecene: The Human Era and How It Shapes Our Planet*, Santa Fe: Synergetic Press, 2014.

64   Cited by Hamilton, *Earthmasters*, 135.

65   Erle C. Ellis, 'Neither Good nor Bad', *New York Times*, 23 May 2011, nytimes.com. For a critical reading of the eco-modernism of the Breakthrough Institute, see Clive Hamilton, 'The New Environmentalism Will Lead Us to Disaster', *Scientific American*, 19 June 2014, scientificamerican.com.

66   Virginie Maris, 'Back to the Holocene: A Conceptual, and Possibly Practical, Return to a Nature not Intended for Humans', in Clive Hamilton,

The discourse of a new geopower

The representation of the Earth and its contemporary disarray proposed by the anthropocenologists must be taken seriously, in two ways. On the one hand, it brings knowledge and warnings that are absolutely essential and indispensable, while on the other, it is a product of Western naturalism and the scientific culture of the Cold War. It cannot be the unique point of view, the unique imaginary of the Earth, or the unique way of inhabiting it collectively and in peace. There are multiple narratives about the change of existential regime under way on our Earth. In Western culture alone it is possible to distinguish at least five: the (naturalist) official narrative that prevails today in the scientific and international arenas (discussed in chapters 3 and 4), the post-nature and 'eco-modernist' narrative of a high-tech 'good Anthropocene' (as mentioned above), an eco-catastrophist narrative that envisions a collapse of industrial civilization and seeks local resilience, an eco-Marxist narrative in which the Anthropocene is better described as a 'Capitalocene' (see Chapter 10) and an eco-feminist one that relates male domination to the degrading of the Earth.[67] But many more narratives, imaginaries, cosmologies and types of knowledge have an essential role to play in order to inhabit the Earth in a proper fashion. We need a variety of civic initiatives and popular alternatives, of transition and abstemiousness, which explore the outlines of 'living better with less', rather than relying upon 'solutions' offered by a circle of planetary eco-technocrats. It is also essential to note in the dominant narratives of the Anthropocene (the first two of the five mentioned narratives) the elements that could form part of a new *geopower*.

What do we mean by geopower? As historians have shown (Michel

François Gemenne and Christophe Bonneuil (eds), *The Anthropocene and the Global Environmental Crisis: Rethinking Modernity in a New Epoch*, London: Routledge, 2015, 123–33; see also Frédéric Neyrat, *Enquête sur la part inconstructible de la terre. Critique du géo-constructiviste*, Paris: Seuil, 2016.

67   For a comparative analysis of the first four of these grand narratives of the Anthropocene, see Christophe Bonneuil, 'The Geological Turn: Narratives of the Anthropocene', in Hamilton, Gemenne and Bonneuil, *The Anthropocene and the Global Environmental Crisis*, 17–31.

Foucault above all), the biological knowledge of the nineteenth and twentieth centuries made possible the constitution of new scientific objects:
'population', 'life' and 'race'. Biological advances heralded a new form of
power, biopower, with the particular property of taking biological life as
an object and political project. This biopower, characteristic of the industrial age and the construction of the nation-state, aimed to optimize the
number, quality (health, physical, intellectual, genetic, etc.), military
'strength' (war becoming total) and productivity of populations.[68]

The new knowledge and imaginaries of the global environment that
have asserted themselves since the Cold War, and the dominant narratives of the Anthropocene, can be read as elements of a new
knowledge-power that bears not only on the 'bio' but also on the 'geo'.
After life, it is the Earth as a whole (from the lithosphere to the stratosphere) that simultaneously becomes the object of knowledge
('geo-knowledge') and government ('geopower'). The advent of new
subjectivities of 'citizens of the planet', the geological turn of our –
previously ecological – understanding of the 'global environmental
crisis', its increased timescale that seems to make the ordinary time of
collective and political action inoperative (if the problem is geological,
what can the mere citizen do except trust experts?), the hyper-
interdisciplinarity of global expertise of Earth socioecological systems
as envisaged by the IPCC (or 'Future Earth', the recent global research
platform launched by the UN), and finally the monitoring systems of
the planet by satellite,[69] are so many indexes of the emergence of a new
geopower that establishes the Earth as a 'system' to know and govern as
a totality, in all its components and all its functions.

It is true that an 'imperial ecology'[70] developed in the nineteenth
century, but it was only well after the Second World War, with atomic
weapons, new international institutions and, above all, a Cold War

---

68   Michel Foucault, *A History of Sexuality. Volume 1: An Introduction*, New
York: Vintage, 1990, 135ff. Paul Rabinow and Nikolas Rose, 'Biopower Today',
BioSocieties, 1, 2006: 195–217.

69   Paul N. Edwards, *A Vast Machine: Computer Models, Climate Data, and
the Politics of Global Warming*, Cambridge, MA: MIT Press, 2010.

70   Peder Anker, *Imperial Ecology: Environmental Order in the British Empire,
1895–1945*, Cambridge, MA: Harvard University Press, 2001.

that conceived the whole globe as the theatre of an imminent conflict, that a new knowledge-power of the entire globe was born, from the submarine depths to the Moon.[71] At the same time, ecology became systemic and global. The biosphere, a concept initially proposed by Vladimir Vernadsky in the 1920s, was thus redefined by UNESCO in 1968 as 'an ancient, extremely complex, multiple, all-planetary, thermodynamically open, self-controlling system of living matter and dead substance which accumulates and redistributes immense resources of energy and determines the composition and dynamics of the Earth's crust, atmosphere and hydrosphere'.[72] Armed with this cybernetic conception of nature, the champions of systems ecology claimed the role of global experts in the governing of the planet's 'biological productivity' – a term frequently encountered in articles of the time, with a view to reconciling short-term economic profitability with the long-term maintenance of the ecosystems that supplied resources.[73]

This understanding of the environment as a global system to control and optimize formed part of a *Weltanschauung* of the 'closed world' forged in each bloc by the culture of the Cold War (Chapter 3). The United States, in particular, saw itself as the guardian of the progress of the whole world and worked for the establishment of a global market. There then emerged a new planetary subjectivity, a new deterritorialized and uniform way of inhabiting the Earth. Whatever

---

71 Ronald E. Doel, 'Quelle place pour les sciences de l'environnement physique dans l'histoire environnementale?', *Revue d'histoire moderne et contemporaine*, 56:4, 2009: 137–64; Yannick Mahrane and Christophe Bonneuil, 'Gouverner la biosphère. De l'environnement de la guerre froide à l'environnement néolibéral, 1945–2013', in Dominique Pestre (ed.), *Le Gouvernement des technosciences. Gouverner le progrès et ses dégâts depuis 1945*, Paris: La Découverte, 2014, 133–69.

72 UNESCO, *Final Report: Intergovernmental Conference of Experts on the Scientific Basis for Rational Use and Conservation of the Resources of the Biosphere*, Paris, 1970, 15.

73 Yannick Mahrane et al., 'From Nature to Biosphere: The Political Invention of the Global Environment, 1945–1972', *Vingtième siècle. Revue d'histoire*, 113, 2012: 127–41, available in English only online at http://www.cairn-int.info/article-E_VIN_113_0127--from-nature-to-bioshpere.htm; Chunglin Kwa, 'Representations of Nature Mediating between Ecology and Science Policy: The Case of the International Biological Programme', *Social Studies of Science*, 17:3, 1987: 413–42.

the place you found yourself, you were subject to the universal struggle of 'freedom versus slavery',[74] prey to new fears and scenarios of planetary catastrophe,[75] and the subject of a 'state of exception' (Giorgio Agamben) justified by the threat of death from attack by the opposing bloc (today by climate disruption or a global collapse). Caring for nature thus became 'managing planet Earth',[76] whether to extract a maximum and sustainable yield, or to limit (and adapt to) its tempestuous disruptions. This is how the Brundtland Report depicted the human condition in the age of this new geopower:

> In the middle of the twentieth century, we saw our planet from space for the first time. Historians may eventually find that this vision had a greater impact on thought than did the Copernican revolution of the sixteenth century . . . This new reality, from which there is no escape, must be recognized – and managed.[77]

Geopower is based on a common matrix and mechanisms in which knowledge, power and subjects of a new type emerge together. This geopower exhorts its subject, the *anthropos*, to 'reconnect with the biosphere' and tends to establish an ever-greater number of human problems as soluble only at a global level and only by way of technological solutions.[78] The nascent geopower is a 'space of calculation' (Foucault) at the level of the Earth system: accounting of flows of matter and energy and of 'natural capital', markets in 'ecosystemic

---

74   Paul Edwards, 'Construire le monde clos. L'ordinateur, la bombe et le discours politique de la guerre froide', in Amy Dahan and Dominique Pestre (eds), *Les Sciences pour la guerre. 1940–1960*, Paris: Éditions de l'EHESS, 2004, 225–6.

75   Joseph Masco, 'Bad Weather: On Planetary Crisis', *Social Studies of Science*, 40:1, 2010: 7–40.

76   The title of a 1989 compilation of *Scientific American*.

77   United Nations Commission on Environment and Development, *Our Common Future*, Oxford: Oxford University Press, 1987.

78   Clark Miller, 'Resisting Empire: Globalism, Relocalization, and the Politics of Knowledge', in Sheila Jasanoff and Marybeth Long Martello (eds), *Earthly Politics*, Cambridge, MA: MIT Press, 2004, 81–102; Arturo Escobar, 'Whose Knowledge, Whose Nature? Biodiversity Conservation and the Political Ecology of Social Movements', Journal of Political Ecology, 5, 1998: 53–82.

services', control and management of the components and processes of the Earth system, instruments of anticipation, prediction and global simulation, and making places commensurable in an isonomic space.

This geopower, faced with the upheavals of the Earth system under way, aspires to regulate the globe's thermostat and, in order to do so, to control the Earth by a new engineering of humanity's envelopes.[79] The project of geoengineering is a concrete embodiment of the nascent geopower. Its aim is nothing less than 'improvement of the environmental characteristics of the atmosphere',[80] or even the entire functioning of the planet, biosphere included. Still more here than with nuclear tests or the imaginary of 'Spaceship Earth', the entire Earth is now explicitly reified as object of experimentation and control.

The project of climate engineering goes back to the Cold War. For example, the technology of 'global management of solar radiation' by dispersal of aerosols in the upper atmosphere finds its origin in a proposal by the Soviet scientist Mikhail Budyko at a conference held in Leningrad in 1961 on 'problems of climate control', warning that human activities could in due course shift the Earth's radiative balance. His colleague M. Ye Shvets then proposed injecting 36 million tonnes of aerosols into the stratosphere in order to reduce solar radiation by 10 per cent.[81] An analogous project can be found in the writings of James Lovelock, who, after working for NASA on a programme for the colonization of Mars, published in 1984 a fiction that imagined the use of intercontinental missiles spreading hundreds of tonnes of chlorofluorocarbons around the red planet in order to create a greenhouse effect that would make it habitable.[82] Born in the post-war United States,

---

79   Peter Sloterdijk, *Règles pour le parc humain. Suivi de La Domestication de l'être*, Paris: Fayard, 2010.

80   G. M. Batanov, I. A. Kossyi and V. P. Silakov, 'Gas-Discharge Method for Improving the Environmental Characteristics of the Atmosphere', *Plasma Physics Reports*, 28:3, 2002: 204–28.

81   James R. Fleming, *Fixing the Sky: The Checkered History of Weather and Climate Control*, New York: Columbia University Press, 2010, 236. See also Hamilton, *Earthmasters*; Sebastian Grevsmühl, *La Terre vue d'en haut. L'Invention de l'environnement global*, Paris: Seuil, 2014.

82   Michael Allaby and James Lovelock, *The Greening of Mars*, London: André

then appearing in the Soviet Union and China, multiple projects of cloud seeding with the aid of balloons, planes or projectiles of all kinds attest to a 'real war waged on the atmosphere', in a culture of manipulation of the Earth system favoured by the context of the Cold War.[83]

After the fall of the Soviet bloc, the project of geoengineering was recycled in 1992 as a means of combating climate change, in a report of the US Academy of Sciences.[84] Similarly, if in the first decade of the new century Paul Crutzen finally rallied to geoengineering, this was also because of his background in this culture of the Cold War that made the entire Earth (and even Mars!) a theatre of large-scale intervention: he had worked in the 1980s on the first scenario of 'nuclear winter' resulting from a nuclear war.[85]

In February 2014, John Kerry presented climate change, along with other threats such as epidemics and terrorism, as 'perhaps the world's most fearsome weapon of mass destruction'.[86] In the age of 'global environmental governance', the logic of warfare, of total control of the planet in the name of a state of exception, seems indeed to have made its return in the face of the possibly violent consequences of global ecological disturbance, fuelling new geopolitical cleavages. Though seemingly very different, projects such as geoengineering, UN-REDD (the official acronym for the programme of Reducing Emissions from Deforestation and Forest Degradation) mechanisms that insert forests into a global carbon market, dreams of terraforming, etc., proceed from the same logic of emergency ('climate emergency'), if not that of a 'state of exception':[87] they manufacture a global nature-system that is no longer a commons regulated by collective debate, practices and rights, but one 'whose exclusive access is strictly regulated as a

---

Deutsch, 1984.

83   Fleming, *Fixing the Sky*, 172.

84   Grevsmühl, *La Terre vue d'en haut*.

85   Paul J. Crutzen and John W. Birks, 'The Atmosphere after a Nuclear War: Twilight at Noon', *Ambio*, 11:2, 1982: 114–25.

86   Simon Denyer, 'Kerry Calls Climate Change a Weapon of Mass Destruction, Derides Skeptics', *Washington Post*, 16 February 2014, washingtonpost.com.

87   On the notion of a 'state of exception', inspired by Carl Schmitt, see Giorgio Agamben, *State of Exception*, Chicago: University of Chicago Press, 2005, and *Homo Sacer*, Stanford: Stanford University Press, 1998.

function of the rights, subject to emergency circumstances, to alter, pilot and optimize the whole of the planet and its atmosphere'.[88]

It is difficult to predict the future of geopower. Will it be multilateral and UN-based? Regional or even private? (There have already been certain corporate experiments with the seeding of oceans.) Combined with logics of sovereignty and a national security imperative, this could very well be exercised unilaterally; combined with contemporary neoliberal doctrine and the extension of the domain of private property, it conceives the market as the best calculator to save the planet by giving a price to 'natural capital' and 'ecosystemic services', and would make financial flows the controllers of biogeochemical ones (at the risk of a crash of the Earth system?).[89]

The dominant narrative of the anthropocenologists already involves an embryonic redefinition of what it is to be human on the Earth. The subject of the Anthropocene and of geopower is caught in a 'geodestiny', of 'humanity as geological force' that is both heroic and unsustainable, arousing both admiration and terror while reinforcing a certain number of socio-environmental injustices under the consensual banner of the species. The subject of the Anthropocene, moreover, appears as an eco-citizen optimizing her carbon credits, managing her individual footprint (and governed by way of her environmental reflexivity). This is a being plugged into the flows of 'ecosystemic services' that the different compartments of the Earth system supply her with.[90] And finally, the subject of the Anthropocene is constructed as a passive public that leaves solutions to geocratic experts.

Right from the 1970s, political ecologists signalled the dangers of such a geopower. André Gorz called it 'eco-fascism', while Ivan Illich,

---

88   Grevsmühl, *La Terre vue d'en haut*, 300. See also Mick Smith, 'Against Ecological Sovereignty: Agamben, Politics and Globalization', *Environmental Politics*, 18:1, 2009: 99–116.

89   Graciela Chichilnisky and Geoffrey Heal (eds), *Environmental Markets: Equity and Efficiency*, New York: Columbia University Press, 2000.

90   Christophe Bonneuil, 'Une nature liquide? Les discours de la biodiversité dans le nouvel esprit du capitalisme', in Frédéric Thomas and V. Boisvert (ed.), *Le Pouvoir de la biodiversité*, Paris: Presses de l'IRD, 2015, 193–213.

in his book *Tools for Conviviality*, saw 'a well-organized elite, vocally promulgating an antigrowth orthodoxy' as 'highly undesirable. By pushing people to accept limits to industrial output without questioning the basic industrial structure of modern society, it would inevitably provide more power to the growth-optimizing bureaucrats and become their pawn.'[91] As for Félix Guattari, he spoke of the knowledge and powers of 'scientific' management of the environment as a 'mechanical ecology', insufficient or even dangerous if it was not complemented and controlled by a 'social ecology' as well as by a 'mental ecology' or 'ecosophy'.[92]

And what if 'Earth seen from nowhere' and the narrative of 'interactions between human species and Earth system' were not the most interesting perspectives for relating what has happened to us in the last two and a half centuries, not to mention predicting the future? Perhaps we should accept the Anthropocene concept without succumbing to its dominant narrative. Without handing full powers to the experts and losing the specific resources that every community has, which in their diversity and local attachments are essential motors for a just ecological transition. In 1949, the poet René Char posed a similar problem in his poem 'Les Inventeurs':[93]

> They have come, the foresters from the other side, unknown to us and
>   rebels to our customs.
> They have come in large numbers.
> Their troop appeared on the dividing line of the cedars . . .
> We have come, they said, to warn you that the hurricane will soon
>   arrive,
> your implacable enemy.

What is this 'hurricane'? Char wrote his poem at a time rich in scientific warnings about the state of the planet: the erosion linked to the

91   Ivan Illich, *Tools for Conviviality*, London: Calder and Boyars, 1973, 107.

92   Félix Guattari, *The Three Ecologies*, London: Bloomsbury, 2008.

93   'Les Inventeurs' (1949), in René Char, *Oeuvres complètes*, Paris: Gallimard, 1983, 322–3.

retreat of forest cover in the mountains of his native Provence, the threat of a nuclear winter, the scarcity of resources discussed at a Food and Agriculture Organization conference in 1949, the destruction of nature denounced by the naturalists who founded the International Union for the Conservation of Nature at Fontainebleau in 1948. But these whistle-blowers, who in Char's poem are represented by the 'foresters' (a leading profession in the conservationist movement of that time), are 'inventors', a term Char had used pejoratively in previous poems, seeing them as mechanical demiurges harmful to social and inner life. The poem continues:

> We thanked them and bade them farewell . . .
> Men of trees and axes, able to withstand any terror
> but unsuited to conduct water, to align houses and daub them in
>   pleasant colours,
> they knew nothing of winter gardening and the economy of joy . . .
> Yes, the hurricane soon will come;
> But was it worth speaking of it and disturbing the future?
> Here where we are, there is no urgent fear.

Let us pursue the parallel. The 'inventors' of the Anthropocene, the scientists of the Earth system who warn of planetary unbalances, are very useful in coming to alert us of danger. But, says the poet, they are 'from the other side', unsuited for a warm presence in the world, for the 'economy of joy' and 'pleasant colours'. If the danger is indeed real ('yes, the hurricane soon will come'), Char proclaims the resistance of a society that refuses to abdicate its autonomy and its culture to bow to the heteronomy of an eco-technocratic government. Are the scientists of the Earth system (whose champions propose a general engineering of ecosystems and climate) not the equivalent of Char's inventors? Are they not bearers of a relationship to the world that has precisely produced the danger that they warn us of and offer to save us from? As opposed to the satellites that orbit the Earth and the experts who travel at great speed from conference to conference, another poet, Henri Michaux, proposes that we should slow down:

By slowing down, you feel the pulse of things; you snore, you have all the time in the world; calmly, all of life . . . We have all the time. We savour . . . We no longer believe that we know. We have no more need to count . . . We feel the curve of the Earth . . . We no longer betray the soil, no longer betray the minnow, we are sisters by water and leaf.[94]

94   Henri Michaux, 'La Ralentie' (1938), in *L'Espace du dedans*, Paris: Gallimard, 1966, 216–18. Our thanks to Clara Breteau for leading us to discover this poem and many others.

PART THREE: WHAT HISTORIES FOR THE ANTHROPOCENE?

CHAPTER 5

Thermocene: A Political History of CO_2

We are all familiar with the curve that is the very emblem of the Anthropocene, tracing the exponential growth of carbon dioxide emissions over the nineteenth and twentieth centuries. But no matter how famous this is, the curious fact is that we lack any history of it – a history sufficiently precise, for example, to distinguish the share of responsibility of different technological choices for the climate crisis: Have cars emitted more or less CO_2 than artificial fertilizers? How many times more CO_2 does road freight represent compared with rail and river freight?

Or again, what are the main institutions that have set us on the road to climate cataclysm? What are the great historical processes (imperialism, wars and war preparations, economic globalization, automobiles, Fordism, suburbanization, etc.) that are most important in relation to this curve? These questions currently remain unanswered and constitute the object of what we propose to call the 'history of the Thermocene'.[1]

Political reflection and public debate suffer from this lack of history. For want of precise knowledge, the spontaneous narratives of the

---

1 Jacques Grinevald and Alain Gras introduced the concept of 'thermo-industrial civilization'. See Alain Gras, *Le Choix du feu. Aux origines de la crise climatique*, Paris: Fayard, 2007. We owe the 'Thermocene' neologism to Thierry Sallantin.

environmental crisis are lost in unfocused criticisms, incriminating capitalism in general, or, worse still, modernity. As for the anthropoce-nologists, we have seen their tendency to propose infra-political narratives that emphasize demography or economic growth.

A history of additions

In what way does the history of the Thermocene that we are aiming at differ from energy history as currently practised?

Because of the climate crisis, energy history is experiencing a revival of interest. According to certain historians, examination of the 'energy transitions' of the past makes it possible to elucidate the conditions that will permit the advent of a renewable energy system.[2] Energy history thus questions the focus of the present debate on production. In past transitions, in fact, demand was the determinant factor: the automobile created the oil industry, the filament lamp created electric power stations, and not the other way round. Energy history also argues for a long-term public support for renewable energies: the first entrepreneurs to adopt a new source of energy played a crucial role in developing engines and improving their performance, and this incre-mental process could only take place in a niche situation. For example, the first steam engines in England had such poor performance that they were only viable at the mouth of coal mines. Finally, this history questions the pertinence of the present objectives of energy efficiency. On the one hand, in relation to the tendency measured since 1880, they do not seem particularly ambitious;[3] on the other hand, energy

---

2   The journal *Energy Policy* recently devoted an issue to this theme. See Arnulf Grubler, 'Energy Transitions Research: Insights and Cautionary Tales', *Energy Policy*, 50, 2012: 8–16; Charlie Wilson and Arnulf Grubler, 'Lessons from the History of Technological Change for Clean Energy Scenarios and Policies', *Natural Resources Forum*, 35:3, 2011: 165–84; Vaclav Smil, *Energy Transitions: History, Requirements, Prospects*, Santa Barbara: Praeger, 2010.

3   Paul Warde, 'Low Carbon Futures and High Carbon Pasts: Policy Challenges in Historical Perspective', *History and Policy Working Paper*, 109, December 2010. Watt's steam engine converted between 3 and 6 per cent of the energy contained in coal, the best combined steam engine of the late nineteenth century converted 20 per cent, the diesel engine from 30 to 50 per cent and the present combined cycle

history confirms William Stanley Jevons's great discovery about steam engines: by becoming more economic with coal, machines became more profitable, their use spread and the national consumption of coal finally increased. Historians have thus observed rebound effects in several sectors. In Great Britain, for example, between 1800 and 2000, the price of light (measured in lumens) fell by a factor of 3,000, but consumption increased 40,000 times.[4] According to goods and their price elasticity, the rebound effect varies, but on the whole, energy efficiency has been more than outbalanced by economic growth.

Despite these practical results, energy history with a managerial approach is actually based on a serious misunderstanding: what it studies under the name of 'energy transition' actually corresponds to the very opposite of the process that needs to be fostered today in the context of the climate crisis and peak oil.

The bad news is that, if history teaches us one thing, it is that there never has been an energy transition. There was not a movement from wood to coal, then from coal to oil, then from oil to nuclear. The history of energy is not one of transitions, but rather of successive *additions* of new sources of primary energy. The erroneous perspective follows from a confusion between relative and absolute, local and global. If, in the twentieth century, the use of coal decreased in relation to oil, it remains that its consumption continually grew; and on a global level, there was never a year in which so much coal was burned as in 2014.

Energy history must therefore free itself first of all from the concept of transition. This was promoted in the space of politics, media and science precisely so as to spirit away worries bound up with the 'energy crisis', an expression that was then still dominant. Between 1975 and 1980, the term 'energy transition' was invented by think-tanks and popularized by powerful institutions: the US Department of Energy, the Swedish Secretariat for Futures Studies, the Trilateral Commission,

gas power stations up to 60 per cent. See Smil, *Energy Transitions*, 9.

4   Roger Fouquet and Peter J. Pearson, 'Seven Centuries of Energy Services: The Price and Use of Light in the United Kingdom (1300–2000)', *Energy Journal*, 27, 2006: 139–78.

the European Community and various industrial lobbies. In most cases, this talk of 'transition' served to indicate an indispensable recourse to so-called 'alternative' fuels: nuclear in particular,[5] but also gas and shale oil, coal and synthetic fuel.[6]

To say 'transition' rather than 'crisis' made the future less generative of anxiety, by attaching it to a planning and managerial rationality.[7] The further success of the notion of transition, as understood particularly in ecological milieus (see the 'solar transition' of the 1980s), also drew on a conception of technology developing in great radical shifts.

On the one hand, however, the notion of transition obscures the persistence of old systems, while on the other hand it overestimates technological determinants to the detriment of economic arbitrage. For example, world coal consumption grew from 7.3 to 8.5 billion tonnes between 2008 and 2012.[8] If China made up the greater part of this growth (from 3.0 to 4.1 billion), there are sectors in which Europe could experience a 'return' to coal. For instance, because of the development of shale gas in the United States, the price of US coal fell so much that it was profitable to substitute it for Russian gas. In Britain, the proportion of electricity produced from coal grew from 30 to 42 per cent between 2011 and 2012; in France, the consumption of coal for electricity generation leapt by 79 per cent.[9] In this sense, coal is not an 'older' energy than oil, but looks more likely to be its successor.

An example drawn from the book by Kenneth Pomeranz, *A Great Divergence*, clarifies the issue for the writing of history. Take two technologies: the steam engine and the Chinese furnace, more economic

5   See for example, A. R. Gloyne et al., *Dynamic Energy Analysis of the EEC Energy Transition Programme*, report of the Energy Studies Unit, Glasgow: University of Strathclyde, 1976, inis.iaea.org.

6   John A. Belding and William M. Burnett, *From Oil and Gas to Alternate Fuels: The Transition in Conversion Equipment*, Washington, DC: Energy Research and Development Administration, 1977.

7   John C. Sawhill, Hanns Walter Maull and Keichi Oshima, *Energy: Managing the Transition*, The Trilateral Commission, 1978.

8   US Energy Information Administration, eia.gov.

9   Department of Energy and Climate Change, *Digest of United Kingdom Energy Statistics 2012*, London: TSO, 2012; and Denis Cosnard, 'Électricité. L'Europe retourne au charbon', *Le Monde*, 28 November 2012, lemonde.fr.

on energy than its European counterpart. How should we judge their historical importance? Why does the first seem worthy of historians' interest, while the second is generally unknown? It is only the abundance of coal that makes the capacity to draw more energy from combustibles appear more determinant, and relegates Chinese furnaces to a footnote.[10] If the English coal mines had shown signs of exhaustion from 1800 on, the hierarchy would have been reversed. The oil peak and climate change thus raise the question of direction in the history of technology, forcing us to reconsider its objects and envisage a 'disoriented' history.

If it is to dispense with the idea of transition, energy history should abandon its classic terrain and study past historical situations in which societies were forced to reduce their energy consumption. The crisis of the 1930s offers some interesting cases: carbon emissions in the United States fell from 520 to 340 million tonnes, and in France from 66 to 55 million. In the latter case, this reduction was not just bound up with the recession, but also with the differential evolution of prices: that of coal rose by 40 per cent during the crisis, while the general price index stagnated. It was also in the 1930s that wood fuel experienced a peak, before a definitive decline after the Second World War.[11] A historian of energy degrowth could also study the case of post-war Germany (from 185 to 32 million tonnes of carbon), or, nearer our own time, the fall of the Soviet Union (606 million tonnes in 1992, 419 million in 2002). In each of these cases, production fell sharply (the GDP of the former USSR falling by half between 1992 and 2002).[12]

The examples of North Korea or Cuba after the fall of the USSR allow us to give a concrete meaning to what may lie concealed behind the pleasant euphemism of 'energy transition'. Between 1992 and 1998, deprived of Soviet oil, North Korean agriculture based on mechanization and chemical inputs saw its yields of maize, wheat and rice fall by half.

10   Kenneth Pomeranz, *The Great Divergence: China, Europe, and the Making of the Modern World Economy*, Princeton: Princeton University Press, 2001, 60–2.

11   Jean-Claude Debeir, Jean-Paul Déléage and Daniel Hémery, *Une histoire de l'énergie. Les servitudes de la puissance* (1986), Paris: Flammarion, 2013, 244.

12   These data on emissions are all taken from the database of the Carbon Dioxide Information Analysis Center, cdiac.ornl.gov.

The North Korean state prioritized fuel supply to the army, leaving between 600,000 and a million of its citizens (3 to 5 per cent of the population) to succumb to famine before deciding to call for international food aid.

In the same period, deprived of Soviet oil and under American embargo, the Cubans confronted for a ten-year *periodo especial*, a situation that presents certain similarities with that awaiting our industrial societies. In order to save on energy, working hours in industry were reduced, domestic electricity consumption was rationed, the use of bicycles and car pools was generalized, the university system was decentralized, solar energy and biogas were developed (supplying 10 per cent of electricity). In agriculture, the cost of pesticides and chemical fertilizers, very greedy in terms of energy, led the Cubans to innovate: biological control of pests by insect predators, organic fertilizers, and urban horticulture that enabled the recycling of organic waste. Finally, food was strictly rationed.[13] Cuban bodies were significantly modified by the special period. In 1993, when the crisis was at its worst, the daily ration was reduced to 1,900 kilocalories. Cubans lost an average of five kilos per person, which had the benefit of reducing cardiovascular disease by 30 per cent.[14] What is most disturbing, given the efforts made by the Cuban population, is that the reduction in CO_2 emissions was in the end rather modest, falling in ten years from 10 million to 6.5 million tonnes, much less than the 40 to 70 per cent reduction of world emissions by 2050 called for by the IPCC that would cap global warming at a two-degree celsius increase.

Nor should we fall prey to illusion as to our technological capacity to reduce the energy shock. The French nuclear power programme of the 1970s and '80s offers a vivid demonstration of this: despite colossal public investment (in the order of 400 billion francs at 1990 prices), French CO_2 emissions continued to rise during these two decades, from 90 million to 110 million tonnes per year.

13   Eliso Botella, 'Cuba's Inward-Looking Development Policies: Towards Sustainable Agriculture (1990–2008)', *Historia Agraria*, 55, 2011: 135–76.

14   Manuel Franco et al., 'Population-Wide Weight Loss and Regain in Relation to Diabetes Burden and Cardiovascular Mortality in Cuba 1980–2010', *British Medical Journal*, 346, 2013: 1,515.

A *history of inefficiency*

In relation to energy history, the history of the Thermocene also needs to free itself from two abstractions that overdetermine results: GDP and the very concept of energy.

The exponential growth curves traced by historians are based on nineteenth-century thermodynamics, that is, an intellectual project that brings every form of work (from brain to blast furnace) into a generalized equivalence, on the hypothesis of a general substitutability of energy sources. The main difficulty is that this history depends on statistics of energy production. It counts the energy theoretically available from a kilogram of coal or oil, rather than the services actually performed by combustion. This has two consequences: since the quantity of energy contained in fossil fuel is immense, it overwhelms renewable energy systems, whether organic or simply economical. The history of energy thus very likely overestimates the upheaval introduced by fossil fuels.

Take the case of gas lighting, for example. This technology, which appeared in London in the 1810s, was extraordinarily inefficient. It consisted in distilling coal – using more coal to heat this – in order to produce a gas designed to light housing or streets. Its energy yield was absolutely disastrous: a third of the coal was burned to produce gas, a third of this gas escaped in pipes that massively leaked, and at the end of the day the light it gave was very poor. Contemporaries had a very clear perception of both the dangers and the waste involved in this technique.[15] In this particular case, the transition from oil lamps to gas lighting, that is, from an organic and locally applied energy to a fossil energy distributed over a network, while massively increasing energy consumption, above all increased the losses.

Secondly, the 'energy consumed per capita' traced by historians actually corresponds to national production of energy divided by population. It includes for example the energy spent on waging wars,

---

15   Jean-Baptiste Fressoz, 'The Gas-Lighting Controversy: Technological Risk, Expertise and Regulation in Nineteenth-Century Paris and London', *Journal of Urban History*, 33:5, 2007: 729–55.

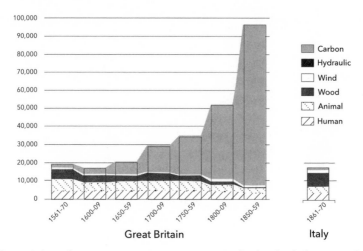

Figure 6: *Annual energy consumption per capita in England and Italy (in megajoules)*

running the navy and controlling the empire, as well as the energy dissipated in inefficient technological systems. What we lack is a history of energy services, which would show the energy actually used by different classes of consumers.

GDP is no less problematic than the concept of energy. In studying the evolution of the ratio between GDP and energy consumed, historians conclude that the energy intensity of industrial economies has steadily decreased from around the 1880s. But what does this result mean?

First of all, it is based on the debatable hypothesis that GDP is a genuine measure of wealth produced. But according to this logic, buying a car that costs £20,000 and does 30 miles per gallon increases the energy performance of the economy more than buying a car that costs £10,000 and does 50 miles per gallon. Secondly, the ratio of GDP to energy aggregates processes that are completely different: the growth in the share of financial services in GDP in the late twentieth century improved energy efficiency only in a completely artificial sense. Thirdly, one of the great lessons of economic analysis in terms of energy, as this was practised in the 1970s, was on the contrary to show the decrease of energy yield in certain sectors, of which the case of agriculture was the best studied. The ecologists David and Marcia Pimentel, for example, showed that the transition from a traditional agriculture to an intensive and mechanized one led to a *fall* in energy yield: more calories (basically derived from oil) had to be used in order to produce each calorie of food. In the case of maize, the shift was from a ratio of ten calories produced for each calorie invested to a ratio of only three to one.[16] The generalization of this type of analysis, that is, a general history of thermodynamic (in)efficiency (taking up Ivan Illich's thesis of counter-productivity), would undoubtedly lead to a far more ambiguous account than that conveyed by energy history and its ascendant curves of energy, wealth and efficiency.

A *history of alternatives*

Finally, and this is its chief objective, the history of the Thermocene will have to *denaturalize* the history of energy. The latter was not written in advance: its transitions and additions follow neither an internal logic of technical progress (the first steam engines were very expensive and highly inefficient), nor a logic of scarcity and substitution (the United States, which possesses immense forests, resorted to coal on a massive scale in the nineteenth century), nor even a logic that was simply economic.

The history of energy is also and above all one of political, military and ideological choices that the historian has to analyse, by relating them to the strategic interests and objectives of certain social groups. This political reading of energy history is particularly important in the present climate context: recourse to unconventional oil and shale gas shows that it is never 'natural' reserves that are allowed to dictate the tempo of energy transition. According to climate models, at least two-thirds of proven reserves of oil and coal would have to be left in the ground in order to limit the rise in temperature to less than two

---

16   David and Marcia Pimentel, *Food, Energy, and Society*, Boca Raton: CRC Press, 2008, 99–119.

degrees by 2100.[17] To prevent runaway climate change, it is absolutely necessary to put a political constraint in place before 'price signals' force us to change models.

In this field as in others, however, history has an extraordinary power to denaturalize. Historical analysis dissolves many prejudices as to the supposedly indispensable character of certain technologies. For example, in 1914 coal made up only 2.7 per cent of French GDP, and 6 per cent of British GDP in 1907.[18] The historian Robert Fogel has also shown that, contrary to accepted ideas, without the railways the United States could have had the same very rapid economic development that it had in the nineteenth century. In 1890, the 'social profit'[19] of the railways as compared with the best available alternative (an improvement in canals and carting) represented only between 0.6 per cent and 1 per cent of American GDP. Given the rapid growth of the United States at this time, Fogel concludes that the absence of railways would only have slowed the development of the American economy by a few months!

In the same way, the historian Nick von Tunzelmann[20] calculated that in 1800, in England, the social profit of steam engines represented less than a thousandth of GDP. Induced effects at this time were all but non-existent. For example, the major innovations in textiles (mechanical loom, spinning jenny) *preceded* the application of steam. Tony Wrigley calls England in the age of the industrial revolution an 'advanced organic economy' oriented primarily to agriculture. The number of horses in fact rose from 1.29 million in 1811 to 3.28 million in 1901.[21]

---

17   No more than 886 gigatonnes (886 x 10^9 tonnes) should be emitted between 2012 and 2050, whereas proven reserves of coal and oil are equivalent to 2,795 gigatonnes. See Carbon Tracker, *Unburnable Carbon*, 2012, carbontracker.org; Michael Jakob and Jérôme Hilaire, 'Unburnable Fossil Fuel Reserves', *Nature* 517 (2015), 150–2.

18   Debeir, Déléage and Hémery, *Une histoire de l'énergie*, 207.

19   Defined as the volume of scarce resources (transport, energy, etc.) that the use of a particular technology can release for other uses. Robert Fogel, *Railroads and American Economic Growth: Essays in Economic History*, Baltimore: Johns Hopkins University Press, 1964.

20   Nicholas von Tunzelmann, *Steam Power and British Industrialization to 1860*, Oxford: Clarendon Press, 1978.

21   Eric A. Wrigley, *Continuity, Chance and Change: The Character of the*

Andreas Malm has similarly shown that the energy potential of English rivers was far from being fully exploited. The switch of the cotton industry to coal that took place in the 1830s was not caused by a scarcity of energy or a simple economic calculation. On the contrary, the 1820s and '30s realized large-scale hydraulic projects that combined reservoirs, dams and mills to ensure the industrialists of Lancashire and Scotland a renewable energy at a lower price than steam. Their defeat was due to the industrialists' refusal to submit to the collective discipline that a common management of hydraulic resources would have imposed: how to be sure that the energy needed would be available at the right moment, how to guarantee paying only for one's own motive power, and how to expand a factory easily. All these problems and many others necessitated a collective coordination and centralization to which the entrepreneurs were unwilling to undergo. The steam engine, on the other hand, despite being more expensive, constituted a flexible, modular and individual source of energy that matched very well the ideology of English textile capitalism of the 1830s.[22]

If we consider the case of shipping, wind energy was still largely dominant in the late nineteenth century: in 1868, 92 per cent of British merchant shipping was powered by sail.[23] In the same year, British dockyards produced 879 sailing ships and 232 steam ships. The second half of the nineteenth century was the age of the clippers, large sailing ships that broke speed records to sell their cargoes ahead of their competitors and profit from higher prices. It was not until the early twentieth century that steam overtook sail in global tonnage. The economic globalization of the late nineteenth century, therefore, was carried out for the most part by wind power.

The focus of historians on energy, the industrial revolution and fossil fuel obscures economic transformations that were equally important. For example, the demographic explosion of the English-speaking

Industrial Revolution in England, Cambridge: Cambridge University Press, 1988, 40.

22   Andreas Malm, *Fossil Capital: The Rise of Steam-Power and the Roots of Global Warming*, London: Verso, 2015.

23   Katharine Anderson, *Predicting the Weather*, Chicago: University of Chicago Press, 2005, 3.

countries in the nineteenth century was based on a 'non-industrial' revolution: on the energies of wind, water, animals and wood. It would be reductive to term these energies 'traditional'. Thanks to selective breeding, livestock were rapidly improved: the American draught horses of the 1890s were 50 per cent more powerful than those of the 1860s. The trotting record for a mile fell from three minutes to two minutes between 1840 and 1880. Historians estimate that in 1850 horses provided half of all American energy. The number of horses in the United States, in fact, reached its peak at the end of the century: in Chicago and New York, in 1900, there was approximately one horse for every twenty-five people.[24] Likewise, in 1870, thanks to new turbines, hydraulic power supplied 75 per cent of industrial energy.[25]

More generally, the history of renewable energy sources – animal, wind and solar – before these were considered as merely 'alternative', shows a past rich in neglected technological paths and unrealized potentialities. The relatively few works on this subject lead to striking results: at the end of the nineteenth century, 6 million windmills, operating the same number of wells, played the historically fundamental role in opening up the plains of the American Midwest to agriculture and husbandry. These windmills were not pre-industrial but rotors built according to the principles of fluid dynamics, capable of following the wind and produced on a mass scale.[26] In the American farmland, decentralized electricity production (using windmills and battery storage) remained dominant until the great programmes of rural electrification of the New Deal and post-war years.[27]

In the same way, in the late nineteenth century, solar energy aroused considerable interest on the part of the French government because of an anticipated shortage of coal and the exploitation of tropical

24   Joel Tarr and Clay McShane, *The Horse in the City: Living Machines in the Nineteenth Century*, Baltimore: Johns Hopkins University Press, 2007.

25   David E. Nye, *Consuming Power: A Social History of American Energies*, Cambridge, MA: MIT Press, 1998, 82.

26   Alexis Madrigal, *Powering the Dream: The History and Promise of Green Technology*, Cambridge, MA: Da Capo Press, 2011.

27   Robert Righter, *Wind Energy in America: A History*, Norman, OK: University of Oklahoma Press, 1996.

colonies. Several technologies were experimented with. In the 1870s, Augustin Mouchot invented the first solar steam engine. He received large subsidies to develop his system in Algeria, a country with no coal resources.[28] In 1885, the engineer Charles Tellier, who had made a fortune in developing refrigeration procedures, developed a solar collector that ran on ammonia.[29] At the start of the twentieth century, in the United States, the Sun Power Company already sold solar engines. Their cost may have been higher than that of classic steam engines, but it was far from prohibitive in appropriate conditions: $164 per horsepower as against between $40 and $90 for coal.[30]

It was in domestic use above all that solar energy almost came to dominate. In California and Florida, the combination of abundant sunshine and distance from collieries explains the rapid development of solar water heaters. In the 1920s, an investment of $20 could save $9 per year in coal.

'Passive house' technologies were developed in the 1930s: making maximum use of orientation, sunshine and shade, large south-facing windows, insulating blind walls to the north and double-glazing (which appeared on the market in 1932). These were in general luxury homes in the American individualist tradition, which sought to free themselves from urban constraints bound up with energy networks.

During the Second World War, the American government financed large-scale research programmes aiming to reduce domestic oil consumption and maximize the share sent to the front. After the war, the fear of exhaustion of resources was an encouragement for solar power. In 1945, MOMA held an exhibition on affordable solar homes (less than $3,000), which seemed at the time the only available option to tackle the country's housing need in the post-war years.[31] In 1948,

28   François Jarrige, '"Mettre le soleil en bouteille". Les appareils de Mouchot et l'imaginaire solaire au début de la Troisième République', *Romantisme*, 150, 2010: 85–96.

29   Frank T. Kryza, *The Power of Light: The Epic Story of Man's Quest to Harness the Sun*, New York: McGraw-Hill, 2003, 229.

30   Ibid., 234–7.

31   Daniel A. Barber, 'Tomorrow's House: Solar Housing in 1940s America', *Technology and Culture*, 55:1, January 2014: 1–39.

Mária Telkes, a physicist at MIT, developed a solar home that was 75 per cent self-sufficient in energy. Physicists who had worked on the Manhattan project, such as Farrington Daniels, switched their interest from civil nuclear power to solar. In 1952, the Paley Commission on US natural resources predicted an oil peak in the 1970s and advised the development of solar, wind and biomass. Finally, resorting to simpler technologies, small companies sold hundreds of thousands of solar water heaters. In Florida in the early 1950s, almost 80 per cent of homes were equipped with these.[32]

A political history of CO_2

B y relativizing the inexorable character of fossil fuels, history enables us to re-politicize their present domination.

The notions of irreversibility ('lock-in') and path dependency make it possible to grasp the importance of political choices in energy policy.[33] 'Initial conditions' such as the abundance of coal or oil, but also political conditions that encourage one source of energy rather than another, determine technological trajectories over a very long term. These decisions are then perpetuated by regulatory frameworks, by the need to protect investments, by the existence of infrastructures bound up with this energy source, as well as by customs, culture, etc. Analysing in this way the decisions that produced our almost exclusive dependence on fossil fuels dispels the illusion of an optimal and efficient contemporary technological world.

In Great Britain in 1935, for example, the industry that consumed most coal was gas for lighting, even above steel. It consumed a fifth of English coal production (or 23 million tonnes). Using coal to produce light, however, is very bad business: 728 tonnes were needed to produce £100,000 in profit, as against 240 tonnes in steel-making and

---

32   Adam Rome, *The Bulldozer in the Countryside: Suburban Sprawl and the Rise of American Environmentalism*, Cambridge: Cambridge University Press, 2001.

33   Paul David, 'Clio and the Economics of QWERTY', *American Economic Review*, 75:2, 1985: 332–7.

only 120 in electricity, the rival technology.[34] Major technological systems such as gas lighting (or nuclear power) have a very great inertia: the volume of capital invested, and the interests involved, explain their survival a half century after the appearance of far more efficient technologies.

Conversely, promising technologies may be killed off at birth. In the 1950s, in the United States, investment in solar energy came to an end with the development of suburbs, the promotion of low-cost prefabricated homes (the famous Levittowns) and very aggressive marketing on the part of electricity companies. In 1968, Congress commissioned a study of these practices. General Electric was even threatening building developers not to connect new estates if they offered alternative sources of power. For such developers, offering only electricity made it possible to reduce construction costs and shift energy expenditure onto the homeowners.[35] This was how, in the 1950s and '60s, the thermodynamic aberration of electric heating was promoted in the United States without any technological necessity for it.

The suburbanization and motorization of Western societies are certainly the most massive example of a technological and civilizational choice that is profoundly suboptimal and harmful. In the United States between the two world wars, suburbanization was a political project: the one-family house seemed the best rampart against Communism, and President Herbert Hoover deliberately encouraged it so as to stimulate the property instinct. In 1926, in order to protect property values, the Supreme Court legitimized the practice of zoning, separating residential spaces from both industrial activity and ethnic minorities. During the Great Depression, construction and suburbanization were perceived as an essential factor for economic revival.

After the Second World War, an economicist and free-market vision of urban development came to dominate, based on the rational choice

---

34   H. W. Singer, 'The Coal Question Reconsidered: Effects of Economy and Substitution', *Review of Economic Studies*, 8:3, 1941: 166–77, table B.

35   Rome, *The Bulldozer in the Countryside*, 45–85. No equivalent study is available of the peculiar choice made by France to develop electric heating in the 1970s.

of consumers who arbitrated between housing and transport expenditure. In this logic, given that the price of mobility was steadily falling and that of housing relatively stable, town planners were bound to project the development of megapolises in synchrony with mass motorization.[36]

In actual fact, if we look more closely, the choice of the individual car corresponds to processes that are far more contingent than is generally believed. American historians have shown that the dismantling of streetcars and suburban railways, and their replacement by individual cars and buses running on petrol, did not follow any technological or economic logic, but considerably increased the costs of mobility, and in the medium term even slowed this down![37]

In 1902, in the United States, streetcars carried 5 billion people on some 35,000 kilometres of electrified lines. This was a safe and relatively comfortable mode of transport. Given the national rail network, the development of urban and interurban electric trams and the lack of good highways, the individual motor car did not seem a particularly promising technology in America at the start of the twentieth century.

The switch from collective to individual transport, which seemed absurd to many contemporaries, was rooted in an old antagonism that opposed local authorities to the streetcar companies. At the start of the twentieth century, the latter were subject to constant attack by the press and public authorities, which presented their monopoly situation as a restriction on business freedom. At the same time, Ford's Model T invaded the streets (the number of cars in New York rose from 40,000 in 1915 to 612,000 in 1927), slowing down streetcars and trolley-buses.

36   Glenn Yago, 'The Sociology of Transportation', *Annual Review of Sociology*, 9, 1983: 171–90.

37   David J. St. Clair, *The Motorization of American Cities*, New York: Praeger, 1986; Glenn Yago, *The Decline of Transit: Urban Transportation in German and U.S. Cities, 1900–1970*, Cambridge: Cambridge University Press, 1984. For a different point of view, see Donald F. Davis, 'North American Urban Mass Transit, 1890–1950', *History and Technology*, 12:4, 1995: 309–26; Dominique Larroque, 'Apogée, déclin et relance du tramway en France', *Culture technique*, 19, 1989: 54–64.

These cars also increased the running costs of public transport, since in the majority of cities the streetcar companies were responsible for maintaining their routes in good shape – in New York, this cost them 23 per cent of their revenue.[38] On top of this were the charges they paid to the local authority. Paradoxically, the streetcar actually subsidized the automobile.

The concessions granted in the 1880s and '90s no longer corresponded to the new economic situation. The sacrosanct 'nickel fare', for example, had not followed the doubling of the hourly wage during the First World War or the compulsory presence of a second employee in each streetcar. The streetcars' competitors, for their part, were not subject to any of these regulations: the 1920s saw the proliferation of the 'jitney bus', collective pirate taxis that picked up passengers at the streetcar stops. This was the decade when investors turned away from the streetcar companies. Streetcars and trolley-buses seemed to be obsolete technologies.

The second act in the tragedy of the streetcars took place in the 1930s. Two great corporations, General Electric and Insull, now owned the majority of the streetcar companies, their interest being to smooth out consumption peaks and optimize the production of their power stations. In 1935, the Wheeler-Rayburn Act compelled local electricity companies to sell their streetcar divisions. Suddenly, hundreds of small and unprofitable companies were placed on the market. General Motors, Standard Oil and Firestone dealt them the final blow, allying themselves with two small transport businesses, the Rapid Transit Company and Yellow Coach, to purchase the streetcar companies in some fifty American cities at rock-bottom prices. Once in control, they closed down the streetcar lines or replaced them with petrol buses, in order to create new outlets for the automobile industry. In 1949, a court decision against General Motors, Firestone and Standard Oil fined them a derisory $5,000.[39]

---

38   Zachary M. Schrag, "'The Bus Is Young and Honest": Transportation Politics, Technical Choice, and the Motorization of Manhattan Surface Transit, 1919–1936', *Technology and Culture*, 41:1, 2000: 51–70.

39   Stephen Goddard, *Getting There: The Epic Struggle between Road and Rail in the American Century*, Chicago: University of Chicago Press, 1996, 102–37.

In the 1930s, in both France and the United Kingdom, cities had a free-market approach to urban transport: trams were compelled to be profitable and could not be subsidized. Companies adopted a Malthusian policy, concentrating on profitable lines and delaying investment. With the economic crisis, many lines closed, and by the 1950s, the majority of cities had lost their networks.[40] The comparison with Weimar Germany is instructive, confirming the importance of politics in the definition of modes of transport. First of all, given the central position of the coal-rail industrial complex and the relative weakness of the automobile industry, the German government had no interest in encouraging suburbanization and motorization. On the contrary, in 1927 the ruling Social Democratic Party (SPD) chose to tax motor cars heavily in order to finance public transport. The creation of the public rail company Deutsche Bahn in 1920, along with the municipalizing of the majority of tram companies, was likewise an element in a social policy aiming to reduce the cost of transport for workers.[41]

The Anthropocene is an Anglocene

The eminently political nature of energy additions is confirmed by the historical statistics of CO_2 emissions: Great Britain and the United States made up 60 per cent of cumulative total emissions to date in 1900, 57 per cent in 1950 and almost 50 per cent in 1980. From the standpoint of climate, the Anthropocene should rather be called an 'Anglocene'.

Comparison between France and Great Britain is instructive. In 1913, the British GDP per capita was 20 per cent higher than the French, while cumulative British emissions were four times that of France (6 billion tonnes of carbon as against 1.5 billion). During the long nineteenth century, therefore, the British emitted four times as much CO_2 to reach a standard of living not much greater than France.

---

40   Frédéric Héran, *Le retour de la bicyclette. Une histoire des déplacements urbains en Europe de 1817 à 2050*, Paris: La Découverte, 2014, 50–1.

41   Yago, *The Decline of Transit*.

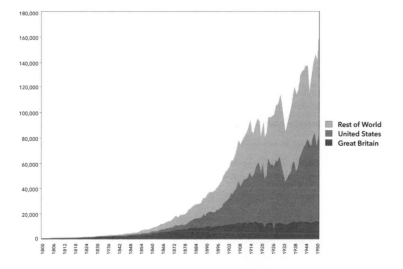

Figure 7: *Annual emissions in thousand tonnes of carbon*

The great historiographical thesis of the plurality of paths of industrialization and the 'soft industrialization' of France, long preserving a dispersed industry inserted into the rural fabric and based on human, animal and hydraulic energy,[42] is thus entirely confirmed by the very different responsibilities of the two countries for the present climate crisis. In 2008, France's cumulative emissions made up 4 per cent of the world total, while those of Great Britain constituted 10 per cent.

The overwhelming share of responsibility for climate change of the two hegemonic powers of the nineteenth (Great Britain) and twentieth (United States) centuries attests to the fundamental link between climate change and projects of world domination.

Coal was indeed the fuel of British hegemony. Besides those territories directly under Westminster's control, Great Britain possessed an immense 'informal empire' based on the export of people, capital, technologies and engineers, an empire founded on free trade, which

42   Patrick O'Brien and Caglar Keyder, *Economic Growth in Britain and France, 1780–1914: Two Paths to the Twentieth Century*, London: Allen and Unwin, 1978.

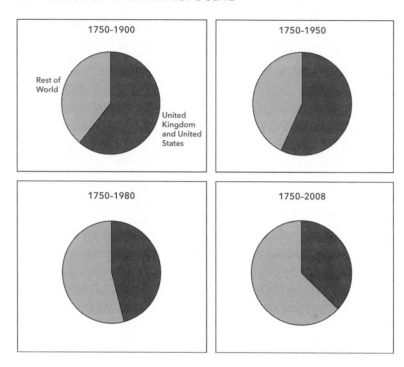

Figure 8: *UK and USA's share in global cumulative CO$_2$ emissions*

systematically worked to its advantage thanks to its control of economic circuits. Coal exports made it possible to fill the holds of ships leaving England[43] and contributed to the exceptional profitability of the British Merchant Navy.

Between 1815 and 1880, five-sixths of the British capital invested abroad was outside the formal empire, chiefly in activities that were high emitters of CO$_2$ (see Chapter 10 on the 'Capitalocene'). Let us take a concrete example that shows the link between the British informal empire and the globalization of coal. After the Napoleonic wars, the British government imposed bilateral trade agreements on the newly independent countries of South America. From the 1820s, British traders and engineers flocked there in droves and bought up many

43   John Darwin, *The Empire Project: The Rise and Fall of the British World-System, 1830–1970*, Cambridge: Cambridge University Press, 2009, 140.

mines, particularly copper mines in Chile and Peru. The city of Swansea in Wales, already specialized in the refining of ore from Cornwall, became the world capital of copper. This was an unprecedented historical phenomenon: raw material was shipped to the other end of the world to be transformed and sometimes re-exported to its country of origin.

Coal lay at the heart of this globalization. Swansea had a competitive energy source in the coal mines of South Wales and an expertise in smelting with coke, while the exported coal served as cargo for the voyage to South America.[44] The export of British expertise led to a new interest in coal throughout the world.

US hegemony in the twentieth century was based similarly on carbon. The energy intensity of American development has been explained in terms of the colonial origins of the country. In the early nineteenth century labour was scarce, while raw materials, wood and coal, were found in great abundance. Employers thus had an interest in reducing the need for labour and using machines instead, irrespective of their productivity in terms of energy.

The historians Bruce Podobnick and Tim Mitchell have recently introduced a new argument into this familiar story. Throughout the twentieth century, oil was constantly more expensive than coal – far more so in Europe, and a little more in the United States.[45] How then are we to explain its extraordinary rise from 5 per cent of world energy in 1910 to more than 60 per cent in 1970?

In their view, social history provides the key to this enigma. In contrast to oil, coal has to be extracted from mines piece by piece, loaded onto conveyors, transported by rail or boat, then again loaded into furnaces that have to be fuelled, overseen and cleaned. The weight of coal gave miners the power to interrupt the energy flow that fuelled the economy. Their demands, after long being suppressed, had finally to be taken into account: from the 1880s, great miners' strikes

---

44 Edmund Newell, 'Copperopolis: The Rise and Fall of the Copper Industry in the Swansea District, 1826–1921', *Business History*, 32:3, 1990: 75–97.

45 Bruce Podobnick, *Global Energy Shifts: Fostering Sustainability in a Turbulent Age*, Philadelphia: Temple University Press, 2006, Figure 4.1.

contributed to the emergence of trade unions and mass political parties, the extension of universal suffrage and the adoption of social insurance legislation.

Once the historical connection between coal and the democratic advances of the late nineteenth century is brought into the equation, the petrolization of America and then Europe gains a new political meaning. It corresponds to a political project, which the United States facilitated in order to defuse working-class movements. Oil is far more capital-intensive than labour-intensive; its extraction is done on the surface and thus easier to control, requiring a great variety of skills and a labour force that fluctuates greatly in numbers. All that makes the creation of powerful trade unions difficult.

One of the objectives of the Marshall Plan was to encourage recourse to oil in order to weaken the miners and their unions, and thereby anchor the European countries to the Western bloc. As with every emergent technological system, oil needed to be massively subsidized. The funds of the European Recovery Program served for the construction of refineries and the purchase of generators. In the post-war decade, more than a half of the petrol supplied to Europe was directly subsidized by the ERP.

Thanks to its fluid nature, oil made it possible to bypass transport networks and the workers who operated these. Pipelines and tankers, by reducing loading breaks, created an energy network that was far less intensive in labour, more flexible and decidedly international. In the 1970s, 80 per cent of oil was exported. With a supply that was now global, industrial capitalism became far less vulnerable to the demands of national labour forces. Finally, the oil network was centred on a few key points (wells, refineries and terminals), and thus readily controllable.[46]

Historians have analysed in the same fashion the 'green revolution' of the 1960s, connecting it with the Cold War and the American policy of stemming Communist influence. The US government, with the aid of the Ford and Rockefeller foundations, then the World Bank, set out to win the hearts of the rural masses of Asia and Latin America by

---

46   Timothy Mitchell, *Carbon Democracy: Political Power in the Age of Oil*, London: Verso, 2011.

modernizing their agriculture and assuring their food security. The green revolution was based on hybrid varieties of rice and maize, along with the use of machines, pesticides and chemical fertilizers, consumption of which rose from 30 million to 110 million tonnes between 1960 and 1980. As a strategy for increasing production, the results were incontestable: production of wheat, rice and maize rose considerably, from Mexico to India. But this agricultural model did not meet the needs of small peasants and led to countless environmental side-effects: water tables were exhausted and polluted, soils salinized and compacted, etc.[47] The green revolution, very demanding in terms of energy, also completed the petrolization of the world.

---

47 Nick Cullather, *The Hungry World: America's Cold War Battle against Poverty in Asia*, Cambridge, MA: Harvard University Press, 2010.

CHAPTER 6

Thanatocene: Power and Ecocide

As the twentieth century progressed, wars became both deadlier and more frequent.[1] The First World War killed more than all the wars of the nineteenth century had together, while the Second World War alone made up half the number of dead in the past 2,000 years of warfare.[2] Advances in productivity and in destructiveness went hand in hand: the cost of destruction steadily decreased throughout the nineteenth and twentieth centuries. In relation to its destructive power, military technology has never been so cheap. Besides, from the eighteenth century on, West European states considerably expanded their tax-raising powers. Historians estimate that Great Britain, particularly precocious in this field, already mobilized 20 per cent of its GDP for war-making in 1800.

War has thus become more affordable, particularly for rich states. Statistical analysis of wars shows that in the twentieth century the richest countries have tended to be at war more often than the poorest: the top third of countries in terms of wealth have been responsible for half the wars of the twentieth century. Before 1914, on the other hand, the richest countries tended to be less frequently involved in

---

1   Mark Harrison and Nikolaus Wolf, 'The Frequency of Wars', *Economic History Review*, 65:3, 2012: 1055–76.

2   Edmund Russell, *War and Nature: Fighting Humans and Insects with Chemicals from World War I to Silent Spring*, Cambridge: Cambridge University Press, 2001, 8.

armed conflicts. The United States, for example, was involved in 9.3 per cent of all wars between 1870 and 1945, and 11.2 per cent in those since then.[3]

In the twentieth century, moreover, the rich states waged wars of a totally different kind from any in the past. Their troops were supported, and to a certain degree replaced, by extraordinarily powerful machines fed by colossal industrial, technological and logistic systems, war machines that required growing quantities of raw materials and energy and had an unprecedentedly heavy impact on the environment.

Even in peacetime, military-industrial complexes destroy. The Cold War, for example, saw a peak in the environmental footprint of armies. By the late 1980s, military training camps, often polluted with radioactive waste, munitions, etc., covered 1 per cent of the Earth's surface (including 2 per cent of the United States). The maintenance and training of Western armed forces consumed enormous quantities of resources: 15 per cent of West German air traffic, for example, was linked to NATO military exercises. In 1987, the American army was responsible for 3.4 per cent of the nation's oil consumption, comparable figures being 3.9 per cent for the Soviet Union and 4.8 per cent for the UK, as well as 1 per cent of all coal and 1.6 per cent of electricity. If we add to this the carbon dioxide emissions bound up with arms production, then between 10 and 15 per cent of American emissions during the Cold War were attributable to the military.[4]

Efficiency has a very different meaning when the object is to kill rather than be killed. The development of contemporary weapons systems illustrates the tendency to energy exuberance that is intrinsic to the military. During the Second World War, General Patton's Third Army consumed one US gallon of petrol (3.7 litres) per man per day. This figure reached nine gallons during the Vietnam War, ten gallons for Operation Desert Storm, and fifteen gallons during the Second

---

3   Harrison and Wolf, 'The Frequency of Wars'.
4   Michael Renner, 'Assessing the Military's War on the Environment', in Lester Brown (ed.), *State of the World 1991*, New York: Norton, 1991. See also John R. McNeill and David S. Painter, 'The Global Environmental Footprint of the U.S. Military, 1789–2003', in Charles Closmann (ed.), *War and the Environment*, Austin: University of Texas Press, 2009, Chapter 2.

Gulf War. Present-day military technologies have reached unheard-of levels of energy consumption. An Abrams tank in the US Army burns four litres per kilometre. A B-52 bomber burns 12,000 litres of jet fuel per hour, and an F-15 fighter 7,000 litres, comparable to the consumption of an average family car in a whole decade. In 2006, the US Air Force consumed a total of 2.6 billion gallons of jet fuel, as much as was used overseas during the whole of the Second World War.[5]

The basic transformation of the Western way of making war, its deep integration in the industrial system, the way in which the military are embedded in research and development,[6] all underlie the argument of the present chapter that the Anthropocene is also (and perhaps above all) a Thanatocene.[7]

A natural history of destruction

On 27 July 1943, at 0100 hours, the Allies dropped 10,000 tonnes of incendiary bombs on Hamburg. By 0120 the city was consumed by a fire-storm that rose to a height of 2,000 metres. The writer Hans Erich Nossak, in one of the rare eyewitness accounts of the immediate post-war years, emphasized the ecological consequences of the Allied 'strategic bombing'. During autumn 1943, in Hamburg,

> rats and flies ruled the city. The rats, bold and fat, frolicked in the streets, but even more disgusting were the flies, huge and iridescent green, flies such as had never been seen before. They swarmed in great clusters on the roads, settled in the heaps to copulate on ruined walls.[8]

---

5   Sohbet Karbuz, 'US Military Energy Consumption – Facts and Figures', resilience.org, 21 May 2007.

6   Amy Dahan and Dominique Pestre (eds), *Les Sciences pour la guerre. 1940–1960*, Paris: Éditions de l'EHESS, 2004.

7   For more long-term historical perspectives on the link between war and environment, see John R. McNeill, 'Woods and Warfare in World History', *Environmental History*, 9:3, 2004: 388–410; Richard Tucker and Edmund Russell (eds), *Natural Enemy, Natural Ally: Toward an Environmental History of War*, Corvallis: Oregon State University Press, 2004; and Joseph P. Hupy, 'The Environmental Footprint of War', *Environment and History*, 14:3, 2008: 405–21.

8   Hans Erich Nossak, 'Interview mit dem Tode', 1948, quoted in W. G. Sebald,

In 1945, after visiting the ruins of Cologne, Solly Zuckerman, a zoologist and one of the founding fathers of British operational research, had the idea of writing an article on the environmental consequences of strategic bombing. In his memoirs, he explains that he abandoned this because the absolute desolation that he had witnessed 'cried out for a more eloquent piece than I could ever have written'.[9] Zuckerman had proposed to his publisher an intriguing title: *The Natural History of Destruction.*

Perhaps out of respect for human victims, historians have generally not taken up this project. So, if specialists in warfare study the environmental circumstances of battles (the role of terrain, the Russian winter, the impenetrable Ardennes Forest, etc.), the environmental consequences of war are far less well known, i.e., the effects of bombing, trench warfare, artillery or incendiary devices. Besides, the distinction is scarcely satisfactory: mud, for example, all-pervasive in the European wars of the twentieth century, is more an effect of the destruction of soil by the passage of military vehicles than a pre-existing characteristic of the terrain.[10] Likewise, it is because forests played a fundamental defensive role (from the war of position in the Ardennes in 1914 to the guerrilla tactics of the Viet Cong) that they have suffered so much from warfare.

Contemporary observers of wars were well aware of the environmental devastation these caused. In France in the 1820s, for example, the Revolutionary and Napoleonic wars were blamed for the reduction in forest cover as well as for the cooling of the climate. If the armed forces of modern times were always very greedy in terms of timber for ships and guns (around 50 cubic metres of wood were needed to smelt one tonne of iron, or the annual sustainable production of ten hectares of forest),[11] the industrial wars of the twentieth century devoured still greater quantities: in 1916–18, when German

---

On the Natural History of Destruction, New York: Modern Library, 2004, 35.

9   Ibid., 32.

10   See Clyde Edward Wood, *Mud: A Military History*, Dulles: Potomac Books, 2006, 10–13.

11   Rolf Peter Sieferle, *The Subterranean Forest: Energy Systems and the Industrial Revolution*, Isle of Harris: White Horse Press, 2001, 64.

U-boats interrupted Britain's trade routes, the country had to fell nearly half of its commercial woodland in order to satisfy military needs.[12] Similarly, during the Second World War, Japan lost 15 per cent of its forests.[13]

Because it came into the calculation of war reparations, French engineers of the 1920s studied very closely the woodland devastation of the First World War. They distinguished between losses due to exceptional felling (two years' production), losses by direct destruction (50,000 hectares),[14] and losses of woodland made unusable by gunfire.[15] A total of 3.3 million hectares of agricultural land were also affected by battles. Trench warfare left a soil that was sterile, full of metal fragments and unsuited for agriculture, though it would be the object of reforestation in the 1930s. The volume of earth churned up by artillery (up to 2,000 cubic metres per hectare) was equivalent to 40,000 years' natural erosion.[16]

On top of these palpable consequences, deliberate environmental destruction and its tactical and strategic role is a subject still in need of exploration. The 'scorched earth' practices of the nineteenth and twentieth centuries, whether offensive (during the American Civil War, the US invasion of the Philippines, the Boer War, the second Sino-Japanese War) or defensive (the German Operation Alberich of 1917 in the Somme, the opening of the Yellow River dikes by Chiang Kai-shek's troops in 1938, Stalin's destruction of Soviet resources in 1941), should be analysed as environmental phenomena.

---

12   A. Joshua West, 'Forests and National Security: British and American Forestry Policy in the Wake of World War I', *Environmental History*, 8:2, 2003: 270–93.

13   William Tsutsui, 'Landscapes in the Dark Valley: Toward an Environmental History of Wartime Japan', *Environmental History*, 8:2, 2003: 294–311.

14   Jean-Paul Amat, 'Guerre et milieux naturels. Les forêts meurtries dans l'Est de la France 70 ans après Verdun', *Espace géographique*, 16:3, 1987: 217–33, and Jean-Yves Puyo, 'Les conséquences de la Première Guerre mondiale pour les forêts et les forestiers français', *Revue forestière française*, 56:6, 2004: 573–84.

15   In the 1960s the French forestry office established a triage system to record timber that was unusable due to munitions remnants.

16   Paul Arnould, Micheline Hotyat and Laurent Simon, *Les Forêts d'Europe*, Paris: Nathan, 1997, 114.

The Vietnam War is certainly the most well known and best documented case in which destruction of the enemy's physical environment constituted a pre-eminent military objective. It was at this time that Barry Weisberg coined the term 'ecocide'.[17] The American infantry could only advance with the aid of 'Rome plows', powerful bulldozers that grubbed up forests and crops. A special six-tonne bomb, the Daisy Cutter, was also developed, with a shock wave that could instantly create zones for helicopter landing in the middle of the jungle. An estimated 85 per cent of the ammunitions used by the US Army were targeted not at the enemy but at the environment sheltering them: forests, fields, cattle, water reserves, roads and dikes.[18] In 1972, the French geographer Yves Lacoste showed how the US Air Force bombed the dikes of the Red River Delta at its widest part in order to maximize the devastating effect on the population.[19] As he put it, geography and environmental sciences were used above all to make war.

Noting the inability of incendiary bombs and napalm to destroy the humid Vietnamese forests, the US Army finally sprayed defoliants developed from agricultural herbicides (Monsanto's 'Agent Orange'), the mutagenic effects of which on the human population still persist nearly half a century after the end of the war.[20]

It is estimated that 70 million litres of herbicide were sprayed between 1961 and 1971, contaminating 40 per cent of Vietnam's arable land, while the country also lost 23 per cent of its forest cover.

Vietnam was also the theatre of a major project of climate engineering. Between 1966 and 1972, in order to cut the Ho Chi Minh trail running from China to South Vietnam, the US Army carried out more than 2,600 aerial missions with the aim of inducing artificial rain by

17   Barry Weisberg, *Ecocide in Indochina: The Ecology of War*, San Francisco: Canfield Press, 1970.

18   Greg Bankoff, 'A Curtain of Silence: Asia's Fauna in the Cold War', in John McNeill and Corinna R. Unger (eds), *Environmental Histories of the Cold War*, Cambridge: Cambridge University Press, 2010, 203.

19   Yves Lacoste, *La géographie, ça sert, d'abord, à faire la guerre* (1976), Paris: La Découverte, 2012: 60–3.

20   Thao Tran, Jean-Paul Amat and Françoise Pirot, 'Guerre et défoliation dans le Sud Viêt-Nam, 1961–1971', *Histoire et mesure*, 22:1, 2007: 71–107.

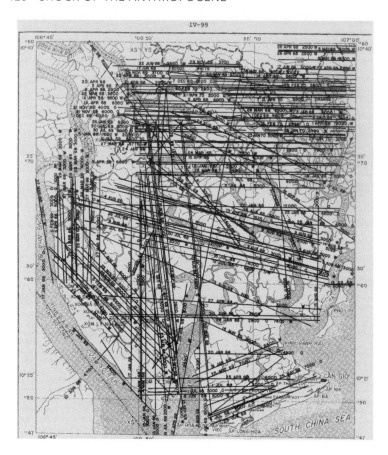

Figure 9: *Defoliant spraying in South Vietnam, 1961–1971*

cloud seeding. At a time when America was mired in the Watergate scandal, revelation of this secret climate war aroused great emotion, and the USSR pressed home its advantage by taking the question to the UN. In 1977, the General Assembly adopted a convention, still in force, forbidding 'the hostile use of environmental modification'. Despite its basic focus on military use, this convention also prohibited 'deliberate manipulation of natural processes – the dynamics, composition or structure of the Earth, including its biota, lithosphere, hydrosphere and atmosphere, or of outer space'. This text is the most solid legal basis for banning experiments of climate engineering that are currently projected with a view to countering climate change.[21]

If the case of the Vietnam War is the best known, it is far from being unique: the destruction of enemy resources and environment was a constant in Cold War conflicts. In 1950, the British Army began to experiment with defoliants in Malaysia, to prevent their Communist opponents from carrying out agriculture in the jungle. During the Korean War, the US Air Force systematically bombed dams and irrigation systems. North Korea lost 75 per cent of its water supply. In Afghanistan, Soviet forces also targeted irrigation systems, and close to half the Afghan cattle were killed during this war.[22]

Napalm, an incendiary mixture of oil and gelling agent invented by the Harvard chemist Louis Fieser in 1942 with support from the DuPont company, played a central role in the ecocides of the Cold War, by its capacity to burn vegetation – as well as the people this sheltered – over large areas. Used already in the Pacific War, it was employed on a massive scale in Korea (32,000 tonnes), by the French army in Vietnam and in Algeria (where two-thirds of French planted forests were destroyed) and by the British against the Mau Mau Rebellion in Kenya.[23]

Brutalizing nature

Generalizing somewhat, we could hypothesize that war, by creating a state of exception, has justified and encouraged a 'brutalizing' of relations between society and environment.[24] If nuclear weapons are the most palpable example of this, the 'scorched earth'

---

21   James R. Fleming, *Fixing the Sky*, New York: Columbia University Press, 2010, 179–88.

22   Bankoff, 'A Curtain of Silence', 226.

23   Robert M. Neer, *Napalm: An American Biography*, Cambridge: Belknap Press, 2013, 91–108.

24   The concept of brutalization was introduced by George L. Mosse to describe the banalization of violence brought about by the First World War. See *Fallen Soldiers: Reshaping the Memory of the World Wars*, Oxford: Oxford University Press, 1990.

policy of modern war should also be studied as both ideology and practice. In 1940, British MPs pressed Kingsley Wood, the air minister, to destroy the Black Forest by incendiary bombs. And it was likewise in terms of biotopes that Churchill explained the meaning of the total war he was waging: to 'make Germany a desert'.[25] It is a revealing fact that the most severe punishment envisioned for Germany was an environmental one: Henry Morgenthau, the US Treasury secretary, proposed to convert Germany into a country 'primarily agricultural and pastoral in character'.

Besides the immediate theatre of operations, war preparations and the organic link between the military, R&D and technological choices have played a fundamental role in the arrival of the Anthropocene.

Certain connections are so self-evident that they have scarcely been studied up till now. By learning to kill humans in an efficient fashion, the military have also learned to kill living things in general.

In the second half of the twentieth century, for example, fishing techniques were indirectly revolutionized by the military. Nylon, which made it possible to manufacture nets several kilometres long, was closely linked with the Second World War – developed by the DuPont company to replace Japanese silk in producing parachutes, bulletproof vests and special tyres. After the Second World War, mechanisms for detecting enemy ships and submarines were applied to industrial fishing. Acoustic detection, radar and sonar, followed by GPS (a Cold War creation), multiplied fishing capacities exponentially and made deep waters and ocean trenches accessible. Moreover, this expensive equipment started a vicious circle, as it was necessary to capture ever more fish to make it profitable.[26] World catches increased by an annual 6 per cent in the 1950s and '60s before declining from 1990, when the application of technology no longer

25   Quoted in Jörg Friedrich, *The Fire: The Bombing of Germany 1940–1945*, New York: Columbia University Press, 2007, 61.

26   Philippe Cury and Yves Miserey, *Une mer sans poissons*, Paris: Calmann-Lévy, 2008, 112–13, and Paul R. Josephson, *Industrialized Nature: Brute Force Technology and the Transformation of the Natural World*, Washington, DC: Island Press, 2002, 197–253.

compensated for the reduction in fish stocks. In the early 2000s, stocks of large fish were down to a mere 10 per cent of their level before the Second World War.[27]

Military machines, by their particular power applied to destructive capacity, constitute archetypes of what Paul R. Josephson proposes to call 'brute force technologies'. Tanks, for example, provided a developmental model for a range of tracked vehicles used in forestry (clear-cutters, harvesters, forwarders)[28] or civil engineering (bulldozers). Indirectly, therefore, they contributed to damaging the lithosphere: mining, the proliferation of forest tracks to render the natural resources of Siberia or Amazonia accessible, the development of suburbias, etc. An interlinked history of mining and military technologies could be written: from the black powder used by German miners in the seventeenth century through to Alfred Nobel's dynamite which made mountain-top removal possible.

The 'peaceful' use of nuclear weapons could also be included in this category. In 1949, the Soviet ambassador to the UN justified his country's first nuclear tests by invoking civilian aims: 'We want to put atomic energy to blowing up mountains, changing the course of rivers, irrigating deserts, laying new lines of life there where the human foot has rarely stepped.'[29] This inaugurated the 'atoms for peace' discourse that Eisenhower took up in 1953. The following year, Camille Rougeron, considered the great French strategist of the Cold War, published a monograph describing the possible applications of the bomb: to alter climate and the course of rivers, melt glaciers, build underground power stations, mine otherwise inaccessible minerals, etc.[30]

In the United States, the secret 'Project Plowshare' was launched in 1957 by the Atomic Energy Commission. Edward Teller, father of the H-bomb, proposed the construction of a second Panama canal with the help of 300 nuclear explosions. Another option involved 764 bombs for

27   Cury and Miserey, *Une mer sans poissons*, 83–5.

28   Josephson, *Industrialized Nature*, 88–91.

29   Francis W. Carpenter, 'United Nations Atomic Energy News', *Bulletin of the Atomic Scientists*, 6:1, 1950: 19.

30   Camille Rougeron, *Les Applications de l'explosion thermonucléaire*, Paris: Berger-Levrault, 1956.

a canal route across Colombia. In 1958, the US administration studied the possible use of the H-bomb in building an artificial port on Cape Thompson in Alaska. In 1963, the AEC and the Californian highways department proposed constructing a freeway across the Bristol Mountains in the Mojave Desert by exploding twenty-two nuclear devices.

The most promising use for nuclear explosions seemed to be for extracting bituminous oil from Alberta. A hundred underground explosions were planned, to liquefy the oil and make it extractable by existing technologies. This project was well advanced in 1962 when Canada changed its mind on the desirability of nuclear tests. In Colorado, on the other hand, the Americans did use the bomb to extract gas, but it turned out to be too heavily contaminated with radioactive elements to be marketable. The growing opposition to radioactive contamination led to Plowshare being abandoned in 1977. Altogether, over twenty years, the US spent $770 million and conducted twenty-seven explosions for civilian aims. The equivalent Soviet programme (Programme no. 7 on Nuclear Explosions for the National Economy) was still more destructive, with a total of 128 explosions to test thirteen possible civilian uses.[31]

Transfers between war and agriculture, both technological and ideological, have become better known thanks to the work of historians Sarah Jansen and Edmund Russell. The development of chlorinated gases during the First World War demonstrated the insecticidal properties of certain organochloride compounds. The US Army's Chemical Warfare Service, in particular, showed the effectiveness of chloropicrin in the battle against typhus. In 1916, the chemist Fritz Haber proposed using the gases developed for warfare by the German Army for exterminating pests. Together with entomologists and foresters, he tested different compounds and different forms of spraying on fields, in flourmills and in barracks. In 1925, this application to forestry served as a pretext for Haber and the German Army to conduct experiments with

---

31   Scott Kirsch, *Proving Grounds: Project Plowshare and the Unrealized Dream of Nuclear Earthmoving*, New Brunswick: Rutgers University Press, 2005.

chemical shells that were forbidden by the Versailles Treaty.[32]

In the United States, the chemical industry underwent a change of scale during the First World War, as a result of the need to substitute for German imports and the demand for explosives. DuPont, Monsanto and Dow grew into powerful corporations. The income from confiscated German patents financed a trade association, the Chemical Foundation,[33] which particularly promoted the conversion of the gas warfare industry to pesticides. The biplanes of the First World War, symbol of the alliance between military technologies and agriculture, were used to spread herbicides.

But it was especially after the Second World War and the invention of DDT, another organochloride compound, that the damaging dream of a purified nature entirely subjected to agricultural needs took concrete form. DDT, invented by the Swiss chemist Paul Hermann Müller in 1939, was used on a massive scale by the US Army from 1942 on, to struggle against typhus and malaria during the Pacific War. Very rapidly, farmers were faced with the problem of resistance. In Korea, the US Army also noted the ineffectiveness of DDT against certain mosquitoes. This was the start of an endless battle between innovation and evolution. The 1950s were marked by the rapid development of the American chemical arsenal, centred on organophosphate compounds such as Sarin, gases known as 'innervating' on account of their capacity to block an enzyme in the nervous system. As they had a similar effect on insects, phytosanitary and military inventions reciprocally fuelled one another. For example, it was working on the basis of the pesticide Amiton that British researchers at the Defence Science and Technology Laboratory at Porton Down perfected the powerful battle gas VX.[34]

War and chemistry powerfully contributed to the development of a culture of annihilation: from the First World War to the Second, the transition was steadily made from a control of pests based on

32   Sarah Jansen, 'Histoire d'un transfert de technologie', *La Recherche*, 340, 2001.

33   Benjamin Ross and Steven Amter, *The Polluters: The Making of Our Chemically Altered Environment*, Oxford: Oxford University Press, 2010, 20.

34   Brian Balmer, *Britain and Biological Warfare: Expert Advice and Science Policy 1930–65*, Basingstoke: Palgrave, 2001.

entomology (protecting crops by the use of predators on insects, or by natural substances) to a logic of extermination. Stephen Forbes, one of the great American ecologists, explained in 1915: 'The struggle between man and insects began long before the dawn of civilization, has continued without cessation to the present time, and will continue, no doubt, as long as the human race endures.'[35]

During the Second World War, insect phobia and racism mutually fuelled one another: Japanese and Germans were often caricatured with the features of insects, beetles or vermin to be exterminated by means of chemical insecticides. Nazi Germany took this process of dehumanization to its culmination. Connections both ideological (degeneration, purity, species health) and technological (Zyklon B was a pesticide developed by Haber) linked the extermination of pests with that of Jews and others in the death camps. We should finally note that, from the Second World War to the publication of Rachel Carson's *Silent Spring* (1962), the chemical industry in the US enjoyed a great prestige thanks to its involvement in the war effort, despite awareness of the danger of pesticide residues in foodstuffs and their acute toxicity for agricultural workers.[36]

Figure 10: *A Japanese depicted as a louse in a wartime US magazine*

---

35   Quoted in Russell, *War and Nature*, 23.
36   Linda Nash, *Inescapable Ecologies: A History of Environment, Disease, and Knowledge*, Berkeley: University of California Press, 2006, 134–51.

Autarchic technologies

Along with the invention of brutal technologies for killing people and, by extension, life forms in general, we have also to examine a set of more complex historical phenomena that indirectly link war and the Anthropocene. For example, the imperative of supplying a war economy leads to the duplication of productive infrastructure and finally the build-up of excess industrial capacity in many fields. Or again, industrial mobilization, war emergency, blockades and the imperative to substitute imports play a role in the establishment of autarchic productive systems that are particularly polluting and devouring of energy.

The first major industrial chemical system based on the Leblanc process for synthesizing soda, using sulphuric acid and sea salt, appeared during the Napoleonic Wars: in 1808–09, deprived of natural soda that had been imported from Spain (the ash of marine plants, indispensable to the textile, soap-making and glass industries), French chemists succeeded in synthesizing this 'artificial soda'. The process was very likely the most polluting industry of its time: the production of two tonnes of soda emitted one tonne of hydrochloric acid vapour, which corroded everything in its vicinity and particularly destroyed crops and trees.

Beside its direct environmental effects, the historical consequences of this artificial soda are very important, as it was to protect these extraordinarily polluting chemical works, often owned by industrialists close to ruling circles (Jean-Antoine Chaptal above all, who was at the same time chemist, industrialist and interior minister) that the 1810 decree on classified establishments was issued. This decree caused a fundamental shift in the logic of environmental regulation: from now on, factories were subject to administrative jurisdiction (the *préfectures* and the Conseil d'État), in other words by institutions swayed by national considerations, and thus far more industrialist in their mentality than local jurisdictions or the town police of the ancien régime.[37] Since in 1810 the empire was at its

---

37   Thomas Le Roux, *Le Laboratoire des pollutions industrielles. Paris 1770–1830*, Paris: Albin Michel, 2011, and Jean-Baptiste Fressoz, *L'Apocalypse joyeuse. Une histoire du risque technologique*, Paris: Seuil, 2012.

apogee, this industrialist shift in environmental regulation had repercussions throughout Europe.

The second major chemical system born from war and the project of national autarchy was based on a reaction discovered in 1896 by the French chemist Paul Sabatier: hydrogenation. By way of a catalyst, hydrogen can be added to a number of organic and inorganic compounds.[38] The hydrogenation of nitrogen to obtain ammonia (NH_3) was perfected by the German chemical firm BASF just before the First World War, and turned out to be of prime importance during the war, since nitrate was an essential component of explosives and the Germans were cut off from guano supplies coming from Chile and Peru. It was still more important in agriculture, making possible the production of artificial fertilizers to replace imports of guano or the effort of recycling organic matter.

The synthesis of ammonia is certainly a key piece in the historic jigsaw of the Anthropocene: artificial fertilizers have deeply disturbed the natural biogeochemical cycle of nitrogen on a global scale, leading to the eutrophication of estuaries and the release of nitrous oxide, a powerful greenhouse gas, into the atmosphere. Ammonia synthesis also requires extreme conditions of pressure and temperature (400°C and 200 bars), thus consuming great amounts of energy.

The other major hydrogenation process involved carbon and the production of synthetic fuel. Once again, the context of national self-sufficiency and war preparation was the determining factor. One of the great priorities of the Nazi four-year plan of 1936 was self-sufficiency in fuel. Hermann Göring was in charge of supervising fuel production, and the IG Farben company was commissioned to produce artificial petrol. In 1944, the Germans produced 25 million barrels in this way. In energy terms, the process was highly inefficient, requiring six tonnes of coal to obtain one tonne of petrol. After the war, this technology was abandoned except in East Germany, cut off from the international oil market, and South Africa under apartheid. China is currently interested in the technology in order to increase its strategic

---

38   David Edgerton, *Shock of the Old: Technology and Global History since 1900*, London: Profile Books, 2008.

oil reserves. In the perspective of peak oil, coal hydrogenation would make possible a continuation of the Thermocene in the medium term, and accordingly an aggravation of climate change with incalculable consequences.[39]

Mobilizing the world

War, by disturbing or interrupting trade relations, forces states and businesses to explore new supply solutions. If autarchic technologies are the response of the dominated, the hegemonic powers – Great Britain and the US – preferred a geographical expansion of the material base of their economy. Historically, wars have contributed to the discovery of new sources of strategic materials and thus to integrating new spaces into the industrial exploitation of nature.

In this light, it is highly significant that long-distance trade first grew to mass proportions during the Napoleonic Wars. Up till then, it was only high-value products that crossed the Atlantic: above all, sugar (50,000 tonnes per year in the late eighteenth century), followed by rice, tobacco and precious metals. In 1808, the continental blockade imposed by Napoleon cut off the British supply of timber from the Baltic, a resource indispensable to the Royal Navy. Britain turned therefore to North America. Timber exports rose from 21,000 tonnes in 1802 to 110,000 in 1815. This exploitation of American timber created trading habits, and far from going into reverse at the end of the war, it continued its sharp increase in peacetime. Before the war, only 6 per cent of British timber imports came from America, a figure that rose to 74 per cent after 1815. This transformation in the timber trade was a major historical phenomenon, as in a few years it tripled the capacities of transatlantic shipping and thus made possible the waves of mass emigration of the nineteenth century.[40]

---

39   Alexander Gladstone, 'Coal Emerges as Cinderella at China's Energy Ball', *Financial Times*, 1 May 2013.

40   James Belich, *Replenishing the Earth: The Settler Revolution and the Rise of the Anglo-World, 1789–1939*, Oxford: Oxford University Press, 2009, 106–14.

War also imposes an increased mobility on men and things. It requires new infrastructures whose economic and environmental effects persist long after the return of peace. Thus it was to resolve logistic problems bearing on the supply of army and navy that the Grand Junction Canal between London and the Midlands was inaugurated in 1805, then the Grand Union Canal the following year. The most well-known example is that of the German motorways. If Nazi propaganda vaunted the modernity of these great infrastructure projects and their contribution to economic revival, the precocious development of motorways in a country still only little motorized actually aimed at resolving Germany's strategic dilemma, i.e., its vulnerability to a coordinated attack on both eastern and western fronts. In 1933, Fritz Todt was charged by Hitler with constructing 6,000 kilometres of motorway in five years. The justification of this programme was drawn from the First World War and the famous 'taxis of the Marne' that had saved France from defeat in September 1914. Thanks to Todt's motorways, 300,000 men could cross the Reich from east to west in just two days.[41]

By extension, it would be possible to argue that the petrolization of Western societies in the 1950s and '60s was prepared during the Second World War. The British case is a striking example. Before the war, this country was the world's leading exporter of energy. The war and the massive resort to American oil made it the leading importer by the 1950s. Besides, the war required the construction of refineries and a network of pipelines to take oil to military airfields. This infrastructure, extremely expensive and financed largely out of public funds, made possible the mass expansion of the automobile in the post-war years.[42]

After the war, American suburbanization (and thus motorization) was encouraged by the nuclear threat. Strategists saw US cities from

---

41   Adam Tooze, *The Wages of Destruction: The Making and Breaking of the Nazi Economy*, London: Penguin Books, 2008, 46; Thomas Zeller, *Driving Germany: The Landscape of the German Autobahn, 1930–1970*, New York: Berghahn, 2007, 51–66.

42   David Edgerton, *Britain's War Machine: Weapons, Resources, and Experts in the Second World War*, Oxford: Oxford University Press, 2011, 181.

the point of view of strategic bombing. Given the success of the German policy of industrial dispersion from 1942 to 1944, they deemed it indispensable to spread the US industrial system more widely in order to make it more resilient to the nuclear threat. In 1951, a national policy of 'industrial dispersion' began. The government granted tax reductions, as well as favourable access to strategic resources, low-interest loans and military contracts, to businesses that agreed to relocate away from industrial centres. Satellite towns and ring roads (such as Route 128 around Boston) emerged during this time as the preferred locations for strategic industries. The suburb was officially promoted as a pleasant context for life, far from pollution and traffic jams.[43]

Eisenhower, who had been very impressed by the German *Autobahnen*, launched under his presidency one of the most ambitious civil engineering projects of the twentieth century: the construction of 70,000 kilometres of freeway in fifteen years, at a cost of $50 billion (the total cost of the Marshall Plan was $15 billion).[44] This colossal investment was justified to Congress for reasons of national defence: the freeways would permit the evacuation of cities in case of nuclear attack. In 1956, after years of negotiation, Congress passed the National Interstate and Defense Highways Act. The routes of these interstate highways partly followed military objectives, crossing regions that were thinly populated so as to serve the 400 American military bases. The width of the roads, tunnels and bridges was fixed to accommodate military vehicles.[45]

The war also played a fundamental part in establishing the infrastructure of economic globalization in the second half of the twentieth century. The global nature of the war raised tremendous logistic challenges for merchant shipping. In Suez in 1941, 117 ships were waiting to be discharged, and 171 in Bombay in May 1942. The ports of the Middle East were transformed in order to receive American war

---

43   Peter Galison, 'War against the Center', *Grey Room*, 4, 2001: 5–33.

44   Stephen B. Goodard, *Getting There: The Epic Struggle between Road and Rail*, Chicago: University of Chicago Press, 1996, 184.

45   John R. McNeill and Corinna R. Unger (eds), *Environmental Histories of the Cold War*, Cambridge: Cambridge University Press, 2010, 7.

Figure 11: *German motorways in 1936*

material. Because the war was global, it reconfigured the conditions of globalization.[46] In January 1941, the United States launched an emergency programme of cargo construction, the 'Liberty ships'. Over 2,700 were built between 1941 and 1946. The result was that the volume of global merchant shipping was greater in 1946 than in 1939, despite the loss or obsolescence of half of all pre-war ships. The destruction of war and the Liberty ships explain the conversion of world shipping to oil: from a level of 30 per cent before the war to 52 per cent after.[47]

The history of containerization, which deeply shaped the economic globalization that we have seen since the 1980s, has also been linked to the history of war. In 1956, Malcolm McLean, the

46   Michael B. Miller, *Europe and the Maritime World: A Twentieth-Century History*, Cambridge: Cambridge University Press, 2012, 276–88.

47   Edgerton, *Britain's War Machine*, 82.

head of a major road transport business, bought two Second World War tankers which he converted into container carriers. The business stagnated until the Vietnam War opened an immense new market. In 1965, the US Army was faced with logistic disaster: defective ships, theft, losses, etc. Lacking trained dockers and suitable cranes, ships awaiting discharge piled up in the port of Saigon.[48] Their contents had to be offloaded into small boats, which increased both costs and losses. In 1966, McLean persuaded the Pentagon to entrust him with logistics, and by 1973 the Sea-Land Service's income from the military was $450 million. McLean, not wanting his container ships to make the inward journey empty, decided to seek port facilities in Japan, then experiencing rapid economic growth. The Japanese government grasped the opportunity, and the ports of Tokyo and Kobe were rapidly equipped with the necessary infrastructure. The reduction in transport costs increased Japanese exports (electronic products and vehicles) bound for the United States, beginning what is now called 'globalization'.

Burn, kill

One of the major historical challenges for the Anthropocene is to study the many connections to be made between Thermocene and Thanatocene. The military played a major role in the deployment of high-energy technologies, in which power mattered far more than efficiency.

During the Napoleonic Wars, European governments paid increased attention to coal. The proliferation of cannon foundries accelerated the development of mines. In France, the legal framework was simplified, the rights of concessionaires strengthened, while the state financed mineral prospecting on a major scale. In 1811, mining engineers conducted large-scale surveys in the region of Saint-Étienne with a view to locating sources of ore and tracing the boundaries of

---

48 Marc Levinson, *The Box: How the Shipping Container Made the World Smaller and the World Economy Bigger*, Princeton: Princeton University Press, 2006, 175.

concessions. While coal was still rejected for domestic consumption on account of its dirtiness and bad smell, the army signed large purchasing contracts that stabilized and encouraged mining investment. According to Chaptal, coal production in France rose from 250,000 tonnes per year in 1794 to 820,000 in 1814.[49] Suddenly it became a strategic resource. The Saar, annexed to France by the Treaty of Campo Formio in 1797, underwent an expansion of its iron mines and an initial development of coal.

The British navy played a historically fundamental role in the globalization of coal. In 1824, the East India Company used steamships in Burma in its war against the kingdom of Mandalay. From the 1830s, they were used on the China coast by British opium traffickers. These small gunboats gave the traffickers tremendous assurance. When threatened by the governor of Canton, William Jardine, a large shipowner and an opium trafficker on the side, replied haughtily: 'Our commerce must not be subject to arbitrary rules that gunboats could break by a few rounds of mortar on this town.' The first Opium War (1839–42) demonstrated the superiority of steamships over the Chinese military junks. As well as steam propulsion, their metal hulls enabled the British gunboats to navigate in shallow waters and thus proceed up rivers to pursue enemy embarkations or threaten inland cities.[50]

It was at that point that the Admiralty, along with the British Geological Survey, organized a global survey of coal resources suitable for ensuring its supply lines: Bengal, Australia, Java, New Guinea, Malaysia, Brunei, Palestine, Syria, Nigeria, Socotra, Aden, Natal, etc. The British Empire developed a dense network of coal mines and supply points that were the basis of its naval domination until the twentieth century. For those countries already in the British orbit,

---

49   Jean-Antoine Chaptal, *De l'industrie française*, vol. 2, Paris: Renouard, 1819, 113. Denis Woronoff gives higher figures: 600,000 tonnes in 1789 and 900,000 by the end of the empire. See *Histoire de l'industrie en France*, Paris: Seuil, 1994, 194.

50   Daniel Headrick, *The Tools of Empire: Technology and European Imperialism in the Nineteenth Century*, Oxford: Oxford University Press, 1983, 17–58.

asking for geological expertise was also the most rapid and effective way of attracting British capital and engineers.[51]

The British Admiralty also played a major role in the conversion of world shipping to oil and, more generally, in the harmful union between the military and oil in the twentieth century. In July 1911, the German warship *Panther* was cruising off the coast of Agadir. According to Churchill, appointed First Lord of the Admiralty in September, the superiority of the Royal Navy vis-à-vis its German rival was an absolute imperative, with the survival of the empire at stake. Pressed by oil interests, he was also convinced of the tactical interests of oil: more concentrated than coal in terms of energy, it gave ships a greater radius of action and a faster speed; it saved both space and manpower, and could be more rapidly loaded. But the empire had no oil of its own and had to provide this. The British government bought a 51 per cent share in the Anglo-Persian Oil Company and signed a twenty-year contract for supplying the British navy. This decision inaugurated a century of rivalries and wars in the Persian Gulf.[52]

The First World War confirmed the strategic importance of oil. In 1914, the British Expeditionary Force in France had only 827 motor vehicles; by the end of the war, it had 56,000 lorries, 23,000 cars and 34,000 motorbikes. The war was perceived by the general staff as a victory of trucks over locomotives.[53] It accelerated research into oil combustion, and the speed, performance and power of engines doubled in four years. With state support, automobile constructors renewed their equipment, introduced assembly-line work and generalized the application of Taylorism, making it possible to use semi-skilled workers. In France, the automobile industry quadrupled its capacity.[54] More than 200,000 combat aircraft were produced by the belligerent states.

---

51   Robert A. Stafford, *Scientist of Empire: Sir Roderick Murchison, Scientific Exploration and Victorian Imperialism*, Cambridge: Cambridge University Press, 1989.

52   Daniel Yergin, *The Prize: The Epic Quest for Oil, Money and Power* (1991), London: Simon & Schuster, 2008, 137–47.

53   Ibid., 156.

54   Jean-Pierre Bardou et al., *La Révolution automobile*, Paris: Albin Michel, 1977, 114.

War and the Great Acceleration

It was the Second World War, however, that made for the decisive break, marking a leap forward in energy terms in relation to its predecessor. The average American soldier in the Second World War consumed 228 times more energy than in its predecessor. The main strategic advantage of the Allied armies lay in their almost unlimited supply of American oil. The new role of aircraft sharply increased demand. US Air Force statistics indicate a consumption of aircraft fuel of close to 50 billion litres, of which 80 per cent was consumed within the United States, underlining the major importance of logistics and the military-industrial complex in military consumption.[55] The share of oil consumption represented by the US military rose from a pre-war level of 1 per cent of the national total to 29 per cent in 1944. In parallel with this, the United States strongly developed its extractive capacity from 1.2 to 1.7 billion barrels per year.

Oil logistics were transformed in the course of the war: pipelines and refinery capacity were steeply increased in response to military needs. The production of aircraft fuel (100-octane aviation spirit) formed one of the most important industrial research projects of the Second World War. Investment in the process of alkylation rose to $1 billion, half the total of the Manhattan Project. By the end of the war, the United States could produce 20 million tonnes of aircraft fuel per year, followed by Great Britain with only 2 million.[56] Similarly, two gigantic pipelines (Big Inch and Little Big Inch) were constructed at breakneck speed in 1942 to connect the oilfields of Texas to New Jersey, from where oil was shipped to the European front. These pipelines, initially conceived to ensure safe transport immune from German U-boats, are still in service today.

The 'Great Acceleration' of the 1950s should naturally lead us to investigate the key role of the Second World War in the history of the Anthropocene, and the US war effort in particular. More precise quantitative studies could show that the Great Acceleration was the

---

55   http://www.usaaf.net/digest/operations.htm
56   Edgerton, *Britain's War Machines*, 185.

result of the industrial mobilization for the war, followed by the creation of civilian markets designed to absorb the excess industrial capacity.

Between 1940 and 1944, US industrial production increased more rapidly than in any other period of history. Whereas it had grown by an annual 7 per cent during the First World War, it tripled between 1940 and 1944 (production of raw materials increasing by 60 per cent).[57] Businesses that had been crippled by the problem of over-production in the 1930s were reticent to develop their productive capacity as much as military needs demanded. Investment in production was thus largely financed out of public funds: the US government paid for infrastructure, equipment and machinery, leaving the management of production to private companies. The share of industrial investment in US public expenditure also reached an absolute historical record in 1943 of 70.4 per cent (it is now less than 10 per cent).[58] The result of this orgy of public investment in productive infrastructure or transport was a fifteen-fold multiplication of aircraft and munitions production, tenfold for shipping, three times for chemical products and bauxite, twice for rubber, and so on.[59] Road transport measured in kilometre-tonnes more than doubled, air transport multiplied by six, and the volume of oil transported by pipeline increased five times.

The problem of productive over-capacity and its reconversion in peacetime may be illustrated by the case of aluminium. Production of this metal is both very polluting and highly energy-intensive: the bauxite has first to be converted into alumina (aluminium oxide), then alumina into aluminium. Today, aluminium production consumes 4 per cent of global electricity. In France, which was the cradle of the aluminium industry between the wars, the industry took root in the Alps on account of the abundance of hydro-electricity. Before the Second World War, the uses for this costly mineral were very limited.

---

57   Alan S. Milward, *War, Economy and Society, 1939–1945*, Berkeley: University of California Press, 1979, 63.

58   Alan Gropman (ed.), *The Big 'L': American Logistics in World War II*, Washington, DC: National Defense University Press, 1997, 150.

59   Milward, *War, Economy and Society*, 69.

The development of military aviation during the Second World War radically changed the situation. In the United States, production increased from 130,000 tonnes in 1939 to 1.1 million in 1945, and in Canada from 66,000 tonnes to 500,000 tonnes. World production grew three times during the war, with North America supplying three-quarters of the total. As a result, the geography of bauxite itself changed: France, Greece and Italy, which had been the main sources, were replaced by Suriname, British Guyana and Jamaica.[60] Bauxite production is very polluting on account of the heavy metal residues that contaminate ground-water, and the shift of sources of ore to poor countries simplified the extraction process.

After the war there were several initiatives to find outlets for the aluminium industry. In Britain, a law passed in 1944 provided for the emergency construction of 500,000 prefabricated houses. The aircraft industry saw in this a possibility of reconversion and produced en masse both family homes and schools, using aluminium and asbestos.[61] In the United States, the Beech aircraft company asked the architect Buckminster Fuller to design aluminium houses. The aluminium industry went on to conquer several markets for industrial equipment, automobiles, transport, turbines, etc. Despite health warnings, it was sold as a material for cookware par excellence, neither rusting nor giving off a taste, a good conductor of heat, a preservative and emulsifier in food, an anti-agglomerant in cosmetics, etc.

The history of Volkswagen and its flagship post-war product, the 'Beetle', well illustrates the connections between warfare and civil consumption. In 1933, Hitler charged the Austrian engineer Ferdinand Porsche with developing a 'people's car' for less than 1,000 Deutsche Mark. To finance the factory, the Nazi regime set up a Volkswagen savings plan that people had to subscribe to for several years before being able to obtain a car. No Volkswagen was delivered to individual

---

60   Germaine Veyret-Verner, 'Une industrie en pleine expansion: l'aluminium', *Revue de géographie alpine*, 44:2, 1956: 311–42; Matthew Evenden, 'Aluminium, Commodity Chains and the Environmental History of the Second World War', *Environmental History*, 16:1, 2011: 69–93.

61   Brian Finnimore, 'The A.I.R.O.H. House: Industrial Diversification and State Building Policy', *Construction History*, 1, 1985: 60–71.

customers during the war. On the other hand, the Wolfsburg factory produced more than 70,000 'Kübelwagen' for the Wehrmacht on the basis of Porsche's designs. After the war, Volkswagen converted the Kübelwagen into the Beetle.[62]

The contemporary aircraft industry is likewise a product of the Second World War, both technologically (aluminium, radar, jet engines) and institutionally: in Chicago in 1944, fifty-two countries signed the convention that founded the International Civil Aviation Organization, the aim of which was to promote 'the development and international expansion of trade and travel'. One article of the 1944 convention prohibits the taxation of aircraft fuel and so makes it hard to realize current projects to tax air travel as a means of combating climate change. Despite the increase in oil prices, travelling by plane is still extremely cheap in terms of cost per kilometre. Aviation is the economic sector whose emissions of CO_2 are rising most rapidly, doubling approximately every ten years.

The Second World War thus prepared the technological and legal framework for mass-consumption society.

---

62   Winfried Wolf, *Car Mania: A Critical History of Transport*, London: Pluto, 1996, 87–101.

CHAPTER 7

Phagocene: Consuming the Planet

Human identity is no longer defined by what one does, but by what one owns. But we've discovered that owning things and consuming things does not satisfy our longing for meaning. We've learned that piling up material goods cannot fill the emptiness of lives which have no confidence or purpose.

–Jimmy Carter

On 15 July 1979, before a TV audience of 65 million, Jimmy Carter delivered a major anti-consumerist speech. If its immediate context was the second oil shock, its key idea was that the energy crisis could not be combated without a profound change in values. Americans were summoned to renounce consumerism and individualism, in a 'rebirth of the American spirit'.

If Carter's defeat by Ronald Reagan in 1970, who called for a restoration of US hegemony and the deregulation of polluting activities, showed the limits of this appeal, his speech does illustrate the influence, since unequalled, that criticism of the consumer society had acquired in the public sphere. During the 1960s and '70s, the themes of 'commodity fetishism' and 'cultural alienation' dear to the Frankfurt School invaded the periodical press. Herbert Marcuse's *One-Dimensional Man* (1964), Jean Baudrillard's *The System of Objects* (1968), Guy Debord's *Society of the Spectacle* (1967) and Marshall Sahlins's *Stone Age Economics* (1974) were all bestsellers. Daniel Bell, the theorist of post-industrial society, explained in *The Cultural Contradictions of Capitalism* (1976) how the consumer society undermined the Protestant work ethic that had been the bedrock of

American capitalism. In 1979 Christopher Lasch published *The Culture of Narcissism*, in which he lambasted consumerist and hedonist subjectivity. This cultural critique of consumption was closely bound up with an environmental critique. In 1974, two years after the famous Club of Rome report on *The Limits to Growth*, the biologists Anne and Paul Ehrlich published a successful work, *The End of Affluence*, which predicted the coming exhaustion of mineral and agricultural resources.

If the 1960s and '70s saw the apogee of this criticism, it had already been substantial at the height of the Cold War, the very time when the expression 'consumer society' was coined. The 1950s were marked by David Riesman's *The Lonely Crowd* (1950), which denounced the rise of individualism and the consumer society. This was in fact one of the most popular sociological works of all time, selling 1.4 million copies. In 1958, with *The Affluent Society*, John Kenneth Galbraith showed the contradictions between private consumption and national prosperity: the exuberance of private consumption (artificially stimulated by advertising) limited public investment in education, health and transport. And in *The Hidden Persuaders* (1957), Vance Packard denounced the cynicism of advertising and the immense material waste it produced.

If we go further back in time, in the early years of the century, authors such as Thorstein Veblen were alarmed by the development of advertising, marketing and conspicuous consumption. And in 1925, Stuart Chase published *The Tragedy of Waste*, a scathing pamphlet against planned obsolescence and the proliferation of poor-quality products that forced repeated purchase.[1]

While noting these age-old criticisms, we must also note their inability to sway the historical trajectory. The consumer society is a perfect example of this: criticism of it is as old as the target itself, yet consumerism remains more than ever the motor of capitalism. Worse,

---

1   Daniel Horowitz, *The Morality of Spending: Attitudes toward the Consumer Society in America, 1875–1940*, Baltimore: Johns Hopkins University Press, 1985, and *The Anxieties of Affluence: Critiques of American Consumer Culture, 1939–1979*, Amherst: University of Massachusetts Press, 2004.

history seems to have set out to confirm the majority of these analyses. The fall of the Berlin Wall has even been interpreted as the triumph of democracy *through* consumerism, the 'evil empire' succumbing to the empire of the commodity.

During the decades that followed, the rich countries stimulated their economies, despite wage stagnation, by an excess consumption made possible by the low price of oil, raw materials and Asian labour power. In the United States, household debt rose from 60 per cent of annual income in 1980 to 130 per cent in 2005. Housing expanded by 55 per cent in the same period, which was clearly not enough to cope with the tide of objects, as the 'self-storage' sector grew in the 2000s at the dizzying rate of 81 per cent per year. Before the crisis of 2008 a new profession appeared, that of 'home organizer', helping families to manage the overabundance of their possessions. And yet, during the same period, indicators of well-being deteriorated: both the 'happiness index' and more material measurements such as life expectancy stagnated, and healthy life expectancy actually began to decline.[2] Among the rich countries, the human development index (education, health, income) diverged from GDP, the former stagnating from the late 1970s while the latter, a wretched indication of real well-being, continued to rise.[3]

How can this incapacity to escape from consumerism be explained historically? How can we explain, despite certain heralds of 'reflexive modernity' (see chapters 4 and 8), our absolute lack of reflexivity? The issue for the historian of the Anthropocene is to understand the making of consumerism and its power.

---

2   André Cicolella, *Toxique planète. Le scandale invisible des maladies chroniques*, Paris: Seuil, 2013.

3   Clive Hamilton, *Requiem for a Species: Why We Resist the Truth about Climate Change*, London: Routledge, 2010, 66–77.

Is it desire that led us into the Anthropocene?

From the 1980s on, an increasing number of historians showed that certain elements generally attributed to the 'consumer society' could be already observed in England and the Netherlands in the late eighteenth century. This thesis, initially controversial, aroused a rich bundle of research, which has upwardly reassessed the material density of 'advanced organic economies' in Western Europe.[4] According to Neil McKendrick, English society of the eighteenth century displayed a powerful desire for the consumption of commodities (porcelain, textiles, watches, as well as colonial products such as sugar, tea, coffee and precious woods). A royal census of 1759 counted 141,700 shops in England and Wales, a density of 240 per 10,000 inhabitants (as against 45 per 10,000 at this time in France).[5]

At the source of this phenomenon was a less rigidly defined social status, which generated social emulation between the middle classes and the landed aristocracy. If the expression 'conspicuous consumption' was coined by Thorstein Veblen, the actual idea is very old, formulated among others by Adam Smith. Smith's anthropology naturalized the instinct of enrichment: individuals were moved by a powerful acquisitive passion that needed to be controlled and enlisted so that it acted in the sense of the common good.

These historians went on to show the causal link between this 'consumer revolution' and the industrial revolution. According to Jan de Vries, the latter was prepared by a long 'industrious revolution', from the late seventeenth century to the 1800s.[6] This period was marked by a rise in production, but without a technological break or a gain in productivity. Growth was therefore basically realized by an

---

4   Neil McKendrick, John Brewer and John Plumb, *The Birth of a Consumer Society: The Commercialization of Eighteenth-Century England*, London: Europa Publications, 1982.

5   Hoh-Cheung Mui and Lorna Holbrook Mui, *Shops and Shopkeeping in Eighteenth-Century England*, London: Routledge, 1989, 36–7.

6   Jan de Vries, *The Industrious Revolution: Consumer Behavior and the Household Economy, 1650 to the Present*, Cambridge: Cambridge University Press, 2008, 3.

intensification of labour: the working year in England rose from 2,700 hours to 3,300, chiefly by the suppression of religious festivals. In parallel with this was a new involvement of women and children in productive activities oriented to the market.

How should we explain this acceptance of 'working more to earn more' in the eighteenth century? It is here that desire and the appearance of new and attractive goods come into play. For example, the spread of watches and clocks in Western Europe in the eighteenth century was rapid and general. In the Netherlands, while clocks had been extremely rare in inventories drawn up after the death of farmers in the late seventeenth century, fifty years later they were to be found in 86 per cent of such lists. In Paris, in 1700, only 13 per cent of servants possessed a watch, but this figure rose to 70 per cent by the 1780s. For Jan de Vries, the desire to consume becomes the deus ex machina of European economic dynamism. It is what reoriented productive activity from subsistence agriculture to the sphere of commodities and money.

If this thesis complements explanations in terms of production or environment (innovation, coal and the 'ghost acres' of the British Empire), it nonetheless has the defect of naturalizing the desire for consumption. It neglects several indications that attest, contrary to this, the difficulty of inculcating in artisans or new arrivals from the countryside a labour discipline involving whole days and weeks of work. For example, 'Saint Monday' (i.e., absenteeism) was considered a privilege well into the nineteenth century by well-paid artisans who opted in favour of leisure.[7]

Under the law of pre-revolutionary France, artisans were subject to a contract of hire by the job. They committed themselves to the entrepreneur or commissioner to supply a product at a given date but remained responsible for the methods and rhythms of labour. This freedom legally distinguished them from servants.[8] The rhythm of

---

7   Edward P. Thompson, 'Time, Work-Discipline, and Industrial Capitalism', *Past and Present*, 38:1, 1967: 56–97.

8   Michael Sonenscher, *Work and Wages: Natural Law, Politics and the Eighteenth-Century French Trades*, Cambridge: Cambridge University Press, 1989, 69–72.

labour under the ancien régime, whether agricultural or handicraft, was characterized by a great irregularity: intense periods were followed by those of relative idleness. Many contemporary authors suggested that the motivation to work *declined* with a rise in wages. This rational behaviour attests to the hold of a culture of sufficiency.[9]

The infrastructures of the consumer society

A different historiography, whose roots go back to the critique of the consumer society in the 1970s, has shown the importance of the material and institutional arrangements that forged the first mass-consumption society, particularly in the United States at the turn of the twentieth century.[10]

This period was marked by large-scale social conflicts, followed by major strike waves after the First World War. The issue was not just the level of wages but the wage relation itself, as a principle and for the subordination of the worker that it involved. At the start of the twentieth century, entrepreneurs complained of workers' absenteeism. Even during the First World War, skilled workers in munitions factories refused to abandon the custom of 'Saint Monday'.

This period also saw major increases in productivity, bound up with the introduction of electricity and Taylorist methods in factories. In the United States, the power of industrial machines quadrupled between 1899 and 1927.

Finally, this was the period in which economic globalization was completed: radio, refrigerated ships, and railways followed the telegraph to link up a unified world market for the first time. This phenomenon, closely bound up with the consumer society, had particularly deleterious consequences for the environment of tropical countries. Between 1870 and 1920, American consumption of tropical products (coffee, sugar, bananas, rubber) grew steeply: that of sugar

---

9   Gary Cross, *Time and Money: The Making of Consumer Culture*, London: Routledge, 1993, 16–20.
10   Stuart Ewen, *Captains of Consciousness: Advertising and the Social Roots of the Consumer Culture*, New York: McGraw-Hill, 1976.

rose from an annual 17 kilograms to 42 kilograms per person, that of coffee by a multiple of seven.[11] In the countries of Central America, subsistence agriculture was pressed back onto the mountain slopes by the latifundia and big estates of the United Fruit Company, causing a disastrous erosion of the soil and accompanying social tensions.[12]

As a result of globalization, commodities also became far more abstract, cut off from their connections with producer and territory. For example, in the great silos that arose in Chicago in the 1860s, wheat could no longer be related to a particular farm. This abstraction made nature far more suited for circulation in the networks of world capitalism. The grain stored in Chicago could be bought in London without concern for its quality. It could even be bought before being produced, as along with the silos came the invention of futures markets for food crops.[13]

Mass consumption was a strategic adaptation of American capitalism to these various mutations. The explicit and paramount aim of politicians, industrialists and advertisers alike was to create markets able to absorb the new productive capacities of Taylorist factories. In the words of Herbert Hoover, 'High wages are the very essence of mass production.'[14] As well as spending power, various innovations also contributed to the creation of mass markets.

First of all, trademarks became general. In the early 1900s, the majority of common consumer goods were not branded: the grocer sold wine from the barrel, sugar from the sack and so on. The choice of mass production was a risky one: it was necessary to be sure that the costly machines it required would be profitable. Entrepreneurs therefore needed commercial outlets that were stable and independent of

---

11   Jon Soluri, *Banana Cultures: Agriculture, Consumption and Environmental Change in Honduras and the United States*, Austin: University of Texas Press, 2005, 219.

12   Richard Tucker, *Insatiable Appetite: The United States and the Ecological Degradation of the Tropical World*, Berkeley: University of California Press, 2000. On Guatemala, see Beatriz Manz, *Paradise in Ashes*, Berkeley: University of California Press, 2004.

13   William Cronon, *Nature's Metropolis: Chicago and the Great West*, New York: Norton, 1991, 97–147.

14   Herbert Hoover in 1923, quoted by Ewen, *Captains of Consciousness*, 28.

intermediaries. Trademarks precisely made it possible to bypass the wholesaler and create a direct relationship with the consumer. And the consumer in turn now demanded a particular brand, imposing stock requirements on the retailer. For producers, the trademark, by stabilizing demand, reduced the impact of economic fluctuations. Protection of trademarks was established in 1890 when the US Supreme Court granted a property of unlimited duration. This decision aroused fierce controversy, as it went against the fourteen-year protection that was given by patent law.[15]

The turn of the century was also marked in the United States by a revolution in the distribution chain. Barter and bargaining were marginalized and credit sale formalized with the transition from the traditional slate to consumer credit. Mail order was also invented, along with grocery chains, followed soon by the self-service supermarket – inaugurated by the Piggly Wiggly chain during the First World War as a response to staff shortage.[16]

Finally, there was a change in the nature of advertising. From a marginal activity more like the present-day classifieds, it became an essential engine of the consumer society. In the 1920s, the advertising sector of the US economy grew from $58 million to $200 million.[17] Madison Avenue in New York City became its centre. More generally, the transition was from advertising a particular product to glorifying consumption as a lifestyle and marker of social normality. Advertisers made the essential discovery that the precondition of being able to sell is to question the perception that consumers have of themselves. In the 1920s, *Printers' Ink*, the advertising trade journal, explained that Americans 'had to be made aware of such things as enlarged nose pores or bad breath'. 'Advertising helps to keep the masses dissatisfied with their mode of life, discontented with ugly things around them. Satisfied customers are not as profitable as discontented ones.'[18] Psychologists,

---

15   Susan Strasser, *Satisfaction Guaranteed: The Making of the American Mass Market*, Washington, DC: Smithsonian Institution Press, 1989, 29–57.

16   Ibid., 58–88.

17   Ewen, *Captains of Consciousness*, 32.

18   Quoted ibid., 39.

psychoanalysts, sociologists and behaviourists invaded this rich new market.

With the development of advertising, the classic concept of the market was turned completely on its head. From the abstract market of the economists, the meeting point between rational individuals seeking to satisfy needs that preceded their entry onto the market, there was now the concrete market of advertisers, a market that could be created from scratch, where needs were malleable and buyers irrational.[19]

Disciplinary hedonism

In 1893, the economist George Gunton explained that new products were indispensable for attaching workers to their job: 'such a conscious need for an object that its absence will cause sufficient pain to induce the effort and sacrifice necessary to its attainment'.[20] With the production of deep and stable markets, the second goal of mass consumption, completely explicit, was to discipline the workers. Henry Ford introduced a daily wage of $5, double that of his competitors, partly so that his workers could buy the cars that they made, but above all to reduce staff turnover. The repugnance of workers for Taylorist methods and assembly-line work was such that Ford had to recruit 963 men in order to add 100 workers to its labour force.[21]

Consumer credit also played a key role in this disciplinary hedonism. Until the 1920s, credit remained informal (the slate) or underground (loan sharks and other 'leeches'). Banks only financed businesses and property acquisitions. New credit techniques such as hire purchase or instalment plan universalized the slogan 'buy now, pay later'. Companies producing consumer goods, such as Ford, General Motors and General Electric, became major suppliers of

---

19   Jackson Lears, *Fables of Abundance: A Cultural History of Advertising in America*, New York: Basic Books, 1994, 196–233.

20   George Gunton, *Principles of Social Economics* (1893), quoted by Cross, *Time and Money*, 25.

21   Matthew B. Crawford, *The Case for Working with Your Hands: Or Why Office Work Is Bad for Us and Fixing Things Feel Good*, London: Viking, 2009, 41–2.

credit. During crisis periods, when investment flagged, banks were also interested in this lucrative market. The development of mass consumption in the United States took place on credit. In 1926, for example, half of American households already owned a car, but two-thirds of these cars had been bought on credit.[22] This was a characteristically American trait: neither Britain nor France, the two European countries most motorized at this time, had more than one car for twenty inhabitants at the end of the 1930s. When consumer credit was first introduced in Britain, it failed to take off.[23]

The 'consumer society' thus refers to a new relationship with objects and the environment, and a new form of social control that makes this relationship desirable. Disciplinary hedonism played (and continues to play) a fundamental role in the acceptance of mass production and its disastrous environmental consequences. It required a transformation of values: repairing, economizing and saving were presented as outdated habits harmful to the national economy, while repeated and ostentatious consumption, fashion and obsolescence became respectable objectives. The rise in wages and above all the introduction of consumer credit were the pillars of a new form of social control, at the heart of the famous Fordist model. In exchange for consumption, individuals had to accept an increased routinization of work and the dependency arising from credit.

From recycling to planned obsolescence

Mass consumption eclipsed the practices of recycling that were absolutely fundamental in the nineteenth century, deeply affecting the cycles of materials.

In France in the 1860s, *chiffonage*, the collection of discarded objects and material, occupied more than 100,000 people. Virtually everything was suitable for recovery: rags for paper and bone used for tablets and

---

22   Lendol Calder, *Financing the American Dream: A Cultural History of Consumer Credit*, Princeton: Princeton University Press, 1999, 19.

23   Victoria De Grazia, *Irresistible Empire: America's Advance through Twentieth-Century Europe*, Cambridge, MA: Harvard University Press, 2005, 90.

buttons, animal charcoal, phosphorous, sal-ammoniac and gelatin. Until the late nineteenth century, human and animal excrement was systematically collected for agriculture.[24] Recycling was integrated into the distribution circuits. In the United States, commercial travellers also acted as recyclers, offering distributors new goods in exchange for worn-out ones, bits of metal, glass or rags, and thus stimulating a general collecting effort.[25]

Good housekeeping minimized the production of waste. Several handbooks with evocative titles such as *The Frugal Housewife* or *The Family Save All: A System of Secondary Cookery* taught the recycling of waste. It was commonplace, for example, to save cooking fat for the production of soap. The massive presence of animals in the city also limited the volume of organic waste, much of which was fed to domestic animals. In New York in the mid nineteenth century, 10,000 scavenging pigs provided sustenance for the poor and aroused the complaints of the middle class. 'Be careful of the pigs if you visit New York', Charles Dickens warned in 1842.[26] Until late in the century, small pigsties and domestic chicken coops were very common in towns.

Several factors explain the general crisis of the recycling economy in the late nineteenth century. First of all, urban transformation: the expansion of cities, followed by the general provision of running water and flush toilets, complicated the collection of human excrement and its application to agriculture. Then there were technological factors: the manufacture of paper from wood pulp, for example, made rags useless. In the same way, the use of artificial nitrate fertilizer from the mid twentieth century ended the agricultural function of excrement and urban mud. More generally, increases in productivity made recycling economically less profitable than manufacture.

The culture of objects also changed. In the 1920s, Christine Frederick, a specialist in household management who was extremely

---

24   Sabine Barles, *L'Invention des déchets urbains. France 1790–1970*, Paris: Champ Vallon, 2007.

25   Susan Strasser, *Waste and Want: A Social History of Trash*, New York: Metropolitan Books, 2000, 70–80.

26   Ibid., 30.

famous at the time, popularized the idea of 'convenience' as the domestic equivalent of industrial efficiency. The meaning of 'waste' changed from rejected matter to lost time.[27] Electrical household devices were marketed under the banner of household efficiency and the emancipation of women. In the 1930s, half of American households possessed a washing machine and a vacuum cleaner.[28] Likewise, ready-made meals became popular in the 1920s for the American middle classes.

A throw-away culture was also developed under the banner of health. Kimberly-Clark supplied the US Army with bandages during the First World War. In 1918, it found itself with surplus stocks of cellucotton, and Kotex, the first disposable menstrual pad, was invented in order to use this material. Industrial packaging was similarly popularized on health grounds.[29]

Finally, psychological obsolescence became an essential tool in the struggle against overproduction.[30] It was first developed in the automobile sector. In 1923, when half of US households already had a car and the Ford Model T dominated a saturated market, General Motors introduced an annual change of model. Obsolescence was bound up with the growing role of industrial laboratories: the electric starter, invented in 1913, showed the ability of R&D to make certain goods obsolete overnight. In 1932, Ford followed this practice, which rapidly became general for all household durables. And when innovation failed to keep pace, which was indeed the general case, the futurist industrial design of the 1950s maintained the illusion of permanent technical progress.[31]

---

27   Ibid., 181–7.

28   Sue Bowden and Avner Offer, 'Household Appliances and the Use of Time: The United States and Britain since the 1920s', *Economic History Review*, 47:4, 1994: 725–48.

29   Strasser, *Waste and Want*, 169–81; Giles Slade, *Made to Break: Technology and Obsolescence in America*, Cambridge, MA: Harvard University Press, 2006, 9–27.

30   Bernard London, *Ending the Depression Through Planned Obsolescence*, New York, 1932.

31   Slade, *Made to Break*, 29–55.

Time rather than money

Consumerism is not simply an economic order. It also defines a temporal order organized around work. Its triumph eclipsed powerful social movements for a drastic reduction in working hours. These alternative voices scarcely had a chance, trapped between crisis and war.

The trade-off between consumption and leisure was fiercely debated during the whole first half of the twentieth century. Alfred Marshall, the most influential economist of his generation, had already explained in 'The Future of the Working Classes' (1873) that productivity gains would increasingly have to be allocated to leisure, given that material needs were not infinitely extendable. He proposed a working day of six hours, and even four hours for unpleasant work.[32] The eight-hour day was the common demand of all European and American trade unions. For the generation of 1910–30, the spectacular increase in productivity had necessarily to lead to a massive reduction in working time. Leisure, rather than consumption, was seen by economists and intellectuals (such as John Maynard Keynes and Bertrand Russell in England, Charles Gide and Gabriel Tarde in France) as the variable that would bring about economic equilibrium and win the struggle against over-production and unemployment.

The First World War and the massive application of Taylorist methods visibly showed the productivity gains being made in the factories. At the end of the war, the British industrialist Lord Leverhulme (founder of Lever Brothers, eventually Unilever) argued for a six-hour day. In the 1920s, the European left supported the scientific organization of work, as this would make possible an increase in free time. The unions recycled the traditional pride of the worker in his trade into a collective affirmation of mass production and productivity.[33] Free time was an important political issue both in the democracies and under the fascist regimes, with the expectation that it would become the centre of social life. Holiday

---

32 Cross, *Time and Money*, 22–4.
33 Ibid., 37.

camps, discussion groups and the practice of sports were encouraged by government. In France, Léo Lagrange symbolized these concerns.[34]

In an initial period, the crisis of the 1930s reinforced this movement for a reduction in working hours. In Europe, trade unions demanded the forty-hour week, which was voted into law in France in 1936. In 1932, the American Federation of Labor called for a thirty-hour week *with* reduction of wages. A law imposing a thirty-hour week was even adopted by the US Senate in April 1933 but rejected by the House of Representatives.[35] The world crisis seemed to have discredited the hymn to consumption of the 1920s.

The triumph of consumerism

How is the resurgence of this powerful current to be explained? For economists trained in marginalist theory, the traditional distinction between natural and artificial needs disappeared in favour of a subjective theory of utility. Paradoxically, the economic crisis led to the idea of growth being naturalized. Previously, growth was bound up with a process of material expansion: it was a question of increasing production of a particular material, opening up new resources or territories for the economy. With the overproduction crisis of the 1930s, growth came to be thought of no longer in material terms but rather as an intensification of the totality of monetary relations. The abandoning of the gold standard in the 1930s (i.e., the end of the idea that bank-notes represented gold) and the invention of GDP for national accounting completed the dematerialization of economic thinking, so that the economy could now be conceived as growing indefinitely without coming up against physical limits.[36]

---

34   Léo Lagrange (1900–40) was France's first minister for sport and leisure, in the Popular Front government of 1936, and particularly associated with the introduction of paid holidays.

35   Ibid., 82–4.

36   Timothy Mitchell, 'Fixing the Economy', *Cultural Studies*, 12:1, 1998: 82–101.

Figure 12: *The post-war world as technological consumerist paradise, General Electric advertisement, 1943*

In the United States, the economists of the New Deal acted on the assumption that the crisis had been caused not by a lack of demand, but rather by a weakness of purchasing power. Franklin D. Roosevelt accordingly made Keynesian revival and an increase in purchasing power the linchpin of his policy of public works.

The war brought the Keynesian boost that the New Deal had lacked. The start of the war, for Americans, coincided with a period of intense consumption: car sales leapt by 55 per cent in the first half of 1941, sales of refrigerators by 164 per cent.[37] The war massively

---

37   Lizabeth Cohen, *A Consumer's Republic: The Politics of Mass Consumption in Postwar America*, London: Vintage, 2004, 63.

enriched Americans, their purchasing power rising by 60 per cent between 1939 and 1944. It is true that official propaganda called for recycling and saving, but simply to consume more later on. The purchase of well-remunerated war loans made it possible to benefit from technological advances. A propaganda campaign titled 'Why we are fighting' promised post-war abundance. Advertising presented the world to come as a technological paradise. As the manufacturer of Sparton radios explained: 'Home will be truly a House of Wonders in this after-Victory world. Science already knows how to make it comfortable beyond our dreams. Invention will fill it with conveniences we have never known.'[38] It was during the Second World War, in fact, that the dream of the 'American way of life' based on the family home in the suburbs was constructed, along with its panoply of electrical equipment.

In the aftermath of the war, the United States experienced once again a major strike wave. In the words of Charles E. Wilson, president of General Electric and adviser to President Eisenhower, the problems of the United States could be summed up in a few words: 'Russia abroad, labour at home.'[39] The employment law of 1946 and the Taft-Hartley Act on industrial relations established a new order often referred to as Cold War Keynesianism. The employment law stipulated that the government had to promote full employment and maximize production and purchasing power. The Taft-Hartley Act restricted the right to strike. Trade unions abandoned a reduction in working time in exchange for an increase in consumption. From now on, their main demand was for an indexing of wages in relation to prices. In exchange, capitalists obtained the social stability they needed for their investments. They also accepted state intervention into the economy, on condition that this guaranteed their opportunities of profit. Hence the option for military expenditure to fill order books, for highways rather than public transport, for the single-family home rather than public

38   Donald Albrecht (ed.), *World War II and the American Dream: How Wartime Building Changed a Nation*, Cambridge, MA: MIT Press, 1995, 27.
39   Quoted by David Noble, *Forces of Production: A Social History of Industrial Automation* (1984), New Brunswick: Transaction Publishers, 2011, 3.

housing, loans to veterans (the G.I. Bill) and private pensions rather than the financing of public education and universal health coverage.

In Europe as well as the United States, the post-war decades were marked by a very sharp rise in GDP, which quadrupled in thirty years. Median and average incomes tripled. In the United States, consumption increased still more rapidly, thanks to the credit explosion. The guaranteed loans for veterans and the appearance of credit cards massively expanded household debt. By 1957, two-thirds of Americans were in debt.

A good part of this economic dynamism was based on the expansion of suburbs and motorization. The return of 14 million G.I.s and the 'baby boom' intensified the housing crisis. To stimulate supply, the housing developer William Levitt proposed applying to the construction sector the production methods of the arms industries: mass production to negotiate prices with suppliers, the division of tasks (twenty-six in the building of a house), specialization of labour, massive use of prefabrication, vertical integration and a simplification of construction with everything being electrical (see Chapter 5). Before the war, between 200,000 and 300,000 houses per year were built in the United States; in 1949, the figure was 1 million. Levitt became a national hero.

Suburbanization encouraged the purchase of consumer durables: refrigerators, cookers, washing machines and televisions, particularly since these items were often integrated into the house itself. In 1965, in the United States, car production reached a historic peak of 11.1 million per year. One job in six was bound up with automobile construction.

To stimulate demand, the state guaranteed housing loans. Thirty-year mortgages brought the suburban dream within reach for less than $60 per month, or the equivalent of three days' wages. Suddenly, for millions of Americans, buying in the suburbs became less expensive than renting in town. The move to the suburbs was accompanied by public investment in roads. During the 1950s, 80 per cent of new homes in the US were built in the suburbs, which gained an extra 30 million inhabitants between 1947 and 1953. Suburbanites overtook city dwellers and country folk together by 1960. By that time, half of the economically active population lived in the suburbs, and three-quarters of those under forty.

State-supported suburbanization redefined the political and social world of the worker: it dissolved the ethnic and social solidarities that had been the support of working-class solidarity, and in combination with television it domesticated and privatized leisure, which shifted from the urban public space to the suburban living room. The share of household income spent on cinema and public entertainment fell by an annual 2 per cent between 1947 and 1955.[40]

Cold War Keynesianism gave consumerism a moral and political meaning, linking it with national prosperity and civic virtue, as well as with competition with the USSR and the defence of freedom. Mass consumption was presented as an alternative to Communism: the United States would beat the Soviet Union at its own game by effacing the traditional barriers of class society. In 1951, the sociologist David Riesman published 'The Nylon War', a satirical essay in which a US colonel decides to bombard the Soviet Union with nylon hose, cigarettes and watches with the aim of convincing Russians to embrace capitalism. Unfortunately, the Soviet government responds with its own 'aggressive generosity' in the form of caviar, fur coats and copies of Stalin's speeches. The pertinence of the essay was confirmed a few years later with the famous 'kitchen debate' between Nixon and Khrushchev at the US exhibition in Moscow on 29 July 1959.

In Europe, the Nazi and fascist regimes sought to forge a consumerist culture in the service of political stabilization.[41] The Nazis demonstrated a certain ambivalence towards the consumer society: on the one hand, this appeared as an American invention, decadent and Jewish; on the other, they recognized the role it could play in winning the support of the middle and working classes. The solution was to promote an Aryan consumer society that preserved certain elements

40   Lynn Spiegel, 'Installing the Television Set: Popular Discourses on Television and Domestic Space, 1948–1955', *Camera Obscura*, 16:1, 1998.

41   S. Jonathan Wiesen, *Creating the Nazi Marketplace: Commerce and Consumption in the Third Reich*, Cambridge: Cambridge University Press, 2010; Victoria De Grazia, *The Culture of Consent: Mass Organisation of Leisure in Fascist Italy*, Cambridge: Cambridge University Press, 1981.

of its American exemplar (the 'Fordism' that Hitler greatly admired) while differentiating itself from this by the state organization of the market, the promotion of healthy products, and the despoliation of non-Aryans. To this end, the Nazi regime drew up a list of 146 products designated as 'people's products' (*Volksempfänger* – radio, *Volkswohnung* – apartment, *Volkswagen*, etc.), production of which was to be rationalized. According to the German historian Götz Aly, the abundance of consumer goods was more decisive than ideology in winning popular support for the regime; tracing the Nazi origins of the 'German miracle', he shows that the pillage of occupied countries and the plunder of Jewish goods made it possible to establish the consumer society, welfare state and social market economy that post-war West Germany inherited.[42]

In Western Europe, productivism and the consumer society similarly took root as the cement of a social compromise promoted by the Marshall Plan.[43] In 1944, the general secretary of the French Communist Party, Maurice Thorez, declared to the miners of Waziers: 'Produce, that is today the highest form of class duty.'[44]

After the war, American films launched a semi-official propaganda campaign for the 'American way of life'. Modern domestic life and the world of abundance were presented as self-evident, and the natural stage for romantic or criminal plots.[45] The pioneering writings of Henri Lefebvre and Roland Barthes (*Mythologies*, 1957), then George Perec's acrid novel *Things* (1965), mapped the entry of French society into a consumerist culture with its own icons and temples: the Salon de l'automobile and the 'Arts of Housekeeping' show, the 'motor' ever-present in New Wave films, the talk of the emancipation of women

---

42   Götz Aly, *Hitler's Beneficiaries: Plunder, Racial War, and the Nazi Welfare State*, New York: Henry Holt, 2005.

43   De Grazia, *The Culture of Consent*. On the Americanization of French society and the reactions it aroused, see Richard Kuisel, *Seducing the French: The Dilemma of Americanization*, Berkeley: University of California Press, 1993.

44   Marc Lazar, 'Damné de la terre et homme de marbre. L'ouvrier dans l'imaginaire du PCF du milieu des années trente à la fin des années cinquante', *Annales*, 1990, 45:5, 1071–96.

45   Kristin Ross, *Fast Cars, Clean Bodies: Decolonization and the Reordering of French Culture*, Cambridge, MA: MIT Press, 1996, 38.

by consumer durables, the hypermarkets that sprang up in the 1960s.[46] As in all industrialized countries, the consumerism that fuelled strong economic growth was made possible by drawing on the planet's finite natural resources and by unequal exchange with the countries that produced raw materials, the terms of trade shifting against these by 20 per cent between 1950 and 1972. As far as oil was concerned, this shift came to an end with the 'oil shock' of 1973, but for renewable and mining materials it continued until the 1990s.[47]

The Anthropocene body

The entry into consumerist society that was the foundation of the 'Great Acceleration' not only degraded environments; it also deeply affected the bodies and physiology of consumers.

In 1947, the Rockefeller Foundation sent a team of researchers to study European nutrition. The people of Crete, despite being relatively tall, were described as suffering from deficiencies on account of a consumption of meat and dairy products that was insufficient by American standards.[48] This study formed part of a broad movement of imposing on Europe after 1945, and on the whole world in recent decades, a new dietary model high in meat and sugar and dominated by industrial foodstuffs. This model, actively constructed by the major agricultural and food corporations,[49] has gone hand in hand with a degradation of the planet's ecosystems: overfishing, specialization and monoculture that undermine biodiversity, pollution by fertilizers and pesticides, the shrinking of tropical forests in favour of

---

46   Claire Leymonerie, 'Le Salon des arts ménagers dans les années 1950. Théâtre d'une conversion à la consommation de masse', *Vingtième siècle. Revue d'histoire*, 91, 2006: 43–56.

47   Paul Bairoch, *Mythes et paradoxes de l'histoire économique*, Paris: La Découverte, 1999, 161.

48   Martin Bruegel, 'Alimentary Identities, Nutritional Advice, and the Uses of History', *Food and History*, 2:2, 2004: 105–16.

49   Roger Horowitz, *Putting Meat on the American Table: Taste, Technology, Transformation*, Baltimore: Johns Hopkins University Press, 2006; William Boyd, 'Making Meat: Science, Technology, and American Poultry Production', *Technology and Culture*, 42:4, 2001: 631–64.

stock-raising, soya and palm oil, with enormous emissions of green-house gases.

Its corollary, too, is a sharp rise in chronic diseases such as cancer, obesity and cardiovascular illness. Ever-earlier puberty in poor American families and the rise in child cancer incidence in Europe (up 35 per cent in thirty years) are a regular cause of concern. But the problem is global. Chronic diseases have become the prime cause of mortality worldwide (63 per cent of the 57 million deaths in 2008), much higher than infectious diseases (27 per cent) and amounting to a real time bomb, especially in India and China.[50] The number of people in the world suffering from overweight and obesity rose from 857 million in 1980 to 2.1 billion in 2013.[51] And now nutritionists explain to us the virtues of the Cretan diet.

The Anthropocene body is also one damaged by thousands of toxic substances. In 2004, when the European Union's Registration, Evaluation, Authorisation and Restriction of Chemicals (REACH) Regulation was being debated, the World Wildlife Fund published blood tests for thirty-seven European parliamentarians showing the presence of an average forty-one persistent and accumulative organic poisons. The malleability of regulations, and particularly the notion of thresholds, has authorized the proliferation of substances produced by synthetic chemistry since the Second World War. In the late 1940s, toxicologists warned governments that even at the lowest doses certain of these molecules increased the risk of cancer, and a consensus formed to ban such substances from foods. In 1958, in the United States, the Delaney Clause prohibited the presence of pesticide residues in food-stuffs. But in the 1970s, regulatory bodies turned to deploying a cost/benefit analysis that allowed risk to be accepted in view of economic importance, along with the definition of thresholds. New international norms such as 'daily acceptable dose' for foodstuffs or 'maximum

---

50   Cicolella, *Toxique planète*. See also Julie Guthman, *Weighing In: Obesity, Food Justice, and the Limits of Capitalism*, Berkeley: University of California Press, 2011.
51   Marie Ng et al., 'Global, Regional, and National Prevalence of Overweight and Obesity in Children and Adults During 1980–2013: A Systematic Analysis for the Global Burden of Disease Study 2013', *The Lancet*, 384:9945, 2014, 766–81.

authorized concentration' for air quality made a subtle deception: given the non-existence of a threshold effect, they confirmed the de facto agreement to an acceptable rate of cancer for economic reasons.[52]

Finally, the Anthropocene body is shaped by the automobile and the suburb. American town-planners and doctors have recently shown the correlation between motorization, urban sprawl and the prevalence of diseases such as diabetes and obesity. Between 1963 and 2003 in the United States, distances travelled by motorcar doubled, while obesity now affects 65 per cent of adults, leading to a rise in cardiovascular diseases.[53]

---

52   Soraya Boudia and Nathalie Jas (eds), *Toxicants, Health and Regulation since 1945*, London: Pickering and Chatto, 2013.

53   Laura E. Jackson, 'The Relationship of Urban Design to Human Health and Condition', *Landscape and Urban Planning*, 64:4, 2003, 191–200; Wesley E. Marshall, Daniel P. Piatkowski and Norman W. Garrick, 'Community Design, Street Networks, and Public Health', *Journal of Transport and Health*, 1:4, 2014, 326–340.

CHAPTER 8

Phronocene: Grammars of Environmental Reflexivity

The great advantage of the concept of Anthropocene is that it abolishes the futile distinction between modernity and reflexive modernity, forcing us to consider the contemporary situation from a historical standpoint, less as a threshold in the acquiring of environmental awareness than as the culminating point of a history of destructions.

The problem with the narrative of ecological awakening, according to which our generation is the first to recognize environmental disturbance and question industrial modernity, is that by obliterating the reflexivity of past societies it depoliticizes the long history of the Anthropocene.

In their defence, the scientists, philosophers and sociologists who proclaim this narrative have hardly been helped by historians. If it is a cliché to say that history is written by the victors, then to say that economic or technological history is written from the standpoint of the modernizers is a euphemism. For a long time indeed, historians in general showed little interest at all in environmental controversies: concerns and alarms were viewed as romantic curiosities or simply 'resistance to progress'.[1]

---

1 Jean-Baptiste Fressoz and François Jarrige, 'L'Histoire et l'idéologie productiviste. Les récits de la révolution industrielle après 1945', in Céline Pessis, Sezin Topçu and Christophe Bonneuil (eds), *Une autre histoire des 'Trente*

As for environmental history, despite being very dynamic since the 1980s, it has still not had the refutation effect that it should have had on the grand narratives of postmodernism. While it describes very convincingly the radical transformation of environments (rivers, oceans, plains) by technology and the market,[2] and shows the fundamental importance of non-humans (viruses in particular) in world history, it has also tended to deprive actors of the capacity that they had to understand and analyse the complexity of the new situation they were creating. Environmental historians have often offered bird's-eye views, deliberately removed from political history, of societies caught in ecological traps or in technological and capitalist logics that have made (or unmade) their environments, without really seeming to account for this process, ending up with a view of the environmental crisis as an unexpected consequence of modernity.

To start out on the right track, the history of the Anthropocene must base itself on the disturbing fact that the destruction of environments has not been carried out inadvertently, as if nature did not count, but despite the environmental prudence (*phronesis* in Greek) of the moderns. If it is anachronistic to view modern societies, or certain of their actors, as 'ecological', it is on the other hand impossible to understand their particular forms of reflexivity by envisaging them in terms of today's categories (global environment, ecosystem, biogeochemical cycles, Anthropocene, etc.), as if this offered the only valid and useful way of being 'environmentally aware'. History provides us

---

Glorieuses'. Modernisation, contestations et pollutions dans la France d'après-guerre, Paris: La Découverte, 2013, 61–79.

2   For example William Cronon's great book, *Nature's Metropolis: Chicago and the Great West*, New York: Norton, 1991; also William McNeill, *Plagues and Peoples*, New York: Anchor Books, 1976, and John R. McNeill, *Mosquito Empires: Ecology and War in the Greater Caribbean, 1620–1914*, Cambridge: Cambridge University Press, 2010. This describes a general tendency, though there are of course many exceptions: Clarence Glacken, *Traces on the Rhodian Shore: Nature and Culture in Western Thought to the End of the Eighteenth Century*, Berkeley: University of California Press, 1967; Samuel P. Hays, *Conservation and the Gospel of Efficiency: The Progressive Conservation Movement 1890–1920*, Pittsburgh: University of Pittsburgh Press, 1999; or in France, Raphaël Larrère, *L'Utopie forestière de F.-A. Rauch*, Paris: INRA, 1985.

with a space of intelligibility for grasping the localized, changing and disputed character of ways of being in the world and conceiving the place of humans within nature.

The problem posed for history is thus to restore the *conceptual grammars* within which what we now call environmental reflexivity was conceived. The present chapter will analyse six of these: *circumfusa* and environment, climate, nature's economy, society-nature metabolisms, thermodynamics and exhaustion.

Three remarks first of all. Firstly, this list is not exhaustive, and the connections that exist among these different grammars make possible different arrangements. Secondly, if these environmental grammars are expressed in scientific theories, we should not underestimate the importance of 'common environmental decency',[3] i.e., a moral economy of nature on the part of ordinary people. For fishermen managing their resources in common, the notion of nature's economy was an everyday experience that circumscribed their action; for people close to chemical plants, their stench was an unambiguous danger signal. Thirdly, these grammars, rather than systems of propositions, constitute rules of conduct. They differentiate the healthy from the contaminated, the pure from the impure, and sustainable uses of nature from dangerous actions. In this way, they make it possible to give a wider sense to particular or local struggles by connecting them with a public good that combines social uses and natural creatures.

From circumfusa *to environment*

Let us begin quite simply with the word 'environment'. Its recent history seems to confirm the thesis of a contemporary environmental awareness: it was only in the 1970s that the environment became institutionalized, with the establishment of the Environmental Protection Agency in the United States, ministries of the environment in the countries of the OECD, and the UN Environment Programme (1972). It is necessary however to note two points: firstly, these new agencies and ministries were charged with applying laws

---

3   The expression is inspired by George Orwell's 'common decency'.

and regulations (such as clean air acts, for example) that had a longer history, and secondly, the very history of the word shows that the form of reflexivity it denotes is in fact very long-standing, going back at least to the late eighteenth century.

The present-day sense of 'environment' was popularized by Herbert Spencer in the mid nineteenth century, and subsequently adopted in French. George Perkins Marsh does not use it in *Man and Nature*, the great American environmentalist text of its decade, nor does Eugène Huzar in *La Fin du monde par la science* (1855), the first catastrophist philosophy of technology. Herbert Spencer, on the other hand, first in *Principles of Psychology* (1855) and then in *Principles of Biology* (1864), uses it dozens of times to describe the 'circumstances of an organism', in other words all the forces that affect and transform it, and he explores the reciprocal relationships between organism and environment.

In the 1850s, in both French and English, 'environment' was commonly used to refer to such things as the immediate surroundings of a town. But Spencer used the term in a more specific sense, corresponding to a fundamental concept of French public health studies from the late eighteenth century, that of *circumfusa* or 'surrounding things'. By this term, the medics included air, water and place, inspired by Hippocratic medicine and all the elements that held an influence over health. At the same time, materialist philosophers such as Buffon and Diderot were interested in environment and climate as a way of modifying or improving living creatures and, above all, man. The notion of *circumfusa* finally merges, in Lamarck's theories, with the concept of the 'surrounding circumstances' that shape living creatures, in the ideas of Cabanis ('surrounding objects'), then finally in the notion of 'milieu' that was central to Comtean sociology and drawn on by Herbert Spencer in the new sense he gave to the word 'environment'.[4]

The filiation of *circumfusa* and environment is important, as it refutes the common opposition made between the 'old kind' of environment, mere surroundings, an externality out of reach, and the

---

4   On the history of the notion of milieu, see Ferhat Taylan, *La Rationalité mésologique. Connaissance et gouvernement des milieux de vie (1750–1900)*, PhD thesis, University of Bordeaux, 2014.

'environment' of the 1970s as a fragile object to protect, internal to the social and thus eminently political.

In the eighteenth century, surroundings were already viewed as highly fragile. Transformations that were apparently benign could have dreadful consequences. The degeneration of the Romans after the classical period was explained by the destruction of the sewers (the *cloaca maxima*) by the barbarians, and the proliferation of alum mines that spoiled the city's air.[5] An epidemic in the Dutch Moluccas was attributed to the destruction of the clove trees, whose aromatic particles healed the air corrupted by the fumes of a volcano. Smoke from manufacturing aroused similar concerns among the urban bourgeoisie: in the eighteenth century, cities were seen as extremely unhealthy, on a par with swamps, prisons and ships.[6]

According to the medical and philosophical thinking of this century, human societies evolved in relation with the atmospheric envelopes that they shaped. The *circumfusa* were the sum of all possible environmental transformations; human action reverberates in the things surrounding it, which in turn modifies human constitutions.

From the eighteenth century into the early nineteenth, pollution was seen as extremely dangerous. Neighbours accused polluting factories of fomenting epidemics and leading to a degeneration of the population. The police paid scrupulous attention to air quality, since the health, number and even shape of the inhabitants seemed to depend on this.[7] They kept a close eye on workshops, their smoke and discharge. Overly polluting trades, in particular those that involved work on organic materials (tanners, tripe butchers, candle-makers, etc.), were not allowed in built-up areas.[8]

---

5   Jean-Baptiste Dubos, *Réflexions critiques sur la poésie et sur la peinture* (1714), vol. 2, Utrecht: Étienne Neaulme, 1732, 152–7.

6   Alain Corbin, *Le Miasme et la jonquille. L'odorat et l'imaginaire social, XVIIIe–XIXe siècles*, Paris: Aubier, 1982; Sabine Barles, *La Ville délétère. Médecins et ingénieurs dans l'espace urbain, XVIIIe–XIXe siècles*, Paris: Champ Vallon, 1999.

7   Jean-Baptiste Fressoz, *L'Apocalypse joyeuse. Une histoire du risque technologique*, Paris: Seuil, 2012, 111–14.

8   Thomas Le Roux, *Le Laboratoire des pollutions industrielles*, Paris: Albin Michel, 2011.

In the mid nineteenth century, it seemed that industrial pollution was even disturbing the large-scale equilibrium of the atmosphere. In 1845, when crops were attacked by cryptogamic diseases, farmers accused the big chemical works. According to one agronomist, 'from Genoa to Grenoble, from Lyon to Dijon and as far as Strasbourg and Metz . . . people ascribe the vine disease to gas lighting'.[9] In 1852, when the potato harvest failed in the Charleroi region of Belgium, peasants demanded that the authorities suspend production in soda factories. At one demonstration, soldiers fired and two people were killed. Léon Peeters, a Charleroi pharmacist, was imprisoned for publishing a short book seeking to demonstrate that bad harvests were not caused by cryptogams but by the hydrochloric acid fumes that poured out from these plants. As the fumes paid no heed to national borders, 'To obtain a radical cure of the plague that has been desolating Europe for ten years, it is necessary for all governments to come to agreement'.[10] As a calming influence, Corneille Jean Koene, a chemistry professor at the University of Brussels, gave a series of popular science lectures on this subject. According to him, chemical plants helped to regulate the overall composition of the atmosphere. He argued that the increase in human population, and in the number of cattle and buildings, had fixed carbon and increased the proportion of oxygen in the atmosphere. Industry maintained a stable level of carbon in the atmosphere by burning coal; chemical plants, by emitting hydrochloric acid, destroyed alkaline miasmas and reduced the risk of epidemics.[11] And so it was not only the detractors of industry but also its defenders who saw it as a major environmental factor.

In the 1850s, human technology seemed to have reached a global scale. As Eugène Huzar wrote in 1857, the modern age was marked by

---

9   Louis Leclerc, *Les Vignes malades. Rapport adressé à M. le comte de Persigny, minister de l'Intérieur*, Paris: Hachette, 1853, 15.

10   Léon Peeters, *Guérison radicale de la maladie des pommes de terre et d'autre végétaux ou moyen d'en faire dispaître la cause*, Namur, 1855.

11   Corneille Jean Koene, *Conférences publiques sur la création à partir de la formation de la terre jusqu'à l'extinction de l'espèce humaine ou aperçu de l'histoire naturelle de l'air et des miasmes à propos des Fabriques d'acide et des plaintes dont leurs travaux font l'objet*, Brussels: Larcier, 1856.

a transformation of our responsibilities. Earth and science had followed opposing paths; the first had shrunk while the second was stretching:

> I would understand how a South American savage who had never left his forest could tell me that the earth was infinite, and that man therefore could not disturb it. Today, with science, the proposition is completely reversed; it is man who is infinite, thanks to science, and the planet that is finite.[12]

The fragile climate of modernity

The notion of climate, equally essential for understanding the reflexivity of modern societies, is closely bound up with that of *circumfusa*. In the seventeenth century, climate was already understood on a global scale. Natural theology conceived the Earth as a perfect system on which the great masses of matter were balanced. Water in particular circulated permanently from the equator to the poles, following a divine plan that ensured the fertility of temperate zones.

European colonial expansion played a key role in the emergence of reflection on anthropic climate change. It raised right away the question of the considerable differences in temperature and precipitation between territories situated on the same line of latitude at either side of the Atlantic. In line with neo-Hippocratic medicine, climate thus acquired a certain plasticity. If it remained partly determined by position on the globe, natural philosophers were increasingly interested in its local variations, its transformations, and the role of human action in its improvement or deterioration. And as climate maintained its ability to determine human and political constitutions, it became the epistemic site where the consequences of technological action on the environment were conceived. What determined social health and organization was no longer simply position on the globe, but everyday things (the atmosphere, forests, the forms of cities) on which it was possible to act for good or ill.[13]

---

12   Eugène Huzar, *L'Arbre de la science*, Paris: Dentu, 1857, 113.
13   Jean-Baptiste Fressoz and Fabien Locker, 'L'agir humain sur le climat et

Figure 13: Thomas Burnet, 'Ideas of Different Stages in the Formation of the Earth' from *Sacred Theory of the Earth*, 1690

Take for example Buffon's *Epochs of Nature* (1778). This magnificent text, a culminating point of modern rhetoric, presents the historical conditions for a reversal. The seventh and final epoch of the planet's history corresponds to the advent of man as global force: 'the entire face of the Earth today bears the imprint of human power', Buffon tells us. Humanity has transformed plants and animals, brought new breeds into being, acclimatized and improved. For Buffon, this role is completely positive: Europe's 'civilized nature' is more productive than the 'raw' and hostile nature left abandoned by 'the savage little nations of America'. But if human work is not guided by science, if people act short-sightedly, the consequences may be disastrous:

la naissance de la climatologie historique', *Revue d'histoire moderne et contemporaine*, 62:1, 2015: 48–78.

The most contemptible condition of the human species is not that of the savage, but that of those nations, a quarter civilized, that have always been the real plagues of nature . . . They ravaged the land . . . these nations simply weigh on the globe without relieving the land, starve it without making it fertile, destroy without building, use everything up without renewing anything.[14]

Buffon's utopia was a climatic one: united by a universal peace, humanity would rationally transform the planet. By foresting and deforesting judiciously, it would be able to 'modify the influences of the climate it inhabits and set the temperature, so to speak, to the point that suits it'.[15]

By placing climate within human reach in this way, the modernist project of controlling nature created the conditions for superseding it. From the 1770s, European societies underwent a great debate on the climatic consequences of deforestation. Meteorologists referred to the works of Stephen Hales on the physiology of plants and their gaseous exchanges with the atmosphere (*Vegetable Staticks*, 1727) to blame climate disturbances (cold, drought, storms and rain) on the destruction of vegetation: trees, by the relationship they maintained with the atmosphere, dried out wet land and moistened dry land; they also warded off storms, erosion and floods. Deforestation was conceived as a rupture in the natural and providential order that balanced cycles of matter between Earth and atmosphere.[16]

Climatic disasters, therefore, became politicized. In France in the 1820s, for example, after a series of bad harvests, blame was put on the revolution, the division of communal lands, the sale of national forests and their short-term exploitation by a new bourgeoisie. In England,

---

14   Georges-Louis Leclerc de Buffon, *Histoire naturelle générale et particulière*, vol. 5 ('Des époques de la Nature'), Paris: Imprimerie royale, 1778, 237.

15   Georges-Louis Leclerc de Buffon, *Histoire naturelle générale et particulière*, supplément, vol. 5 ('Des époques de la Nature'), Paris: Imprimerie royale, 1778, 244. See Jean-Baptiste Fressoz, 'Eugène Huzar et la genèse de la société du risque', introduction to Eugène Huzar, *La Fin du monde par la science*, Alfortville: Ère, 2008, 24–6.

16   Richard Grove, *Green Imperialism: Colonial Expansion, Tropical Island Edens and the Origins of Environmentalism, 1600–1860*, Cambridge: Cambridge University Press, 1995.

the question of enclosures was discussed in terms of climate: the proliferation of hedges and pasture allegedly made the English climate still wetter and colder.

Two remarks may be made here. First of all, from the early nineteenth century onwards, we clearly see climate knowledge and discourse establishing global climatic connections. According to the engineers François-Antoine Rauch and Jean-Baptiste Rougier de la Bergerie, for example, or Joseph Banks, secretary of the Royal Society, deforestation in the United States and Europe increased humidity in the atmosphere, which condensed at the poles, expanding the ice caps and causing bad weather in Europe. Secondly, climate change was conceived as an *irreversible* phenomenon that challenged the very direction of civilization. Deforestation transformed the climate and undermined the forest's very conditions of existence. From the 1820s on, a powerful discourse of what could be called 'climatic orientalism' warned the European states against deforestation and climate change by recalling the ruins of brilliant civilizations now surrounded by desert.[17]

The economy of nature

Historians of scientific ecology have identified the concept of 'economy of nature' as the starting point of the contemporary notion of ecosystems and shown its centrality in the natural philosophy of the eighteenth and nineteenth centuries.[18] This concept constitutes a third grammar of reflexivity in the face of environmental destruction.

From Carl Linnaeus to Thoreau, naturalists marvelled at the systemic relations among living things. One of the aims of natural history was to discover interdependencies and thus show the

17   Jean-Baptiste Fressoz and Fabien Locher, *Le Climat fragile de la modernité*, Paris: Seuil, 2016.

18   Donald Worster, *Nature's Economy: A History of Ecological Ideas*, Cambridge: Cambridge University Press, 1977; Jean-Paul Déléage, *Histoire de l'écologie. Une science de l'homme et de la nature*, Paris: La Découverte, 1991; Jean-Marc Drouin, *L'Écologie et son histoire. Réinventer la nature*, Paris: Flammarion, 1997.

symphonic precision of nature. The natural theology that underlay this research rested on the religious conviction that every living thing has a function in the natural order. In Linnaeus's words:

> If even a single [species of] earthworm were missing, stagnant water would damage the soil and the moisture would rot everything. If a single important function were lacking in the animal world, we could fear for a very great disaster in the universe. If all the sparrows perished in our lands, our crops would fall prey to crickets and other insects.[19]

Gilbert White wrote in a similar vein in *The Natural History of Selborne* (1789): 'The most insignificant insects and reptiles are of much more consequence, and have much more influence, in the economy of nature, than the incurious are aware of.'[20]

In this nature pervaded by connections, chains of dependence and reciprocities, catastrophe always threatened. In the words of Bernardin de Saint-Pierre: 'The harmony of this globe would be partly destroyed, if not entirely, were one to suppress even the smallest species of plant.'[21]

This view of an infinitely connected nature may have been guided either by a theology that postulated 'the wise disposition of beings by the Creator' (Linnaeus) or by a mechanistic view of material exchanges, but in both cases it gave rise to modesty and awe in the face of the world's infinite complexity. According to Jean-Baptiste Robinet, in 1766: 'We [humans] and the other large animals are no more than parasites on that greater animal that we call the Earth.'[22]

It was on the basis of this economy of nature that scientists started to take a systematic interest in the extinctions of species caused by what the clergyman and zoologist John Fleming called in 1824 the

---

19   Carl Linnaeus, 1760, quoted in Drouin, *L'Écologie et son histoire*, 40.

20   Quoted in Worster, *Nature's Economy*, 7.

21   Jacques-Henri Bernardin de Saint Pierre, *Voyage à l'île de France* (1773), Paris: La Découverte, 193, 136.

22   Jean-Baptiste Robinet, *De la nature*, vol. 4, Amsterdam: Van Harrevelt, 1766, 25.

'destructive warfare' waged against them by humans.[23] The geologist and priest Antonio Stoppani, herald of the Anthropozoic age in 1873, rejoiced to see an old nature give way to a 'new nature' in which humans had completely recast the distribution of species between continents.[24]

On reading such texts, the question arises as to how the economy of nature fitted into the concrete management of environments. What knowledge of relationships structured the uses of nature? Major topics of historiography such as the question of the commons could be revisited with greater attention to this knowledge and the concerns expressed in the theoretical grammar of the economy of nature.

In Normandy, for example, when a controversy broke out in the 1770s on the management of foreshore resources, the fishermen's guild complained about the stripping of wrack (seaweed that was burned for ash used in producing soda for glass-works) precisely by appeal to its role in the survival of young fish and the natural economy of the marine world. In a memoir sent to the Academy of Sciences, they explained that fish came to spawn in the wrack, as the seaweed held the fish eggs together, protecting them from tides and currents and increasing their density and chances of fertilization. Such popular knowledge of environments, despite being little formalized and thus generally invisible to historians, was very important as the basis of the communal management of resources.[25]

In the second half of the eighteenth century, fear of an exhaustion of fish stocks was general.[26] The medic Tiphaigne de la Roche described

23   John Fleming, 'Remarks Illustrative of the Influence of Society on the Distribution of British Animals', *Edinburgh Philosophical Journal*, 11, 1824: 288; on the emergence of studies on the extinctions of species, see Mark V. Barrow Jr., *Nature's Ghosts: Confronting Extinction from the Age of Jefferson to the Age of Ecology*, Chicago: University of Chicago Press, 2009.

24   Antonio Stoppani, *Corso di Geologia*, vol. 2, *Geologia stratigrafica*, Milan: G. Bernardoni, 1873. (An extract from this on the 'Anthropozoic era' is translated in Valeria Federighi and Etienne Turpin (eds), 'The Anthropozoic Era: Excerpts from *Corso di Geologia*', trans. Valeria Federighi, *Scapegoat*, 5, 2013, scapegoatjournal.org.)

25   Fressoz, *L'Apocalypse joyeuse*, 132–40.

26   Alain Corbin, *Le territoire du vide. L'Occident et le désir du rivage (1750–1840)*, Paris: Aubier, 1988, 226–9.

the seas as 'exhausted', 'now only providing fish on a scale that leads us to regret their former fecundity'.[27] He particularly accused drag-nets that destroyed the marine environment: 'What is the consequence of tearing plants out of the sea? A considerable damage, very likely . . . They are the retreat of large fish and many small ones, and food for the majority of them.'[28] In 1769, the famous naturalist Henri-Louis Duhamel du Monceau ended the first volume of his *Traité des pêches*[29] with a 'dissertation on what can have led to the scarcity of fish, particularly in the sea'. He reviewed several hypotheses: a cyclical phenomenon without tangible cause; an epidemic disease attacking fish; too great a consumption of fish and too large a number of fishermen. But he particularly blamed drag-nets that destroyed the natural economy.

In the same way, from the late eighteenth century to the 1830s, it was by basing themselves on the idea of natural harmony that French agronomists and foresters undertook a great crusade against deforestation. In March 1792, for example, attacking a law that proposed the sale of national forests, the civil engineer François-Antoine Rauch recalled that

> forests have a visible influence on the harmony of the elements, in terms of the weather that they enliven . . . the animals that they shelter and preserve, the clouds that they attract, the springs that they nourish and the rivers that they feed.[30]

The economy of nature played a key role in the nascent political economy. In the mid eighteenth century, the aim of this science was to study the interface between human societies and nature. The project of the physiocrats was to extend the laws of natural economy into positive laws governing human organization. According to François Quesnay, the

---

27 Charles-François Tiphaigne de la Roche, *Essai sur l'histoire œconomique des mers occidentales de la France*, Paris: Bauche, 1760, 117.

28 Ibid., 142.

29 Henri-Louis Duhamel du Monceau, *Les trois premières sections du traité des pêches et l'histoire des poissons. Description des arts et métiers*, 1763 and 1776, 683, note 169.

30 François-Antoine Rauch, *Harmonie hydro-végétale et météorologique*, Paris: Levrault, 1801, i.

latter were simply 'laws of maintenance in relation to the natural order'.[31] The same was true of Carl Linnaeus, a great champion of political economy in Sweden, for whom the study of nature had to be the basis of this discipline. It was important above all else to analyse natural economy in order to learn how to derive wealth from it for the national good. Linnaeus's great project of acclimatization of tropical plants in Scandinavia represented the summit of political economy.

The notion of economy of nature also led to a renewal of the organicist view of the Earth. Carolyn Merchant has shown how during antiquity, the Renaissance and up to the scientific revolution, our planet was conceived as a living being with its veins and fluids, its palpitations and sickness. Earth was a nourishing mother that it was important to respect.[32] According to her, the scientific revolution and the emergence of capitalism led to an inexorable decline in organicist theories. Nature became a great mechanism that had to be explained, exploited and transformed.

By way of the economy of nature, in fact, the view of the Earth as a living being persisted well after the scientific revolution. In 1795, the philosopher Félix Nogaret published a popular essay with the title *La Terre est un animal*,[33] in which he systematically compared the phenomena of terrestrial physics with their physiological and corporal counterparts. Major geologists such as Eugène Patrin and Philippe Bertrand criticized such analogies as overly simplistic (according to Patrin, the Earth was 'very likely an organized body, but with an organization that is neither that of an animal nor of a vegetable; it is that of a world'), but argued nonetheless for the introduction of organicist interpretations into their discipline, since viewing Earth as a living being made it easier to grasp 'the intimate connectedness of all phenomena on the globe'.[34]

31   François Quesnay, *Physiocratie, ou constitution naturelle du gouvernement*, Yverdon, vol. 2, 1768, 25.

32   Carolyn Merchant, *The Death of Nature: Women, Ecology and the Scientific Revolution*, New York: Harper and Row, 1983, 2–41.

33   Félix Nogaret, *La Terre est un animal, ou conversation d'une courtisane philosophe*, Versailles: Colson, 1795.

34   Eugène Patrin, 'Remarques sur la diminution de la mer et sur les îles de la mer du sud', *Journal de physique, de chimie et d'histoire naturelle*, 60, 1806: 316.

It was in this vein, in 1821, that Charles Fourier diagnosed a 'decline in the health of the globe'. He called for a new science, a planetary medicine or 'sidereal anatomy', based on an analogy between the human body and the planetary body. In Fourier's writing, volcanoes are equivalent to the planet's boils, earthquakes its shivers, magnetic fluid its blood and (more curiously) the aurora borealis the planet's nocturnal emissions, 'tormented by the need to copulate'. Flooding and silting up of rivers, pollution of springs, erosion and deforestation were so many epidermal symptoms.[35] Under Fourier's inspiration, Eugène Huzar similarly elaborated the image of a planet as living and fragile superorganism. Man, by his industry, believed he could scratch the Earth without heed that such scratches, according to the law of small causes and large effects, could very well cause its death.[36]

The history of systemic reflexivity is all the more complex, given that the notion of nature's economy was profoundly reconfigured by the development of the natural sciences and the emergence of Darwinism in particular. For Darwin, a great opponent of natural theology, it was clear that living beings no longer had their function in a natural order defined by God. Nonetheless, the laws of evolution (and co-evolution) of living beings, and the Malthusian law of the geometrical progression of populations, produced a nature that was intensely connected and completely filled, a continuous world in which species exploited all possible resources: 'The face of nature may be compared with a friable surface on which ten thousand sharp wedges are pressing, impelled by incessant blows.'[37] In an early draft of *The Origin of Species*, Darwin added that the 'jar and shock' of these blows could be 'often transmitted very far to other wedges in many lines of direction'.[38]

---

35   Charles Fourier, 'Détérioration matérielle de la planète', in René Schérer, *L'Écosophie de Charles Fourier: Deux textes inédits*, Paris: Anthropos, 2001, 31–125, quotes from 37–44; these were preparatory notes for *Traité de l'association domestique-agricole*, later titled *Théorie de l'unité universelle*, first published in *La Phalange* in 1847.

36   Huzar, *L'Arbre de la science*, 103.

37   Charles Darwin, *The Origin of Species* (1859), London: Penguin, 1985, 119.

38   Quoted by Sharon E. Kingsland, *Modeling Nature: Episodes in the History of Population Ecology*, Chicago: University of Chicago Press, 1985, 10.

Thus the term 'ecology' (*ökologie*), proposed by Ernst Haeckel in 1867, did not indicate a terra incognita but renamed and reorganized established traditions of thought.[39] By coining this word, Haeckel had two main objectives in mind: on the one hand, to suggest that living beings made up a home, an *oikos*, which despite being conflictual, as Darwin had shown, also benefited from symbiosis and mutual aid; on the other hand, he sought to integrate the study of interactions between organisms and their environments into a single discipline that would include both the physical conditions of existence (climate, soil . . . again the idea of *circumfusa*) and biological conditions, i.e., interactions with all other organisms. The rather long time that it took for the term 'ecology' to become accepted (the contemporary spelling was first used at the International Botanical Congress of 1893) does not mean that it was hard for the natural sciences to grasp the systemic aspect of nature, rather that the concept of nature's economy was still quite persistent until the late nineteenth century.

Cycles and metabolisms: the chemistry of nature–society relations

Chemistry, with its concern for the exchange of matter and energy between human society and nature, was a fourth grammar of environmental reflexivity. These exchanges of matter, Lavoisier wrote, ensured 'a marvellous circulation between the three realms', vegetable, animal and mineral, on a planetary scale:

> Vegetables draw water from the atmosphere, and the materials needed for their organization from the mineral realm. Animals feed either on vegetables or other animals that themselves feed on vegetables . . . Finally, fermentation, putrefaction and combustion constantly return to the air and the mineral realm the principles that vegetables and animals have borrowed from them.[40]

---

39   Worster, *Nature's Economy*, 191–5.
40   Antoine Lavoisier (1789), quoted in Jean-Paul Deléage, *Histoire de l'écologie*, Paris: La Découverte, 1991, 51.

Drawing on the discoveries of chemistry, the nineteenth century was marked by very strong worries about the metabolic rupture between town and country. Urbanization, in other words the concentration of humans and their excrement, prevented mineral substances indispensable to fertility from being returned to the land. All the major materialist thinkers, from Liebig to Marx, warned against both urban pollution and the exhaustion of soil, as did agronomists, public health officials and chemists. In the third volume of *Capital*, Marx criticized the environmental consequences of capitalist agriculture's great spaces empty of people, which broke the material circulation between society and nature. According to Marx, there could be no getting away from nature: whatever the mode of production, society would remain dependent on a historically determined metabolic regime; what was particular about capitalist metabolism was its unsustainable character.[41]

From the late eighteenth century to the mid twentieth with its generalized use of artificial fertilizer, a reflexive tradition persisted that was bound up with a chemical and bookkeeping view of agriculture, the principle of which was that each harvest reduced the fertility of the soil, so that the durability of production rested on the ability of the farmer to replace these nutritive chemical elements. Arthur Young in his *Rural Economy* (1770) sought to establish by experiment the correct relationship between pasture and tillage and discover the best ways of circulating matter between animals and plants. The stakes were immense, since 'if one of these proportions is broken', Young wrote, 'the whole chain will be affected'.[42]

The development of chemical agronomy in the nineteenth century, with Liebig, Boussingault and Dumas, increased the complexity of this system in a way that gave rise to increased concern. Liebig's famous 'law of the minimum' expressed a far more pessimistic view of the fate of the soil, as its fertility was now seen as determined by whatever

---

41   John Bellamy Foster, *Marx's Ecology: Materialism and Nature*, New York: Monthly Review Press, 2000.

42   Arthur Young, *Rural Economy* (1770), quoted in Paul Warde, 'The Invention of Sustainability', *Modern Intellectual History*, 8:1, 2011: 166.

chemical element (nitrogen, phosphorous, potassium, calcium, magnesium, sulphur, iron, etc.) was least present. For Liebig, urbanization and the lack of recycling were leading the European societies to suicide. Analysis of agricultural metabolism, for Liebig, was the basis for a general critique of capitalism and globalization. In a passage of his *Organic Chemistry* he compared Britain, a great importer of guano and mineral fertilizer, to a vampire: 'Great Britain seizes from other countries their conditions of their own fertility . . . Vampire-like, it clings to the throat of Europe, one could even say of the whole world, sucking its best blood.'[43]

We can understand why the socialists of the mid nineteenth century were so closely interested in the work of chemists and the question of metabolism. In 1843, Pierre Leroux, who coined the word 'socialism', founded in Boussac, in the department of Creuse, a colony by the name of 'Circulus' that put into practice the agricultural recycling of human excrement: 'Nature has established a *circulus* between production and consumption. We do not create anything, we do not destroy anything: we effect changes . . . Consumption is the aim of production, but it is also the cause.'[44]

This circular view of the material relationship between society and soil was also the basis for a radical critique of work that dissipated the material riches transiting around the circulus in useless movements and unproductive capital. Against the accumulation and plunder of the capitalists, a society in homeostasis should be established, engaged chiefly in maintaining the circulus and minimizing loss.[45]

Leroux's circulus was simply one example of countless technical, technocratic and public health projects that aimed to make proper use of excrement. To the degree that European countries urbanized, the question of human fertilizer became crucial for the fertility of the soil.

---

43   Justus von Liebig, *Organic Chemistry in its Applications to Agriculture and Physiology*, London: Taylor and Walton, 1840.

44   Quoted by Claude Harmel, 'Pierre Leroux et le circulus. L' engrais humain, solution de la question sociale', *Cahiers d'histoire sociale*, 14, 2000: 117–28.

45   Dana Simmons, 'Waste Not, Want Not: Excrement and Economy in Nineteenth-Century France', *Representations*, 96:1, 2006: 73–98.

The rising fees for leases on Paris refuse collection (conceded to private entrepreneurs who sold dried excrement to farmers) during the first part of the nineteenth century attest to the economic importance of 'human fertilizer'. Chemical analysis of water from the sewers and comparison of this with the precious guano from Chile and Peru incited local authorities in the mid nineteenth century to see their waste water as a resource. Rather than emitters of waste, towns were thought of as fertilizer factories. Health officials who promoted the development of sewerage, such as Edwin Chadwick in Britain, also used this economic argument to convince municipalities that the sale of waste water to farmers would enable them to finance completely this major infrastructural work.[46] Other solutions were also proposed, less grandiose but more practical, such as the dry toilets promoted in 1861 by Henry Moule, vicar of Fordington, which used a mixture of earth and ash to deodorize and produce fertilizer.[47] In the late nineteenth century, a Michigan entrepreneur, William Heap, produced dry toilets on an industrial scale, with a certain success in Canada and the US Midwest.

In the nineteenth century, therefore, there was a fundamental project to restore material cycles. The fate of excrement lay at the heart of some profound debates. It was bound up with the social question, inasmuch as the impoverished soil of the countryside provoked famines, pauperism and revolutions; with the fate of civilizations (Rome, according to Liebig, fell on account of its inability to manage its excrement properly); with geopolitics, e.g., the seizure of Peruvian guano by the British state; with public health and the degeneration of populations; and even with the divine order: in Victorian England, the metabolic rupture put in question the moral status of urbanization.[48]

---

46   Nicholas Goddard, 'A Mine of Wealth? The Victorians and the Agricultural Value of Sewage', *Journal of Historical Geography*, 22:33, 1996: 274–90.

47   Henry Moule, *National Health and Wealth Instead of the Disease, Nuisance, Expense, and Waste Caused by Cess-Pools and Water-Drainage*, 1861.

48   Christopher Hamlin, 'Providence and Putrefaction: Victorian Sanitarians and the Natural Theology of Health and Disease', *Victorian Studies*, 28:3, 1985: 381–411.

This metabolic view of agriculture persisted for a long time into the twentieth century. Inspired by the ideal of self-sufficiency developed by the anarchist Pyotr Kropotkin, the German architect Leberecht Migge integrated it into his project of self-sufficient co-operatives. In his pamphlet *Jedermann Selbstversorger* (Everyone Self-Sufficient, 1918) and his article 'Das grüne Manifest' (1919, the first occurrence of the term 'green' in a political sense), he developed a political and urbanistic theory based on garden cities that would be self-sufficient thanks to solar and wind power, horticulture and the strict recycling of organic waste. Recycling was the essential lever to escape from the great technological networks of capitalism and establish self-management, 'the smallest form of government possible – according to the will of the people'.[49]

From the 1900s to the 1920s, Albert Howard, working in the agricultural service of colonial India, studied Indian agricultural systems. This agronomist was particularly impressed by the efficiency of recycling practices that allowed the long-term preservation of soil quality. In *Farming and Gardening for Health or Disease*, a founding text of organic agriculture, he emphasized the 'great law of return' and criticized the replacement of organic fertilizers by mineral ones.[50] Finally, it was with explicit reference to such metabolic theories that the Indian minister of agriculture, K. M. Munshi, rejected the logic of the 'green revolution' based on chemical fertilizer, proposing instead to 'study the life's cycle in the village under your charge in both its aspects – hydrological and nutritional. Find out where the cycle has been disturbed and estimate the steps necessary for restoring it.'[51]

---

49   Quoted by Fanny Lopez, *Le rêve d'une déconnexion. De la maison autonome à la cité auto-énergétique*, Paris: Éditions de la Villette, 2014, 94. On Migge, see David H. Haney, *When Modern Was Green: Life and Work of Landscape Architect Leberecht Migge*, New York: Routledge, 2010.

50   Albert Howard, *Farming and Gardening for Health or Disease*, London: Faber and Faber, 1945 (republished in 1947 as *The Soil and Health: A Study of Organic Agriculture*), Chapter 2.

51   Quoted in Vandana Shiva, *The Violence of the Green Revolution: Third World Agriculture, Ecology and Politics*, London: Zed Books, 1991, 25.

The analysis of flows of material was thus inspired by the desire to maintain closed cycles on both local and national scale. It was also applied on a world scale. For Lavoisier, Boussingault and Kliment Timiriazev, through to the biogeochemistry of Vladimir Vernadsky in the 1920s, study of the chemical relations connecting the vegetable, animal and mineral worlds with human societies aimed at understanding the functioning of the Earth as a whole. In 1845, for example, the French chemist Jacques-Joseph Ebelmen established the major principles of the global carbon cycle by identifying the processes that tended to increase or reduce the quantity of carbon dioxide in the atmosphere. According to him, the atmosphere was co-produced by living beings:

> Variations in the nature of the air have most likely been always in relation with the organized beings who lived at each different epoch . . . has the composition of our atmosphere reached a permanent state of equilibrium? . . . We leave to future generations certain elements for this important question.[52]

This global approach to cycles of matter would be taken up by Vernadsky in the 1920s, by Evelyn Hutchinson in the United States in the 1940s, then by systems ecology, and would form the framework of the Gaia hypothesis put forward by Lynn Margulis and James Lovelock.[53]

From entropy to degrowth

In the late nineteenth century, thermodynamics, the study of the properties of energy and its transformations, formed a new grammar for the general apprehension of relationships between nature and society. Historians of science have shown how the works of James Joule

---

52 Jacques-Joseph Ebelmen, 'Recherches sur les produits de la décomposition des espèces minérales de la famille des silicates', *Annales des mines*, 7, 1845: 66.

53 Jean-Paul Deléage, *Histoire de l'écologie*, Paris: La Découverte, 1991, 202–44.

and William Thomson (Lord Kelvin) still fell largely into the English tradition of natural theology. The focus on loss, waste and dissipation was bound up with the project of continuing the work of God in the world below: a Christian society should organize itself so as to maximize use of a stock of energy that, despite being constant, was in constant dissipation (entropy).

Thermodynamics was also anchored in the British political economy of the 1840s, which based itself on labour value. At the Glasgow Philosophical Society (whose members included William Thomson), the desire to optimize the profit derived from both men and machines led to comparing the efficiency of human and mechanical engines, and to proposing the equation: mechanical effect = labour value (in money) = bread,[54] consequently conceiving an entity that was converted and conserved in the productive process. Energy, therefore, was from its origin a concept seeking to apprehend economic and social problems.

In the 1860s, accordingly, it was possible to elaborate a quantitative view of energy flow, intercepted by plants or extracted from coal, and of its circulation in the economy. One of the first to conduct an analysis of this kind was the Ukrainian socialist Sergei Podolinsky. By comparing pasture to wheat, he showed that the agricultural yield in terms of energy grew with the proportion of animal or human input, and declined with the use of machines using coal.[55]

Many writers at the turn of the century proposed a reform of economic analysis, and of the economy itself, based on the study of energy: Eduard Sacher, *Foundations of a Mechanics of Society* (1881); Patrick Geddes, *John Ruskin, Economist* (1884); Rudolf Clausius, *On the Energy Stocks in Nature and their Valorization for the Benefit of Humankind* (in German, 1885); and somewhat later Frederick Soddy, *Cartesian Economics* (1921). All of these shared a very critical view of a political economy that was content to study the monetary value of

---

54   M. Norton Wise and Crosbie Smith, 'Work and Waste: Political Economy and Natural Philosophy in Nineteenth Century Britain, III', *History of Science*, 28:3, 1990: 221–60, and Crosbie Smith, *The Science of Energy: A Cultural History of Energy Physics in Victorian Britain*, Chicago: University of Chicago Press, 1998.

55   Joan Martínez Alier and Klaus Schlüpmann, *Ecological Economics: Energy, Environment and Society*, Oxford: Blackwell, 1987, 45–53.

things. A mere 'chresmatics' of this kind obscured the real problem, which was the provisioning of human societies in terms of material and energy. These writers also emphasized the divergence between the appearance of growing financial wealth and the truth of energy dissipation. Geddes, for example, remarked that only the energy obtained from a steam engine was taken into account by economics, whereas the 90 per cent of energy dissipated and permanently lost remained invisible. In *Cartesian Economics*, Frederick Soddy, professor of chemistry at Oxford University and Nobel laureate for chemistry, explained that the rate of interest was a contingent human invention, which could never contradict for too long the principle of entropy to which capital remained subject. According to him, investment, far from increasing wealth, actually accelerated the exhaustion of fossil resources.[56] Clausius, Thomson and Bernard Brunhes also drew the most general implications for the progress of the world from the second law of thermodynamics: though the quantity of energy is conserved, it degrades in form, inexorably increasing the entropy of any isolated system. Brunhes concluded from this in 1909 that 'if the world progresses like a wound clock whose spring relaxes by the minute, what tells us that the spring, once unwound, would not be in a state of complete instability?'[57]

Analysis and critique of economics in terms of thermodynamics thus follows a long heritage and could give rise to quite technocratic views in writers such as Eugene Odum, Kenneth Boulding or Vaclav Smil, for example, as well as more radical ones with Ivan Illich, Nicolas Georgescu-Roegen and the present-day theorists of degrowth.

Resources and finitude

The question of exhaustion of resources constitutes the sixth and last grammar of environmental reflexivity in modern societies. It emerged in the seventeenth century in the context of natural

---

56   Ibid., 127–44.
57   Bernard Brunhes, *La dégradation de l'énergie* (1909), Paris: Flammarion, 1991, 401.

theology: What moral meaning to give to the 'corruption of nature' or the limits of natural wealth, to the growing scarcity of woodland around English towns, for example? Was it a defiance of providence to seek to preserve resources in order to delay the Last Judgement?[58] The famous example of the silver mines of Potosí led to inferences on the exhaustion of the world in general. This theme was sufficiently well known for the satirist Edward Moore to depict in 1754 a young mathematician who had after long calculations discovered 'that the profusion of man consumes faster than the Earth produces. Vast fleets, and enormous buildings have wasted almost all our oak . . . What shall we do when the coal, iron and lead mines are exhausted?'[59]

The question of limits was fundamental in the political economy of the early nineteenth century, which should be understood in the context of an organic economy and the perception of an asymptotic limit to resources.[60] If coal made it possible to envisage an economy in continuous growth, this did not prevent the problem of exhaustion of coal stocks being raised right from the beginnings of industrialization. In 1819, for example, on the subject of gas lighting, the renowned chemist and industrialist Jean-Antoine Chaptal estimated French coal resources as too low to be wasted in this way: better to reserve them for the production of iron, which was far more useful for national defence.[61] In the same vein, at the start of the railway age in France, the engineer Pierre-Simon Girard argued against steam engines and for animal traction, estimating that the price of coal was bound to increase as mines were gradually exhausted.[62] In England in the 1820s, the exhaustion of certain mines, combined with parliamentary

58   Rolf Peter Sieferle, *The Subterranean Forest: Energy Systems and the Industrial Revolution*, Isle of Harris: White Horse Press, 2001, 181–200; Carolyn Merchant, *Reinventing Eden: The Fate of Nature in Western Culture*, London: Routledge, 2004, 71–7.

59   Edward Moore, *The World*, vol. 3, London: Dodsley, 1755, 262.

60   E. A. Wrigley, 'Two Kinds of Capitalism, Two Kinds of Growth', in *Poverty, Progress and Population*, Cambridge: Cambridge University Press, 2004.

61   Fressoz, *L'Apocalypse joyeuse*, 209.

62   Pierre-Simon Girard, *Mémoire sur les grandes routes, les chemins de fer et les canaux de navigation*, Paris: Bachelier, 1827, cxxv.

debates on the export of coal, led to the first assessments of national reserves. The House of Lords set up commissions on this subject in 1822 and 1829.

Jevons's well-known treatise on *The Coal Question* (1865) can be placed in a particular English political context, that of debates on free trade (Should coal exports be encouraged?) and the reduction of the public debt (What burden should we leave to future generations deprived of cheap energy?). Three new aspects were emphasized by Jevons. First of all, that of a fundamental difference between the asymptotic development of organic economies (the stationary state) and the logic of collapse specific to mineral economies:

> A farm, however far pushed, will under proper cultivation continue to yield forever a constant crop. But in a mine there is no reproduction, and the produce once pushed to the utmost will soon begin to fail and sink to zero. So far, then, as our wealth and progress depend upon the superior command of coal, we must not only stop – we must go back.[63]

In the organic energy system, marginal returns fall to zero and production stabilizes at the limit of sustainable exploitation. In a fossil fuel economic system, it is production itself that collapses towards zero.

Secondly, the debate on exhaustion shifted from the geological question to the estimate of future consumption: should the hypothesis of geometrical growth be accepted (based on the fundamental notion of the rebound effect that Jevons proposed) or simply that of an arithmetical one?

Thirdly, this period was marked by a general questioning on the subject of exhaustion of nature. We have seen the very marked concern raised by the metabolic rupture between town and country. In the same period, geologists worried about the scarcity of copper, zinc and tin, in the context of the development of the world telegraph network. In 1898, the president of the British Association for the Advancement

---

63   William Stanley Jevons, *The Coal Question: An Inquiry Concerning the Progress of the Nation, and the Probable Exhaustion of Our Coal-Mines*, London: Macmillan, 1866, 155.

of Science, William Crookes, warned against the exhaustion of nitrate from guano, and the risk of a global crisis for an agriculture that had suddenly become dependent on non-renewable resources.[64] The disturbing fact had to be acknowledged that the transition from an organic economy and the rupture of metabolic cycles had been undertaken despite a sharper attention to the future and despite a clear awareness of the unsustainable character of the new regime that was coming into being in the late nineteenth century. For Jevons, the coal question amounted to a 'momentous choice between brief greatness and longer continued mediocrity'[65] and, contrary to current interpretations that would see Jevons as a precursor of 'sustainability', he argued for this 'brief greatness'!

The historical choice of a 'brief greatness' that was made at the end of the nineteenth century is clearly reflected in the sudden contraction of the temporal horizon of contemporary political actors. In 1860, in the House of Commons, Disraeli, opposing the free-trade treaty with France (the Cobden-Chevalier Treaty), maintained that, since English reserves would cover no more than three or four centuries of national consumption, it was imperative for the long-term survival of the empire that exports should be taxed. Gladstone, on the other hand, a champion of free trade, mentioned other geological studies that estimated reserves at 2,000 years' consumption. A scarcity foreseeable in three centuries seemed to justify a course of action that was economically damaging in the present. The long term of English politicians managing their empire, instilled with classical references and quoting Edward Gibbon, was in the order of millennia.

Oil exploitation confirmed the historical choice of a 'brief greatness'. The first debates about oil reserves were marked by a spectacular shortening of time frames in relation to the debate about coal. In the United States, the explosion of consumption linked to the automobile and the First World War took place despite warnings as to the coming exhaustion of national reserves. In 1918, a report by the Smithsonian Institution explained that it was unlikely that major new oilfields

---

64   Vaclav Smil, *Enriching the Earth*, Cambridge, MA: MIT Press, 2001, 58.
65   Jevons, *The Coal Question*, 375.

would be found in the United States. During the First World War, the director of the US Fuel Administration anticipated a decline in US military power arising from the increasing scarcity of oil. In 1921, the US Geological Survey estimated the economically exploitable oil reserves as twenty years at the most.[66]

With the Second World War and then the Cold War, a new political attention focused on the sites of strategic materials and their limited stocks. With the universalization of oil, the question of exhaustion became structural. In December 1945, in a celebrated article titled 'The War and Our Vanishing Resources', Interior Secretary Harold Ickes warned his fellow-countrymen that

> the prodigal harvest of minerals that we have reaped to win this war has bankrupted some of our most vital mineral resources. We no longer deserve to be listed with Russia and the British Empire as one of the 'Have' nations of the world. We should be listed with the 'Have-nots' such as Germany and Japan.[67]

Circumfusa, climate, metabolism, economy of nature, thermodynamics, exhaustion: these six grammars of environmental reflexivity of which we have sketched a typology need to be pursued in historical studies, particularly to show their articulation to concrete practices (maintenance of clean air, soil fertility, recycling, etc.), as well as the interaction between their theoretical formalization and political problems. From a preliminary analysis, however, it is clear that the moderns possessed their own forms of environmental reflexivity. The conclusion that forces itself on us, disturbing as it may be, is that our ancestors destroyed environments in full awareness of what they were doing. Industrialization and the radical transformation of environments that it caused by its string of pollutions went ahead despite environmental

---

66   Aaron Dennis, 'Drilling for Dollars: The Making of US Petroleum Reserve Estimates, 1921–25', *Social Studies of Science*, 15:2, 1985: 241–65; Jérôme Bourdieu, *Anticipations et ressources finies. Le marché pétrolier americain dans l'entre-deux-guerres*, Paris: EHESS, 1998, 170.

67   Quoted by Daniel A. Barber, 'Tomorrow's House: Solar Housing in 1940's America', *Technology and Culture*, 55:1, January 2014: 1–39, 15.

medicine; the ever more intensive use of natural resources continued despite the concept of economy of nature and the perception of limits. The historical problem, therefore, is not the emergence of an 'environmental awareness' but rather the reverse: to understand the schizophrenic nature of modernity, which continued to view humans as the products of their environment at the same time as it let them damage and destroy it.

CHAPTER 9

Agnotocene: Externalizing Nature, Economizing the World

The Anthropocene societies did not destroy their environments inadvertently, or without considering – sometimes in terror – the consequences of their actions. How did we enter the Anthropocene despite the environmental grammars studied above? In sociology and the history of science, a new field of research has recently developed, that of 'agnotology', which studies the production of zones of ignorance. How are the damages of 'progress' made invisible (think of the effects of asbestos, known since 1906 and ignored at the cost of hundreds of thousands of deaths)? How are opposition and criticisms against technoscientific projects managed?[1] In this vein, the present chapter offers a history of some of the agnotological processes that accompanied the Anthropocene.

It likewise analyses the great adjustments to the world picture that accompanied the commodification of man and nature, enabling environmentalist critique to be disqualified and the finitude of the Earth to be denied. It starts from the hypothesis that the cultural history of the Anthropocene cannot be that of some fundamental breaks that pre-existed it (the destructive destiny of *Homo sapiens*, Christianity as

---

1   Robert N. Proctor and Londa Schiebinger, *Agnotology: The Making and Unmaking of Ignorance*, Stanford: Stanford University Press, 2008; Robert N. Proctor, *Golden Holocaust: Origins of the Cigarette Catastrophe and the Case for Abolition*, Berkeley: University of California Press, 2012.

domination of nature, the great division between nature and culture, the mechanistic world picture of the scientific revolution, etc.), but that it is borne by cultural and ideological devices that are contemporary with it and still active today. The history of the Anthropocene is not one of a frenetic modernism that transforms the world while ignorant of nature, but rather of the scientific and political production of a modernizing unconscious.

The infinite world of fossil capitalism

At the threshold of the Anthropocene, the *Homo economicus* of liberal political economy, moved by self-interest and material appetites, required in exchange a world made to his measure.[2] Nature had to be profoundly redefined, as well as its influence on human societies, its capacity to reproduce itself and the wealth it offered to industry, in order to leave free rein to *Homo economicus*. The sciences accordingly composed a nature that liberalism and industry could mobilize, a *mundus economicus* to the measure of its industrious master.

In the eighteenth century, Europe, like the rest of the world, lived in an organic economy in which the limits of agricultural land and forests formed a strong constraint on growth. Mechanical force derived from muscular energy (human and animal), from water and from wind, all drawing their source in the last instance from the energy of the sun. For the United Kingdom, the historian E. A. Wrigley has calculated that vegetation cover fixed a part of this solar energy in the production of biomass equivalent to between 20 and 40 million tonnes of coal.[3] It was within this limit (extendable as a function of colonial territories) that human activities developed. The

2 Jean-Baptiste Fressoz, *L'Apocalypse joyeuse*, Paris: Seuil, 2012, 285–302, and 'Mundus oeconomicus. Révolutionner l'industrie et refaire le monde vers 1800', in Kapil Raj and Otto Sibum (eds), *Histoire des sciences et des savoirs*, vol. 2, Paris: Seuil, 2015, 369–89.

3 E. A. Wrigley, 'Two Kinds of Growth, Two Kinds of Capitalism', in *Poverty, Progress and Population*, Cambridge: Cambridge University Press, 2004, 68–86.

organic economy was thus embedded in a very constrained energy budget: four hectares of forest, for example, were needed to produce a tonne of iron, two hectares of pasture to feed a horse, etc. Every development of one kind of production had a negative effect on the growth capacity of others. The rise of forges and glass-works as new consumers of wood came into conflict with the needs of village and urban communities for fire-wood, threatening the quality and docility of the labour force. After more than two centuries of shrinking forests, Western Europe thus experienced a serious energy crisis at the turn of the nineteenth century, connected to social tensions and fears of global climatic disturbance. The price of wood doubled in France between 1770 and 1790.[4] In 1788, the *intendant* of Brittany predicted that 'within twenty years all the present manufactures will fail for want of wood to fuel them'.[5] The growth of the population, the development of manufacturing and the rank of the nation all seemed to depend on the future of the forests.

The initial response to this sense of permanent limitation was to foster 'rational' forestry. By organized annual cutting (with rotation of up to two centuries for the masts of warships), it was possible to guarantee the monarch and his army a stable and predictable supply of wood and at the same time an increased income for the forest proprietors. This mathematical forestry, the forerunner of the contemporary idea of sustainable development, was founded on an iterative conception of nature, which reproduced itself uniformly and whose future could be securely predicted. Developed under Louis XIV and in the German court science of the early eighteenth century, rational forestry conquered Europe at the start of the nineteenth, followed by the colonial territories in the second half of the century.[6] In the 1850s, however,

---

4   Ernest Labrousse, *Esquisse du mouvement des prix et des revenus en France au XVIIIe siècle*, vol. 2, Paris: Dalloz, 1933, 343; Jérôme Buridant, *Le premier choc énergétique. La crise forestière dans le nord bassin parisien, début XVIIIe–début XIXe siècles*, thesis HDR Paris 4, 2008.

5   Quoted by Henri Sée, 'Les forêts et la question du déboisement en Bretagne à la fin de l'Ancien Régime', *Annales de Bretagne*, 36:2, 1924: 355–79.

6   Henry E. Lowood, 'The Calculating Forester: Quantification, Cameral Science, and the Emergence of Scientific Forestry Management in Germany', *The*

foresters noted the extreme fragility of the ecosystems they had created. Forests of uniform age and species were very vulnerable to parasites, storms and meteorological accidents. The introduction of the word 'Waldsterben' (forest death) in Germany in the late nineteenth century attests to the seriousness of foresters' concerns.[7] German foresters developed a new 'forest hygiene' that aimed to recreate the soil and the symbioses that existed before the introduction of forest monoculture. Despite its negative ecological effects and the social conflicts it aroused, the mathematical management of the forest was a promise, a scientific guarantee of the future, making it possible to circumvent the fears bound up with the scarcity of wood that were so forcibly expressed in the late eighteenth century.

Naturally, the main factor that relieved the energy constraint and reversed the shrinkage of European forests was the exploitation of coal. Coal was even presented as a sort of 'green energy' by many foresters, such as François-Antoine Rauch in France, who called for a 'generalized use of these fuels' in order to spare 'our depopulated forests'.[8] Yet coal did arouse sharp disquiet. On the one hand, its toxicity was feared. Coal's sickening fumes were shunned by bourgeois and aristocratic homes, and it was perceived as the fuel of the poor. On the other hand, there was concern for its rapid exhaustion. In 1792, a French deputy explained that the conservation of the forests was of utmost importance, since coal mines 'are not as common as is thought. It is noticeable that those of the Auvergne are becoming exhausted, and the prospections that have multiplied around the capital have not been successful.'[9] The Scottish geologist John Williams expressed

Quantifying Spirit in the Eighteenth Century, Berkeley: University of California Press, 1990, 315–43; Gregory Barton, *Empire Forestry and the Origins of Environmentalism*, Cambridge: Cambridge University Press, 2004.

7   James C. Scott, *Seeing Like a State: How Certain Schemes to Improve the Human Condition Have Failed*, New Haven: Yale University Press, 1998, 11–22.

8   François-Antoine Rauch, *Harmonie hydro-végétale et météorologique, ou recherches sur les moyens de recréer avec nos forêts la force de températures et la régularité des saisons, par des plantations raisonnées*, Paris: Frères Levrault, 1802, 51–2.

9   *Archives parlementaires de 1787 à 1860*, vol. 39, Paris: Paul Dupont, 1892, 292.

similar fears at the same time.[10] At its beginnings, coal seemed only a temporary solution.

The rise of geology then played a major anxiolytic role. In the 1800s, William Smith, an English geometer working in the construction of mines and canals, used fossils as markers of geological strata and showed that the study of their succession made it possible to predict the presence of coal in a given subsoil. By indicating probable deposits, guiding the digging of pits and avoiding useless work, geologists made investment in the mining sector less risky and more lucrative. Geological maps (of which Smith was the precursor) encouraged the owners of land situated in favourable zones to undertake probes, thereby increasing proven reserves.[11] In a general sense, geology constructed the image of a subsoil organized according to vast mineral strata that were hidden but continuous.[12] By moving from the sporadic view-point of the mine exploiters to a larger and continuous view of the subsoil, it founded reassuring concepts such as 'potential discovery' or 'probable reserves', which authorized far more optimistic estimates than those of the practitioners.

In the second half of the nineteenth century, the globalization of geological prospecting further shored up the confidence of the imperial powers as to the material bases of their domination. One of the effects of Jevons's *The Coal Question* (Chapter 8) was to intensify the activity of the British Geological Survey across the empire.[13] In the same way, international geological conferences (starting in 1877) established a global inventory of energy and metal resources. That of Toronto in 1913, devoted to coal, led to the first quantification of global reserves. A certain vagueness in the definition of 'likely reserves' and

10   Robert Peter Sieferle, *The Subterranean Forest: Energy Systems and the Industrial Revolution*, Isle of Harris: White Horse Press, 2001, 187.

11   Hugh Torrens, *The Practice of British Geology, 1750–1850*, Aldershot: Ashgate, 2002.

12   Martin Rudwick, *Bursting the Limits of Time: The Reconstruction of Geohistory in the Age of Revolution*, Chicago: Chicago University Press, 2005, 431–45.

13   Robert A. Stafford, *Scientist of Empire: Sir Roderick Murchison, Scientific Exploration, and Victorian Imperialism*, Cambridge: Cambridge University Press, 1989.

the extension of the limit of economically exploitable coal to 4,000 feet (instead of the previous 2,200) allowed a massive overestimate – in any case a figure six times higher than contemporary estimates.[14] By the late nineteenth century, worries about the exhaustion of the mineral world had been circumvented by this global construction of resources by the science of geology.

As a fossil fuel from a world long since disappeared, coal also transformed the perception of time in many respects. Above all, it conferred on the capitalist the freedom to store energy and mobilize it at the desired moment and in the degree needed. Sadi Carnot, writing at the dawn of its use, had perfectly glimpsed the temporal power of the steam engine: 'It has the inappreciable advantage of being employable at any time and in any place, and of never suffering an interruption in its work.'[15] The steam engine made it possible to homogenize space, to ignore location, watercourses and gradients. It created a much more competitive and fluid labour market, as entrepreneurs could relocate their activities according to local wages. While production had to be adjusted to a moving nature (the strength of horses, the fluctuations of wind and the flow of rivers), coal, because it could be stored and accumulated, made it possible to smooth out production, to linearize time and subject it to market imperatives. The continuous time of industrial capitalism, imposed on recalcitrant workers, was then projected onto cultural representations of the future, conceived as a continuous progress unfurling to the rhythm of productivity gains.

This linear time was likewise projected onto nature by way of the rise of gradualism in geology. This theory, according to which the terrestrial globe was shaped by present causes acting over the very long run (rather than by catastrophic events), was anchored in European culture at the same time as the new centrality of coal.[16] Indeed, the

14   Nuno Luis Madureira, 'The Anxiety of Abundance: William Stanley Jevons and Coal Scarcity in the Nineteenth Century', *Environment and History*, 18:3, 2002: 395–421.

15   Sadi Carnot, *Réflexions sur la puissance motrice du feu et sur les machines propres à développer cette puissance*, Paris: Bachelier, 1824, 2.

16   According to James Hutton, for example, the fact that coal is found of different qualities, corresponding to the intermediary stages of its formation,

Earth had to be given an antiquity sufficient to leave the relics of past vegetation time to accumulate in thick layers, providing for centuries of industrial need.

At the threshold of the Anthropocene, the switch from an organic surface energy to an underground fossil energy widened the gap between the temporality of the Earth and the temporality of human history. In return, this discordance of human and natural times favoured a sense of externality in relation to a nature that was infinitely old and thus immensely rich. From the dawn of time, wrote Sadi Carnot, nature had prepared the 'immense reservoir'[17] from which industry could in future prosper. Jean-Baptiste Say went further: 'Happily, nature placed in reserve long before the formation of man immense provisions of fuel in coal mines, as it foresaw that man, once in possession of his domain, would destroy more combustible materials than it could reproduce.'[18] The geologist and theologian William Buckland saw the providential hand of God in the depth of the coal seams: 'However remote may have been the periods, at which these materials of future beneficial dispensations were laid up in store, we may fairly assume, that . . . an ulterior prospective view to the future uses of Man, formed part of the design.'[19] Thanks to its antiquity, the Earth, despite the evident finitude of its surface, became an endless reservoir of resources.

This new vision of the Earth's bounty circulated widely among the Victorian public. For instance, in his *Statistical Account of the British Empire*, John McCulloch demonstrated in 1839 the unchallengeable superiority of Great Britain and the unshakeable stability of its domination. By lengthy tables, the bourgeois Victorian was relieved to discover fabulous amounts of resources. Coal in particular was

---

supported the gradualist thesis and indicated that the process was still under way. See James Hutton, *Theory of the Earth*, from *Transactions of the Royal Society of Edinburgh*, 1788, 33.

17   Carnot, *Réflexions*, 1.

18   Jean-Baptiste Say, *Cours complet d'économie politique pratique* (1828), vol. 1, Paris: Guillaumin, 1840, 262.

19   William Buckland, *Geology and Mineralogy Considered with Reference to Natural Theology*, vol. 1, Philadelphia: Carey, 1837, 403.

described as inexhaustible: 'The coal fields of Durham and Northumberland are adequate to furnish the present annual supply for more than 1,340 years.' The precision of this figure, and the vague expression 'more than', opened the perspective of an almost infinite quantity.[20] In a few decades, geology had thus transformed Malthus's 'dismal science' into a reassuring argument for limitless growth.

But how could atmosphere, vegetation and oceans absorb without damage all the carbon released by the new fossil economy? This concern was not foreign to contemporaries. In 1832, the mathematician and inventor Charles Babbage noted that steam engines 'are constantly increasing the atmosphere by large quantities of carbonic acid and other gases noxious to animal life. The means by which nature decomposes these elements, or reconverts them into a solid form, are not sufficiently known.' But he immediately went on to reassure his readers about the immensity and recycling power of nature 'incessantly at work in reversing . . . acting over vast spaces, and unlimited by time'.[21] In parallel with Lyell's idea that human action was insignificant in the history of the Earth, scientists in thrall to natural theology conceived human action as microscopic compared to the vast cycles of nature. Likewise, precise studies conducted by the chemists Dumas and Boussingault in 1841 showed that the composition of the air was uniform across the globe. The result was reassuring:

The combustions or oxidations that are accomplished on the surface of the Earth, all these events that our imagination is pleased to expand . . . take place as it were unperceived as far as the general composition of the air surrounding us is concerned.[22]

---

20   Elaine Freedgood, *Victorian Writing about Risk: Imagining a Safe England in a Dangerous World*, Cambridge: Cambridge University Press, 2000, 18–28.

21   Charles Babbage, *On the Economy of Machinery and Manufactures*, London: Charles Knight, 1832, 17.

22   Jean-Baptiste Dumas and Jean-Baptiste Boussingault, 'Recherches sur la véritable constitution de l'air atmosphérique', *Annales de chimie et de physique*, 3:3, 1841: 257–304.

In the same way, in 1855, the chemist Eugène Péligot calculated that European industry each year injected 80 billion cubic metres of carbon dioxide into the atmosphere, equivalent to the breathing of 500 million individuals. Even if vegetation could not absorb all this carbon, he argued, 'however considerable these quantities appear to us, they are in all likelihood nothing in relation to the immensity of our atmosphere'.[23] Nature was supposed to guarantee the stability of the atmosphere's composition, whatever critics (local residents, doctors, workers, etc.) might say about industrial pollutants.[24] By universalizing the air into a majestic atmosphere, an immense receptacle in permanent equilibrium, the local and global effects of industry were minimized and nature became a mere externality.

Externalizing natural and human substance

'Machine production in a commercial society,' wrote Karl Polanyi, 'involves, in effect, no less a transformation than that of the natural and human substance of society into commodities'.[25] On the threshold of the Anthropocene, two disciplines had the function of justifying this great transformation and its consequences for men and nature.

Political economy, above all, provided the principal justificatory theodicy of industrial miseries. In the 1820s and '30s, in England, while misery and economic crises led to a general questioning of the benefits of industrialization, and machine breaking was on the rise, economists such as Hugh Torrens, Nassau William Senior, McCulloch, Babbage and William Whewell endowed machines with providential virtues: they countered the fall in productivity and staved off the stationary state predicted by David Ricardo; they increased profit, stimulated investments and created new jobs by replacing those they destroyed; finally, they promoted the moral progress of the workers by

---

23   *L'ami des sciences*, 1, 1855, 174.

24   See Alexis Zimmer, *Brouillards mortels. Une histoire de la production de météores industriels, 19e/20e siècles. Le cas de la vallée de la Meuse*, PhD thesis, University of Strasbourg, 2013.

25   Karl Polanyi, *The Great Transformation*, Boston: Beacon Press, 2001, 44.

freeing them from mind-numbing tasks. Political economy became the great apologetic discourse of the machine.[26] It also accompanied the disembedding of work from the norms, institutions and solidarities that had regulated its exercise. By demonstrating its optimality, it absolved the free market of social disturbances. Vulgarizers spread a providentialist view of the economy that condemned any intervention (limiting bread prices, helping the poor financially, etc.) as contrary to the natural order desired by God. The market was conceived as a vast arena in which God spoke directly to all, a 'great scheme of human redemption' according to the Tory prime minister Robert Peel.[27] In 1826, in a pre-revolutionary context, the theologian and economist Thomas Chalmers recommended political economy as 'a sedative to all sorts of turbulence and disorder'.[28]

In France, the anxiolytic project was taken up by a small group of economists and vulgarizers very active in the new engineering schools of the industrial revolution. The most important of these, Jean-Baptiste Say, enriched the English theories with an essential element: the supposed law that 'supply creates its own demand'. Contrary to the productive world of the ancien régime, preoccupied above all by overproduction and the effects of competition on the quality of products,[29] the law of supply, by neglecting the role of money and saving, explained that production itself created its own outlet. In this way, it abolished one of the main motives for corporative regulation and justified an unbridled productivism.

---

26   This should be contrasted with the economic vulgarization of Ricardo's more ambiguous positions, as he expressly justified the complaints of artisans made unemployed by machines. See Maxine Berg, *The Machinery Question and the Making of Political Economy, 1815–1848*, Cambridge: Cambridge University Press, 1980, 43–111.

27   Quoted by Boyd Hilton, *A Mad, Bad, and Dangerous People?: England 1783–1846*, Oxford: Oxford University Press, 2006, 326.

28   Quoted by Berg, *The Machinery Question*, 163.

29   The statutes of medieval guilds often laid down production quotas in order to avoid excessive competition, maintain the quality of products as well as the reputation of a town's artisans. Thus the hatters of Marseille and Paris were not allowed to produce more than three hats per day. See Michael Sonenscher, *The Hatters of Eighteenth-Century France*, Berkeley: University of California Press, 1987.

In the first half of the nineteenth century, public health responded to a similar anxiolytic function in justifying the externalities of industrial capitalism: the threat to health from world trade, the biological consequences of pauperism and industrial pollution.

In England, the anti-contagionist doctrine that formed the theoretical basis of the 'sanitarian' movement championed the idea that diseases were caused not by transmissible germs (as Koch and Pasteur would later demonstrate) but by dirt and the miasmas it gave off. The debate between contagionism and anti-contagionism opposed two visions of the economy and the role of the state. The former implied maintaining the system of quarantine that industrialists and businessmen wished to have abolished in the name of free exchange. Anti-contagionism absolved commercial globalization and imperialism from the resurgence of the great epidemics (such as cholera) in the first half of the nineteenth century.[30]

This doctrine also justified the liberalization of the labour market. In the 1830s and '40s, Edwin Chadwick, a major figure in public health in Britain, undertook to prove that excess mortality in the industrial districts was due not to poverty or hunger, but to dirt. This was the cause of disease which in turn led to poverty, rather than the other way round. The direction of causality defined a policy: in the wake of the reform of the Poor Laws in 1834, which abolished outdoor relief, the point was to exonerate the free labour market from the disastrous biological consequences of poverty. Thanks to the new public health doctrine, the construction of sewers and the reform of individual behaviour was more important than social reform.[31]

In France, public health in the 1820s and '30s had a different political role, emphasizing on the contrary the economic causes of mortality so as to downplay the environmental ones, with the aim of legitimizing industrial pollution. French public health policy was born in the context of the industrialization of Paris and the complaints against

---

30   Erwin Ackerknecht, 'Anticontagionism between 1821 and 1867', *Bulletin of the History of Medicine*, 22:5, 1948, 562–93.

31   Christopher Hamlin, *Public Health and Social Justice in the Age of Chadwick: Britain, 1800–1854*, Cambridge: Cambridge University Press, 1998.

pollution, with a view to supplanting the environmental medicine of the eighteenth century. Against the town dwellers who demanded the suppression of factories by invoking the *circumfusa* (or 'environmental things'), the first public health experts proved that factories could be inconvenient without necessarily being unhealthy. Even better, by studying the social causes of health (after the model of Louis-René Villermé), they showed that not only were factories not unhealthy, they could portend a prosperous society and therefore a healthier population. In this way, public health accompanied and justified a fundamental shift in French environmental regulation. According to the decree of 1810 on classified establishments (which influenced a large part of European legislation on this subject), the administration subjected factories to rigorous authorization procedures but guaranteed in exchange their permanence, no matter what subsequent complaints were made. Local residents, unable to hope for the suppression of a factory, had no other recourse than suing the polluters for compensation in the civil courts. The government and civil justice were two faces of the same free-market regime of environmental regulation: civil justice, by making the polluter pay the costs of pollution, was deemed to produce financial incentives that would lead entrepreneurs to reduce emissions. From a common good, responsible for health and subject to the police of the ancien régime, the environment became an object of financial transactions.

The dematerialization of the economy

Prevailing economic theory maintains a very tenuous relationship with matter. It envisages goods according to their psychological effects, as purveyors of utility, rather than according to their material characteristics. In the same way, capital is not conceived as a concrete set of productive equipment, rather as assets generating financial flows. This dematerialization has the effect of naturalizing the exponential growth of the economy during the Anthropocene by disconnecting it from any material substratum.

In the first half of the nineteenth century, European elites were still largely agricultural, and the aristocracy was suspicious of industrialization. They preferred the economic and social stability of the rural world to an uncontrolled industrial and urban growth. In England, until the 1850s, the dominant Tory ideology was deeply pervaded by an evangelical idea of economics, conceiving poverty, trade crises and bankruptcies as dispensations of providence. The economy was seen as static and cyclical. The market was more a place of moral retribution, penitence and gratification than an instrument of growth.[32] For the physiocrats, Malthus and classical political economy alike (Ricardo with his law of diminishing returns), the economic theory of the early industrial period ruled out the idea of indefinite growth. It was only in the last third of the nineteenth century that theorists began to view the economy as an object entirely distinct from natural processes and subject above all, if not uniquely, to human laws and conventions.

Marginalist economists turned away from the study of factors of production (labour, capital and land) and focused on the subjective states of consumers and producers seeking to maximize their individual utility.[33] The economy no longer shared an object with the natural sciences (the production of material wealth), but only mathematical tools: the marginalists transposed equations taken from physics so as to create the illusion of a second world as coherent as nature, analogous but external.[34] Natural resources now occupied only a very marginal place in economic theory. Between 1870 and 1970, their study formed only a small subdivision of the discipline, the economics of conservation, which took its ontology and mathematical tools from marginalist theory. A dynamic approach to the economy, which envisaged long-term evolution in a context of increasing scarcity (with Jevons for example), was replaced by a microeconomic and static approach. Thus in 1931, in a fundamental

32   Boyd Hilton, *The Age of Atonement: The Influence of Evangelicalism on Social and Economic Thought, 1785–1865*, Oxford: Oxford University Press, 1997.

33   Daniel Breslau, 'Economics Invents the Economy: Mathematics, Statistics, and Models in the Work of Irving Fisher and Wesley Mitchell', *Theory and Society*, 32:3, 2003: 379–411.

34   Philip Mirowski, *More Heat than Light: Economics as Social Physics, Physics as Nature's Economics*, Cambridge: Cambridge University Press, 1991.

article on the economics of natural resources, Harold Hotelling analysed the situation of a mine-owner in a competitive situation who sought to maximize his actualized income. The problem was no longer that of the long-term future of a national economy, but more modestly how a mine-owner could find the optimal path for extracting an exhaustible resource so as to maximize its financial value. The mine became an abstract entity, disconnected from the rest of the productive system (despite fuelling this), simply a reserve of value that obeyed the same type of calculation as a stock portfolio.[35]

The disembedding of the economy from natural constraints took place also in the study of economic cycles. Until the 1870s, this consisted in analysing the price of commodities in relation to non-economic causes. Climate played a major role, as the importance of agriculture in the economy and the periodicity of business activity suggested a correlation with meteorological data. In the late nineteenth century, however, automatic techniques of price inscription and communication radically accelerated the flow of financial information (the stock ticker appeared at the New York Stock Exchange in 1867). While the old procedures of setting prices showed monthly variations correlated with harvests, weather, natural catastrophes and wars, prices now varied minute by minute. The result of this major transformation was that stock-market quotations now constituted continuous temporal sequences that seemed to vary in an independent manner, unconnected from anything apart from themselves.[36] The globalization of financial information and the establishment of futures markets (starting with corn in the 1860s) further disconnected prices from local and natural conditions of production, tying them to financial rather than natural causes.

---

35   Antonin Pottier, *L'Économie dans l'impasse climatique. Développement matériel, théorie immatérielle et utopie auto-stabilisatrice*, thesis, EHESS, 2014, 112–22; Guido Erreygers, 'Hotelling, Rawls, Solow: How Exhaustible Resources Came to Be Integrated into the Neoclassical Growth Model', *History of Political Economy*, 41, 2009: 263–85.

36   Alex Preda, 'Socio-Technical Agency in Financial Markets: The Case of the Stock Ticker', *Social Studies of Science*, 36:5, 2006: 753–82.

In the 1890s, econometric tools made it possible to study the systemic relationships between different prices. Instead of correlating these with exogenous factors, the price system made the economy into a homogeneous object closed on itself. 'External' causes, whether natural or political, were no more than secondary disturbances to the system. The economy became an autonomous object on which scientific action was possible.

On the macroeconomic side, neoclassical tools such as the production function proposed by Charles Cobb and Paul Douglas in 1928, and the growth theories of Robert Solow, did not allow any place for nature (and its limits), or at best viewed it simply as a production factor that could be substituted for by an increase in capital or by technological innovation. According to Solow, 'if it is very easy to substitute other factors [e.g., labour or capital] for natural resources, then there is, in principle, no "problem". The world can, in effect, get along without natural resources.'[37]

In the same way, mainstream Marxists, by focusing on the labour theory of value and the distribution of the product between two classes, workers and capitalists, essentially saw only two factors of production: capital and labour. Whereas Marx and Engels were particularly concerned with the metabolic rupture between Earth and society that capitalism had produced, and certain Marxists such as Podolinsky sought to refound the labour theory on energy, Marxist economic science – until the recent emergence of a fruitful eco-Marxism – abolished the role of metabolism and energy, rejecting as 'Malthusian' (and thus conservative) any idea of limits to the planet's resources.[38]

The crisis of the 1930s, Keynesianism and the development of systems of national accounting completed the dematerialization of the economy. Before the 1930s, the idea of growth was bound up with a process of material expansion: it was a question of increasing production of a particular material, opening up new resources or new

---

37   Robert Solow, 'The Economics of Resources or the Resources of Economics', *American Economic Review*, 64:2, 1974: 1–14, 11.

38   Nicolas Georgescu-Roegen, 'Energy and Economic Myths', *Southern Economic Journal*, 41:3, 1975: 347–81; Joan Martínez Alier and Klaus Schlüpmann, *Ecological Economics: Energy, Environment and Society*, Oxford: Blackwell, 1993.

territories. With the overproduction crisis of the 1930s, growth was reconceived not in material terms but as the intensification of economic exchange. The abandonment of the gold standard in that decade (i.e., the end of the idea that bank-notes represented gold) was a key turning-point. Keynes, in a famous passage of his *General Theory*, explained that the end of coal would be unimportant; what mattered was the correct circulation of money: it would be enough, therefore, for the British Treasury to bury bank-notes and ask miners to hunt for them, in order to ensure employment and economic prosperity.[39] During the decades of economic crisis and war, a new object of thinking and government was produced: 'the economy' with a definite article, understood as the totality of market transactions on a given territory.[40] As such, and completely dematerialized, the economy could be conceived as growing indefinitely, outside any natural determinisms and without coming up against physical limits, thanks to the good guardianship of economic experts (at the international level, the OECD incarnated this growth imperative for the industrial countries).

At the same period, the idea of national income acquired a whole new importance. If this had long been estimated by economists and journalists concerned to study the distribution of wealth between wages and profits, it was now calculated by official bureaux. In the United States, the economist Simon Kuznets, a Harvard academic appointed to the National Bureau of Economic Research, established in 1936 rules for calculating GDP that would be taken up across the world. First envisioned as a tool for monitoring the economy during recession, the calculation of GDP would serve above all during the Second World War to prime the American military effort, without compromising economic growth. In 1900, only eight countries had published their national income, a figure that grew to thirty-nine in 1946 and eighty some ten years later.[41] The change was also

39   Timothy Mitchell, *Carbon Democracy: Political Power in the Age of Oil*, London: Verso, 2011, 123–4.

40   Timothy Mitchell, 'Fixing the Economy', *Cultural Studies*, 12:1, 1998: 82–101.

41   Adam Tooze, *Statistics and the German State, 1900–1945: The Making of*

qualitative: the new mode of calculation, inherited from the realm of business accounting, was based on an equation between expenditure and income. This had two major consequences: first of all, the calculation of GDP naturalized the idea of the economy as a closed circuit, a circular flow of value between production and consumption cut off from its natural moorings; and secondly, by measuring it with just one figure, national accounting reified the economy and made it possible to erect it into an entity separate from society, politics and nature.

National accounting rested, finally, on the hypothesis of a completely commodified economy. Housework and 'free' services (including those rendered by nature) were absent from the calculation. In 1949, a fascinating debate took place among the inventors of GDP: Kuznets, Milton Gilbert, Colin Clark, François Perroux, George Findlay Shirras and D. H. MacGregor among others.[42] We find here the earliest and most radical critique of national accounting. According to its own progenitors, as GDP was narrowly correlated with military expenditure, it could not simply be used during peacetime conditions. Nor could it be used for less developed countries, as the non-market sphere played too important a role here, falsifying international comparison. Secondly, GDP had to be reduced by the 'costs of civilization', which included among other things pollution, traffic jams, police, judges, freeways, advertising 'that stimulated artificial needs', not to mention 'the work of insurers, trade associations, lawyers, bankers and . . . statisticians'. Thirdly and above all, mining activity had to be counted negatively, since the exhaustion of resources impoverished the nation. In the end, none of these proposals were taken on board, opening an endless discussion on the 'new indicators' of wealth and well-being. But it was a close call: GDP, which actually is corrected for the amortization of capital, could well have been adjusted for the wear and tear of natural capital. If in the end this proposal was not accepted, it was on the pretext that GDP also did not include the discovery of new mines

Modern Economic Knowledge, Cambridge: Cambridge University Press, 2001, 8.

42   See Milton Gilbert et al., 'The Measurement of National Wealth: Discussion', supplement, *Econometrica*, 17, 1949: 255–72.

or oil fields replacing the depleted ones.[43] Had this debate been decided otherwise, this adjusted GDP would have given a completely different view of Western economic development: for instance, the value of oil burned would have led to a steep decline of US GDP from the 1970s on.[44]

The economization of the world

By unburdening itself of nature, economics naturalized the idea of indefinite growth. Its role could have stopped there and been only ideological, if the tools and ontologies it had forged had not been projected back onto a nature that it had so potently externalized. In the course of the twentieth century, the mode of reasoning of marginalist economics, based on the ideas of optimality and equilibrium as well as on market instruments, became central in the definition of the proper uses of the world.

The case of the management of fish stocks is quite exemplary here. After the Second World War, the countries of South America, Peru in particular, sought to forbid the activity of United States trawlers in their territorial waters. In a similar way, South Korea complained of the incursions of Japanese and Russian vessels. In order to preserve the principle of freedom of the seas, essential for its commercial and military power, the United States imposed on international fishery law a new principle, that of 'maximum sustainable yield', according to which fishing had to be authorized as long as the ratio of catch to effort had not yet reached a maximum. In order to apply the optimization principle, the model neglected both relationships between species and marine environments. It conceived fishery resources after the model of a field which would be stimulated by increased catches (since young fish grow quicker). Natural processes were conceived as linear and reversible. If the fishing effort was reduced, the resource would

43   Martínez Alier and Schlüpmann, *Ecological Economics*, 275.
44   See the calculations of a 'genuine progress indicator' for the United States by Mark Anielski and Jonathan Rowe, *The Genuine Progress Indicator – 1998 Update*, San Francisco: Redefining Progress, 1999, which takes account among other things of the costs of pollution, road accidents and the loss of wetlands.

automatically increase. Under this regime of supposedly sustainable fishing, catches rose dramatically from 20 million tonnes in 1950 to 80 million tonnes in 1970, leading to a generalized decline in reserves.[45]

From the 1970s onwards, the notions of sustainability and durability became central in the fundamental ideological battle to circumvent mounting criticisms of the Western growth model. The publication in 1972 of the famous Club of Rome report *The Limits to Growth*,[46] which followed in the wake of major work by Kenneth Boulding, Herman Daly and Nicolas Georgescu-Roegen, should have forced economics to come down to Earth, but it led on the contrary to new constructions of the world that aimed to discredit any idea of a limit to growth.[47]

First of all, orthodox economists accused the report of neglecting technological innovations that enabled the replacement of 'natural' capital by economic capital, or even the invention of new resources (synthetic rubber replacing natural rubber, for example). In economic theory this idea was embodied in the famous Kuznets environmental curve, according to which growth is increasingly less harmful to the environment. The environment is degraded in order to escape from poverty, but the rise in GDP then permits a better conservation. The future studies movement that developed in the 1970s strengthened the hope of a growth that was dematerialized thanks to innovation. The physicist Herman Kahn (who inspired the character of Dr Strangelove in Kubrick's film) explained that within a few decades innovations would make it possible to feed billions of human beings (transgenic cereals capable of fixing atmospheric nitrogen), propelling them into space, etc. Another futurologist, Alvin Toffler, author of the bestseller *The Third Wave*, likewise depicted a dematerialized high-tech future, realising the 'post-industrial society' dreamed of by Daniel Bell. In France, the Groupe des Dix, Joël de Rosnay's book *Le*

---

45   Carmel Finley, *All the Fish in the Sea: Maximum Sustainable Yield and the Failure of Fisheries Management*, Chicago: Chicago University Press, 2011.

46   Dennis L. Meadows et al., *The Limits to Growth*, New York: Universe Books, 1972.

47   Élodie Vieille Blanchard, *Les Limites à la croissance dans un modèle global – Modèles mathématiques, prospectives, réfutations*, doctoral thesis, EHESS, 2011.

Macroscope (1975) that glorified 'green biotechnologies', or again the Nora-Minc report on *L'informatisation de la société* (1978), developed similar perspectives: the next industrial revolution, we were told, would introduce a bio-optimized and dematerialized service economy, enabling the fearless pursuit of economic growth while resolving environmental problems.[48] It was in this vein that biotechnologies were promoted in the 1970s as alternatives to chemical fertilisers and pesticides (whereas 98 per cent of current GMO crops are designed either to produce a biocide or to be used in association with biocides), and new digital technologies as the vector of dematerialization of the economy (whereas the consumption of rare earths and the energy used by the global digital infrastructure have become colossal). At the present time, it is geoengineering and synthetic biology that are promoted as new technological solutions to deal with global warming and the erosion of biodiversity.

Secondly, a new intellectual construction of nature is asserting itself, aligned to the frameworks of neoclassical economics. In this perspective, environmental problems are in fact 'market failures' that can be corrected by setting a price on nature. In the social democratic version of economization, this price should be paid to the state through a tax that enables environment and growth to be reconciled.

From the 1970s, however, a 'free-market environmentalism' came to prevail, based on the theory of Ronald Coase that it is economically optimal to attribute marketable rights to pollute and leave actors to negotiate among themselves. In various guises, the 'law and economics school', the 'new resource economics' or 'green economics', 'solutions' were promoted that depended on market instruments: markets in emissions rights for sulphur dioxide and CO_2, markets in fishing quotas or the extraction of ground water, even markets in 'ecosystemic services' for biodiversity.[49] These markets stimulated a global movement of land

48 Herman Kahn, William Brown and Leon Martel, *The Next 200 Years: A Scenario for America and the World*, New York: Morrow, 1976; Alvin Toffler, *The Third Wave*, New York: Bantam Books, 1980.

49 Nik Heynen et al., (eds), *Neoliberal Environments: False Promises and Unnatural Consequences*, London: Routledge, 2007; Yannick Mahrane and Christophe Bonneuil, 'Gouverner la biosphère. De l'environnement de la guerre

appropriation for the purpose of activities rewarded by the sale of 'carbon credits', 'biodiversity credits', etc., dispossessing rural and indigenous populations from their commons, in the same way that at the dawn of the Anthropocene the pursuit of charcoal and 'rational forestry' had dispossessed rural societies of their common forests.

With instruments such as these, the whole Earth was subjected to an economic calculation of optimization. Economists thus reconsidered the atmosphere and its ecosystems after the model of an economic resource whose present net value could be maximized, for example by defining optimal paths for CO_2 emission. Global climate change was translated into a problem of maximizing economic growth under climate constraint. In the first decade of the new century, negotiations under the aegis of the UN Framework Convention on Climate Change became bogged down in what Stefan Aykut and Amy Dahan call a 'reality schism', with a façade of global governance quite removed from a 'world reality', that of the globalization of markets and the frenetic exploitation of resources'.[50] Carbon credits, for their part, collapsed then revived, and will most likely continue to fluctuate wildly without sufficient examination of their material references, among other factors because the audit companies that assess the CO_2 emissions reductions of 'clean development projects' have no interest in appearing too strict. At all events, their very existence and exchange are enough to create the perspective of an economy at last ecologized.[51]

What view of nature underlies these new mechanisms for governing the biosphere and atmosphere? First, that the best way of conserving the planetary environment is to set a price on it, to serve as a signal and enable the market, deemed cognitively superior to

---

froide à l'environnement neolibéral', in Dominique Pestre (ed.), *Le Gouvernement des technosciences*, Paris: La Découverte, 2014, 133–69; Christophe Bonneuil, 'Tell Me Where You Come from, I Will Tell You What You Are: A Genealogy of Biodiversity Offsetting Mechanisms in Historical Context', *Conservation Biology*, 2015, 10.1016/j.biocon.2015.09.022. See also the special issue of the journal *Conservation and Society* on 'neoliberal conservation': *Conservation and Society* 5:4.

50   Stefan Aykut and Amy Dahan, *Gouverner le climat? 20 ans de négociations internationales*, Paris: Presses de Sciences Po, 2014, 399–401.

51   Benjamin Stephan and Richard Lane (eds), *The Politics of Carbon Markets*, London: Routledge, 2015.

public action, to internalize the value of nature. Second and particularly, since Garrett Hardin's famous article 'The Tragedy of the Commons', some believe that only private property makes possible the proper management of nature, and that the ideal for certain economists is thus to 'securitize the biosphere',[52] i.e., attribute property rights to all the different elements and ecological functions of the Earth system. With nature assimilated to a 'natural capital', it becomes fungible with finance capital. All the 'services' rendered by the Earth system (carbon capture, pollination, water purification, aesthetic or religious services, etc.) can be valued in dollars and made the object of environmental service markets, rewarding the proprietors of the corresponding spaces who would then maintain them as good managers. The old distinction between (natural) wealth and (social) value gives way to a fetishism of nature as 'the biggest business in the world' (in the expression popularized by the International Union for Conservation of Nature in 2009), as itself the producer of an economic value, already existing independent of any human labour or relation of production.[53]

In this perspective, there is no longer a limit to growth: the preservation of the environment, the environmental crisis and the scarcity of resources are actually presented as economic opportunities. As the firm Advanced Conservation Strategies prophesies, 'We enter a new era of scarcity, environmental markets are exploding. This includes not only carbon, but emerging water and biodiversity markets.'[54] In 1997, the scientific journal *Nature* published a preliminary calculation of the monetary value of services rendered annually by nature on the planetary level, estimated at between $16 trillion and $54 trillion dollars, or

---

52 As recently proposed by the economists Graciela Chichilnisky and Geoffrey Heal, 'Securitizing the Biosphere', in Graciela Chichilnisky and Geoffrey Heal (eds), *Environmental Markets: Equity and Efficiency*, New York: Columbia University Press, 2000, 169–79.

53 Christophe Bonneuil, 'Une nature liquide? Les discours de la biodiversité dans le nouvel esprit du capitalisme', in Frédéric Thomas (ed.), *Le pouvoir de la biodiversité. Néolibéralisation de la nature dans les pays émergents*, Paris: Éditions de l'IRD-Quae, 2015, 193–213.

54 advancedconservation.org, accessed 15 March 2013. (The page containing the quote has since been suppressed.)

the same order of magnitude as global GDP. The annual loss of bio-diversity was estimated at $4,400 billion, and the same Advanced Conservation Strategies has no hesitation in promising that 'by 2030, carbon will be the most important commodity exchanged in the world, with a market value of $1,600 to $2,400 billion, or the equivalent of the present value of the oil market'.

At the start of the nineteenth century, industrial modernity constructed the idea of nature as stock, external to the economy and constituting an inexhaustible storehouse. By the late twentieth century, a new phase of capitalism – financial, postmodern, flexible and network-based – came and challenged this industrial-modern ontology of nature. In the new spirit of late capitalism, the issue of valuing diversity replaces the older issue of reducing diversity to standardize production; flows now matter as much as stocks, services as much as material production, relationships as much as entities. The film *Avatar*, counterpoising the extractivist view of nature as resources (in the shape of a capitalist firm hunting for mineral ore) to the 'connected' nature of the Navi, is emblematic of this 'network' turn of Western representations of nature. In our late modernity, the 'invisibilizing' of the limits of Earth is no longer just a result of an externalization (as a great outside that humans can draw from and jettison into without problem), but on the contrary of a radical internalization. This internalization is expressed in the efforts to measure ecosystemic functions in terms of financial flows, making a nature that is liquid and capitalizable even in its most intimate processes. Internalization into the market is backed by the ontological dissolution of nature by constructivist philosophies that deny its alterity in relation to humans, and from the geo-constructivist engineering project of all aspects of the Earth system, from the genome to the biosphere.[55]

We could also remark that the break from the early nineteenth century to the early twenty-first century is not total. The mode of

---

55   Déborah Danowski and Eduardo Viveiros de Castro, 'L'arrêt de monde', in Émilie Hache (ed.), *De l'univers clos au monde infini*, Paris: Dehors, 2014, 221–339; Frédéric Neyrat, *Enquête sur la part inconstructible de la Terre. Critique du géo-constructivisme*, Paris: Seuil, 2016.

regulating environments by compensation (the 'polluter pays' principle) was in fact born in the nineteenth century, and experience shows that it did not prevent pollution but, on the contrary, historically accompanied and legitimized the degradation of environments. Such regulation possesses an intrinsic logic whose consequences were visible already in the 1820s. The principle of compensation for damage, combined with the imperative of economic profitability, produces three results: the employment for the most dangerous tasks of the weakest sections of the population, whose illnesses can remain socially invisible; the concentration of production and pollution in a few localities; and the choice, for these localities, of poor territories lacking in social and political resources, thus minimizing the value of environmental compensation.[56] We cannot fail to note the contemporary persistence of this logic, and even its most likely accentuation made possible by economic globalization. We can also observe that these new markets for nature encourage the illusion that the human presence in the world has been brought under control.

---

56   Jean-Baptiste Fressoz, 'Payer pour polluer. L'industrie chimique et la compensation des dommages environnementaux, 1800–1850', *Histoire et mesure*, 28:1, 2013: 145–86.

CHAPTER 10

Capitalocene: A Combined History of Earth System and World-Systems

If, as Fredric Jameson put it, 'it is easier to imagine the end of the world than to imagine the end of capitalism',[1] this is because capitalism has become coextensive with the Earth. The last three centuries have been characterized by an extraordinary accumulation of capital: despite destructive wars, this grew by a factor of 134 between 1700 and 2008.[2] The dynamic of capital accumulation gave rise to a 'second nature' made up of roads, plantations, railways, mines, pipelines, wells, power stations, futures markets and container ships, financial positions and banks that structure flows of matter, energy, goods and capital on a world scale. It is this profit-oriented technostructure that swung the Earth system into the Anthropocene. The change in geological regime is the act of the 'age of capital' (Eric Hobsbawm), rather than simply the 'age of man' as the dominant narratives claim.

---

1 Fredric Jameson, 'Future City', *New Left Review*, 21, 2003: 76.
2 A calculation in 1990 dollars on the basis of data from Thomas Piketty, *Capital in the Twenty-First Century*, Cambridge, MA: Harvard University Press, 2014, Supplementary Figures and Tables, Table S12.4, 'Private capital in the world, 1870–2100', piketty.pse.ens.fr, and personal communication. From a Marxist perspective it is wealth that is accounted here, rather than capital in the strict sense, which is only a part of this.

Marx saw capitalism as a mechanism for the self-production of money (the formula M–C–M'), resulting from a mode of production that aimed no longer at the manufacture of useful objects but rather that of commodities sold to increase capital. This became an 'automaton subject', to the detriment of human freedom and the integrity of the Earth, hence Marx's metaphor of the Moloch that demands that the whole world be sacrificed to it. Following him, Marxist writers have analysed ecological degradation as a metabolic rift specific to the intrinsic logic of capitalism.[3] They have described the inability of capitalism to reproduce not only the worker, but also the environment, as its 'second contradiction'.[4] But the mobilization of the world by capitalism has taken extremely diverse forms according to place and time, from the agrarian and rent-seeking capitalism that still prevailed in the British countryside in the nineteenth century, based on the differential fertility of soils (and thus on their relative maintenance), through to the fossil, mining and oil capitalism that drilled its wells across the world as resources were exhausted – from the slave trade to nanosecond trading. Thus, instead of the great universals of 'capital' or the 'human species', this chapter sets out to analyse the historical metabolisms of the capitalist 'world-systems' of the last quarter millennium and their effects on the Earth system in a way that illuminates both the history of capitalism and the genesis of the Anthropocene.

The notion of world-system was developed by the work of Fernand Braudel and Immanuel Wallerstein[5] as a way of grasping historically the globalization of the economy and the perpetuation of economic inequalities between regions of the world.[6] In 400 years of accumulation since

---

3   John Bellamy Foster, Brett Clark and Richard York, *The Ecological Rift: Capitalism's War on the Earth*, New York: Monthly Review Press, 2010.

·   4   James O'Connor, 'Capitalism, Nature, Socialism: A Theoretical Introduction', *Capitalism, Nature, Socialism*, 1:1, 1988: 11–38.

5   See Immanuel Wallerstein, *Historical Capitalism*, London: Verso, 1983, and *World-Systems Analysis: An Introduction*, Durham, NC: Duke University Press, 2004.

6   In the course of each of these, we find alongside the hegemonic power that stabilizes and governs the world economic order, drawing the greatest share of profits from this, a small group of countries in key beneficial positions (such as France and Germany during the British century, Europe and Japan in the second

the fifteenth century, four successive world-systems can be distinguished, centred on four successive hegemonic powers: the Italian cities (which financed the American expansion), Holland, Great Britain (from the late eighteenth to the early twentieth century) and the United States.

The notion of world-system has the double advantage of being not only historical and dynamic, but also systemic and global, making it possible to open a constructive dialogue with the sciences of the Earth system that are likewise systemic and global.[7] Vis-à-vis a transformed Earth system we no longer have an undifferentiated 'anthropos', but rather historical systems of domination that each organize in a distinct fashion flows of matter, energy, commodities and capitals on a global scale. As Wallerstein emphasizes, these systems are structurally inegalitarian: the hegemonic nations accumulate capital, guaranteeing the middle classes a certain standard of living and thus maintaining the domestic social order and financing infrastructure, education, health, mobility and innovation. These states, and above all the businesses that they protect, have the economic power and the military strength to extract raw material at low cost in the peripheral countries, to exploit there if necessary a low-paid labour force, to export outdated goods and to pollute their environments.

The notion of world-system is currently being revisited from the perspective of flows of matter and energy, thermodynamics and ecological footprint.[8] These studies have revealed the existence of successive world-ecologies[9] co-generated by each phase in

half of the twentieth century during the American century), semi-peripheral countries, and finally the peripheral ones that are dominated both politically and economically. Giovanni Arrighi, *The Long Twentieth Century: Money, Power, and the Origins of Our Time*, 2nd ed., London: Verso, 2010.

7   Alf Hornborg and Carole L. Crumley (eds), *The World System and the Earth System*, Walnut Creek, CA: Left Coast Press, 2006.

8   Alf Hornborg, 'Ecological Economics, Marxism, and Technological Progress: Some Explorations of the Conceptual Foundations of Theories of Ecologically Unequal Exchange', *Ecological Economics* 105, 2014: 11–18; John Bellamy Foster and Hannah Holleman, 'The Theory of Unequal Ecological Exchange: A Marx-Odum Dialectic', *Journal of Peasant Studies*, 41:2, 2014: 199–233.

9   We owe this term to Jason W. Moore, *Capitalism in the Web of Life: Ecology and the Accumulation of Capital*, London: Verso, 2015.

the history of the world-economy. These equally show that the prosperity of the rich countries is constructed by way of a monopolization of the benefits of the Earth and an externalization of environmental damages by the phenomena of dispossession and 'unequal exchange'.

In *Capital*, Marx already noted that the economically subjugated position of Ireland meant that 'for a century and a half, England has indirectly exported the soil of Ireland'.[10] This asymmetry is produced not only in predation (the concept of 'appropriation by dispossession' proposed by David Harvey)[11] and unequal exchange in terms of embodied labour,[12] but also through the ecological or energy content of the goods exchanged. Exchange is said to be ecologically unequal when the territories of the periphery export products of high ecological use-value against products that have a lesser ecological use-value. This ecological value can be measured in terms of the acreage needed for the production of different ecosystemic services, of 'ecological footprint',[13] of embodied energy or 'emergy' in

10   Karl Marx, *Capital, Volume 1*, London: Penguin, 1973, 868.

11   Extending Rosa Luxemburg's idea, David Harvey has suggested that capitalism, in order to sustain a regime of wage exploitation in the countries of the centre, has needed to repeatedly appropriate human labour and natural production previously outside capitalist relations. David Harvey, *The New Imperialism*, Oxford: Oxford University Press, 2005.

12   Following the studies of Raúl Prebisch, Arghiri Emmanuel and Samir Amin, unequal exchange is characterized by unfavourable terms of trade for the countries on the periphery of the world-system, i.e., the fact that they have to export an increasing amount of goods (typically raw materials) to obtain the same quantity of imported goods (typically industrial goods), so that the number of hours of labour thus exchanged are increasingly unequal.

13   In the 1960s, the Swedish biologist Georg Borgström introduced the idea of 'ghost acres', as the terrain captured by certain countries that consumed more than their own territory's bioproductive capacity by importing products from other regions of the world. This approach influenced the historian of the industrial revolution Kenneth Pomeranz (see below), as well as William Rees and Mathis Wackernagel, who have developed the concept of 'ecological footprint' as a new indicator of sustainability. See William Rees and Mathis Wackernagel, *Our Ecological Footprint: Reducing Human Impact on the Earth*, Gabriola Island, British Columbia: New Society Publishers, 1998. For the method and recent results, see footprintnetwork.org.

international exchange,[14] of matter,[15] entropy,[16] or of the waste and damage generated.

For example, on the basis of Georgescu-Roegen's thermodynamic analysis of the economy, André Gunder Frank and Immanuel Wallerstein have envisaged the world system as a dissipative structure. In each of its phases, the systems of production and exchange export entropy into the Earth system and distribute this entropy unequally across the planet.[17] This new accounting in terms of the hectares, energy, greenhouse gas, entropy or matter (water, biomass, mineral ores, etc.) embodied in world economic exchange has triggered a mushrooming of new statistical methods and series that provide a new and rematerialized understanding of the history of societies by illuminating their metabolism, and the successive world-ecologies that they produce and of which they form part.

At a time when millions of poor people are affected by climate disturbance and come to swell the tide of migrants, this ecological reading of the

---

14   Proposed by the great ecologist Howard T. Odum, 'emergy' estimates the work of the ecosystems embodied in a product measured in terms of the energy mobilized by the ecological processes that contributed to its formation.

15   Specialists in 'material and energy flow analysis' measure world trade in terms of its mass (in tonnes) or energy content. See the pioneering article by researchers from the Institut für Soziale Ökologie in Vienna: Marina Fischer-Kowalski and Helmut Haberl, 'Tons, Joules and Money: Modes of Production and Their Sustainability Problems', *Society and Natural Resources*, 10:1, 1997: 61–85.

16   According to the law of entropy, any economic undertaking transforms natural resources (of low entropy) into products and waste of a higher entropy, thus presenting an entropic cost that is always higher than that of the product alone. In the case of the Earth as an open system, part of this entropy is reduced by the living world, which reconstitutes a more ordered matter (negentropy) by using solar energy (photosynthesis). The transition to a fossil economy that dissipates the free energy of underground stocks more rapidly than this is reconstituted annually in the biosphere thus appears as an entropic marker of the Anthropocene. See Nicholas Georgescu-Roegen, *The Entropy Law and the Economic Process*, Cambridge, MA: Harvard University Press, 1971.

17   Immanuel Wallerstein, 'Crises: The World-Economy, the Movements, and the Ideologies', in Albert Bergesen (ed.), *Crises in the World-System*, Beverly Hills, CA: Sage, 1983, 21–36; André G. Frank, 'Entropy Generation and Displacement', in Hornborg and Crumley, *The World System and the Earth System*, 303–316, especially 304.

history of world-systems also has a resonance in terms of the major issues of geopolitics and environmental justice. Shortly before the Rio Earth Summit of 1992, while the Climate Convention was being negotiated, two Indian ecologists put forward the idea of a historic debt of the rich countries in ecological terms.[18] They proposed to attribute to each inhabitant of the planet an emission right that took account of the past emissions of their fellow-citizens. A senior Chinese leader asserted in 2009 that

> the climate crisis is the result of the very uneven pattern of economic development that evolved over the past two centuries, which allowed today's rich countries to attain their current levels of income, in part through not having to account for the environmental damage now threatening the lives and livelihoods of others.[19]

It is in response to this kind of instrumentalization of the notion of a 'common but differentiated responsibility' that certain historians, such as Dipesh Chakrabarty, have sought to disconnect the history of capitalism from that of the Anthropocene. For him, 'it is thanks to the poor (that is, thanks to the fact that development is unequal and unjust) that we do not emit still higher amounts of greenhouse gases into the biosphere'. He continues, 'Those who link climate change exclusively to historical origins, or to the formation of inequalities of wealth in the modern world, raise questions about historical inequalities' that are not pertinent to cast light on the historical genesis of the new state of the Earth that the Anthropocene is.[20] It is remarkable that after having proclaimed the encounter between human history and that of the Earth as characteristic of the Anthropocene,[21] Chakrabarty now

---

18   Anil Agarwal and Sunita Narain, *Global Warming in an Unequal World: A Case of Environmental Colonialism*, Delhi: Centre for Science and Environment, 1991.

19   Sha Zukang, foreword to *Promoting Development, Saving the Planet*, UN, 2009, viii, un.org. Sha Zukang was UN head of economic affairs at this time.

20   Dipesh Chakrabarty, 'Quelques failles dans la pensée du changement climatique', in Émilie Hache (ed.), *De l'univers clos au monde infini*, Paris: Dehors, 2014, 107–146, 123–4.

21   Dipesh Chakrabarty, 'The Climate of History: Four Theses', *Critical Inquiry*, 35:2, 2009: 197–222.

postulates a separation, a mutual 'indifference', between the history of dominations and inequalities among humans and that of the ecological and geological disturbances inflicted on the Earth. This paradox enables him to conclude that 'from a logical point of view, the climate crisis is not in itself the result of economic inequalities'.[22]

If the argument seems 'logical' from a static point of view (the poorest do indeed have a lighter ecological footprint), in historical terms it is highly questionable. For two centuries, the development of industrial countries has generated a great divergence of incomes between their populations and those of the poor countries: in 1820, the poorest 20 per cent on the planet obtained 4.7 per cent of world income, falling to only 2.2 per cent in 1992.[23] As we shall see in this chapter, the industrial development model and its metabolism in terms of matter and energy, which altered the geological trajectory of our Earth, is inseparable from the history of capitalist world-systems, of unequal ecological exchange, of colonialism and imperialism, of exploitation and underdevelopment.

The rise of industrial capitalism and the swing into the Anthropocene: a global reading

The standard account of the Anthropocene offers a very Eurocentric history, in which global disruption is supposedly a secondary effect of a European wave of innovations leading the world towards growth. Thinking the Anthropocene as a 'Capitalocene' forces us to reconsider the pertinence of this starting-point and propose a more global reading. It was indeed in the early nineteenth century, with the start of the industrial age, that the entire Earth system was affected and humanity became a geological rather than simply a biological force, yet to begin the Anthropocene around 1800 obscures the essential fact that industrial capitalism was intensely prepared for by the

---

22   Chakrabarty, 'Quelques failles', 124.
23   François Bourguignon and Christian Morrisson, 'Inequality Among World Citizens: 1820–1992', *American Economic Review*, 92:4, September 2002: 727–44.

'mercantile capitalism' that begun in the sixteenth century, not least in its destructive relationship to nature. To speak of a 'Capitalocene'[24] signals that the Anthropocene did not arise fully armed from the brain of James Watt, the steam engine and coal, but rather from a long historical process of economic exploitation of human beings and the world, going back to the sixteenth century and making industrialization possible.

The industrial revolution took place in a world that was already capitalist and globalized. Until well into the nineteenth century, British capitalism was far more mercantile, globalized and extraverted than a history focused on production might lead us to believe. Finance, the management of public debt and international trade generated fortunes far larger than those from mining or the textile industry. British imperialism, and the economic globalization of the eighteenth and nineteenth centuries, was fashioned by an assembly of aristocrats, bankers and merchants.

This class of 'gentleman capitalists' acquired a politically preeminent power from its financing of the wars against France. For Britain, the main object of the War of Austrian Succession, the Seven Years War and the American wars was the domination of the Atlantic trading space and the conquest of global hegemony. The financing of the war and the public debt (which for England in 1815 was twice the GDP of the time) rested on the income from global trade, hence the key role for the British state of the East India Company, which channelled tribute from India, of the Navigation Acts that promoted London's import-export activity, and the 'invisible' revenue from shipping and insurance. The importance of mercantile and financial capitalism for the British state can be read from the major political orientations of the nineteenth century: free trade above all, which made London the global entrepôt, then the reduction of public expenditure, which, at the price of increasing poverty, strengthened the pound (which returned to the gold

---

24   We came across this neologism while preparing the English edition of this book, as it was proposed by Jason Moore and other eco-Marxist writers. See in particular Moore, *Capitalism in the Web of Life*.

standard in 1819) and thus aided the 'gentleman capitalists' to export their capital across the world.[25]

The transatlantic trade was undoubtedly the 'spark'[26] that triggered the industrial revolution. Its value quadrupled during the eighteenth century, coming to represent two-thirds of English trade. Similarly, Saint-Domingue made up two-thirds of French international trade at this time.[27] London became the turntable of world trade, with re-export activity (85 per cent of tobacco and 95 per cent of coffee were re-exported to Europe in the 1770s) paying for the import of raw materials from northern Europe: wood, tar, potash.[28] In 1810, for example, Great Britain imported the alkaline ash from wood burning needed for its soap and glass industries from the Baltic countries and North America. This ash was equivalent to 25 million cubic metres of wood per year, or far more than the annual wood production at home.[29] Added to this were the invisible incomes (those not passing through British customs) from the slave trade, Brazilian gold, Mexican silver,[30] and the multilateral trade assured by the British Merchant Navy. The transatlantic commercial revolution stimulated naval construction and thus the metal industry. Copper for the navy provided a key market for the Cornish mines, a crucial sector in the early days of the steam engine.[31]

---

25   P. J. Cain and A. G. Hopkins, 'Gentlemanly Capitalism and British Expansion Overseas. I: The Old Colonial System, 1688–1850', *Economic History Review*, 39:4, 1986: 501–25, and John Darwin, *The Empire Project: The Rise and Fall of the British World-System, 1830–1970*, Cambridge: Cambridge University Press, 2009, 112.

26   Eric Hobsbawm, *Industry and Empire: An Economic History of Britain since 1750*, London: Weidenfeld & Nicolson, 1968, 48.

27   C. L. R. James, *The Black Jacobins: Toussaint L'Ouverture and the San Domingo Revolution* (1938), New York: Vintage Books, Random House, 1963, ix.

28   Phyllis Deane and W. A. Cole, *British Economic Growth 1688–1959: Trends and Structure*, Cambridge: Cambridge University Press, 1967, 87.

29   Our thanks to Paul Warde for this point.

30   According to François Crouzet, Brazilian gold represented as large a sum as official British foreign trade. See 'Angleterre-Brésil, 1697–1850. Un siècle et demi d'échanges commerciaux', *Histoire, économie et société*, 9:2, 1990: 288–317.

31   Joseph Inikori, *Africans and the Industrial Revolution in England: A Study in International Trade and Economic Development*, Cambridge: Cambridge University Press, 2002, 265–314.

Transatlantic trade also accelerated the development of financial institutions, the use of letters of exchange and commercial credit, facilitating the growth of the money volume; it explains the emergence of marine insurance (Lloyds was founded in 1688) and fire insurance (the first companies, Phoenix and Sun Fire, were established to cover risks associated with sugar refining in London). The colonial trade created banking communities in Bristol, Glasgow and Liverpool (the Heywood and Leyland families), central to the financing of manufacture in these industrial regions.[32]

Finally and above all, it ensured a demand for manufactured products that was determinant for the take-off of English industry in the late eighteenth century. This exponential demand was drawn from the demographic explosion in North America, where the white population grew from 300,000 in 1700 to 6 million in 1800. In 1784, textiles represented 57 per cent of British exports, rising to 82 per cent in 1800.[33] In 1801, America absorbed 60 per cent of Lancashire's textile production.[34] This constantly expanding market explains the efforts for greater productivity and rapid mechanization of cotton from 1760 onwards (the spinning jenny, Arkwright's water frame, Crompton's spinning mule).

In 1745, Malachy Postlethwayt described the British Empire as 'a magnificent superstructure of American commerce and naval power on an African foundation'.[35] The centrality of transatlantic trade in the industrial revolution turned on that of the African slaves that formed the fundamental pivot of the world-system then dominated by Great Britain. Firstly, the revenue from the slave trade, which has aroused so many debates among historians, has recently been revised upward: Joseph Inikori estimates the profit rate of the more successful traders of the late eighteenth century at 50 per cent.[36] These profits represented

32   Ibid., 315–61.

33   François Crouzet, 'Toward an Export Economy: British Exports during the Industrial Revolution', *Explorations in Economic History*, 17:1, 1980: 48–93.

34   Nicholas Crafts, *British Economic Growth during the Industrial Revolution*, Oxford: Oxford University Press, 1985, 143.

35   Quoted in Eric Williams, *Capitalism and Slavery*, Chapel Hill: University of North Carolina Press, 1944, 52.

36   Kenneth Morgan, *Slavery, Atlantic Trade and the British Economy, 1660–1800*, Cambridge: Cambridge University Press, 2000, 36–60.

around 40 per cent of British commercial and industrial investment after 1750.[37] Secondly, the sugar produced by slaves was by far the most lucrative trade. In the early nineteenth century, the British colonies produced 177,000 tonnes of sugar per year, as against 33,000 tonnes for the French colonies that remained after the loss of Saint-Domingue.[38] British consumption rose in the eighteenth century from an annual one pound per person to twenty-five pounds, providing a substantial calorie input (4 per cent of the total in 1800) that increased the productivity of British workers. (Rice was a further element.) Thirdly, cotton, produced in the slave-worked South, was by far the main outlet of the British textile industry. Fourthly, until the early nineteenth century, the number of Africans who crossed the Atlantic was higher than the number of Europeans. Agricultural products from North America, and cod from Newfoundland, were imported to the monoculture Caribbean islands to feed the slave population, which kept the white colonies solvent and enabled them to buy British manufactured products. In the late eighteenth century, the slave trade and the plantation system thus formed the foundation of a very hierarchical world-system, with economic satellites entirely organized for the economic needs of the British power.

The fundamentally global nature of what is too simply called the 'industrial revolution' can also be grasped by way of the productive capacity of the spaces that it connected. The historian Kenneth Pomeranz, in *The Great Divergence*, set out to explain why England pioneered the path of industrialization, rather than the Chinese region of the Yangzi Delta.[39] In 1750, the two societies presented a more or less equivalent level of economic and technological 'development' and were faced with similar pressures on their resources of land and wood. In Britain, the price of fire-wood rose by a factor of eight between 1500 and 1630, and by the late eighteenth century forest cover was down to

37   Barbara Solow, 'Caribbean Slavery and British Growth: The Eric Williams Hypothesis', *Journal of Development Economics*, 17, 1985: 99–115.

38   John Richards, *The Unending Frontier: An Environmental History of the Early Modern World*, Berkeley: University of California Press, 2006, 455.

39   Kenneth Pomeranz, *The Great Divergence: China, Europe, and the Making of the Modern World Economy*, Princeton, NJ: Princeton University Press, 2001.

between 5 and 10 per cent of the country's total area. Complaints about the exhaustion of the soil intensified, and the use of clover (Norfolk rotation) failed to resolve the problem.

According to Pomeranz, a doubly favourable 'contingency' explains the English road. First of all, the availability of coal. English mines were relatively easy to exploit and close to centres of consumption, whereas in China these were more than 1,500 kilometres from Shanghai. In 1820, British coal consumption amounted to the equivalent of over 8 million hectares of rationally managed woodland, or more than ten times the country's forest cover. Secondly, Britain's imperial situation, which enabled it to drain resources crucial to its industrial development. In 1830, sugar from the West Indies was equivalent to 600,000 hectares of good land put to cereals, cotton from North America to more than 9.3 million hectares of sheep pasture, and wood (from North America and the Baltic) to more than 400,000 hectares of domestic woodland. In total, even leaving out coal, the total comes to more than 10 million 'ghost hectares' to fuel British machines and workers – the equivalent of two-thirds of the usable agricultural surface of England and Wales. On top of this were the vast areas of land and sea that made possible the capture of carbon dioxide thanks to photosynthesis, Great Britain being responsible for 80 per cent of world emissions by 1825.[40]

Besides, as Alf Hornberg has shown, this exchange was certainly ecologically unequal: in 1850, by exchanging £1,000 of textiles manufactured in Manchester for £1,000 of American raw cotton, Britain gained 46 per cent in terms of embodied labour (unequal exchange) and 6,000 per cent in terms of embodied hectares,[41] thus releasing its own domestic space from the environmental constraint of having to produce that much fibre, which would compete with other needs of grain, wood and animal fodder. The case of the Yangzi Delta also attests to the importance of this type of asymmetry for British

---

40   Andreas Malm, *Fossil Capital: The Rise of Steam-Power and the Roots of Global Warming*, London: Verso, 2015.

41   Alf Hornborg, *Global Ecology and Unequal Exchange: Fetishism in a Zero-Sum World*, London: Routledge, 2013, 85–91.

industrialization. In the eighteenth century, the Pearl River Delta imported immense quantities of primary goods and raw cotton from the upper Yangzi and northern China. But, as opposed to the peripheral regions of the Atlantic world-system, in this century these regions turned towards textile production, depriving the delta of outlets for its production and cheap raw materials. The Chinese economic world, more homogeneous than the Atlantic imperial space, did not permit the ecological and capitalist accumulation that ensured British industrial take-off. Without the empire, the industrial revolution would have been physically impossible. Werner Sombart saw the shortage of wood due to deforestation, and the exhaustion of European soils, as a 'threat of an end to capitalism' around 1800, or even to 'European culture' itself.[42] Pomeranz, without going as far as that, writes that 'without the dual boon of coal and colonies, Britain would have faced an ecological impasse with no apparent internal solution'.[43]

If the externalization of the environmental constraint relieved Great Britain, it overturned the ecologies of the periphery. The availability of immense spaces, 'empty' thanks to the elimination of 90 per cent of the Amerindian population between 1492 and 1700, initiated a relationship to the environment far more predatory than in Europe. Tobacco cultivation, for example, exhausted the soil so rapidly (after only three or four harvests) that in the course of the eighteenth century production had to move from Maryland and Virginia towards the Appalachians.[44] The transformation of the Caribbean into a sugar monoculture led to deforestation, erosion and exhaustion of the soil.[45] Sugar-cane plantations introduced yellow fever into the American tropics; the terra-cotta vessels needed for drying molasses meant a proliferation of stagnant water and proved excellent incubators for the

---

42   Werner Sombart, *Der moderne Kapitalismus*, vol. 3, Munich: Duncker & Humblot, 1928, 1,137–55, quotations from 1,137 and 1,153.

43   Pomeranz, *The Great Divergence*, 218.

44   Carolyn Merchant, *The Columbia Guide to American Environmental History*, New York: Columbia University Press, 2002, 49.

45   Richards, *The Unending Frontier*, 459; William Beinart and Lotte Hughes, *Environment and Empire*, Oxford: Oxford University Press, 2007, 36–9.

yellow-fever-carrying *Aedes aegypti* mosquito, imported from Africa.[46] As for the fabled silver mines of Mexico and Peru, these were exhausted in only a few decades, leaving intensely polluted environments. Two hundred thousand tonnes of mercury had been used here by 1900, the greater part of which evaporated into the atmosphere.[47] We could also mention the virtual extinction of the beaver, the American bison and the bowhead whale by the late nineteenth century, also bound up with industrialization, as bison skin made excellent transmission belts, and whale oil an excellent lubricant for machines.[48]

In 1999, the African World Reparations and Repatriation Truth Commission demanded payment from the Western powers of $777 trillion to compensate Africa for the slave trade and the wealth plundered during the colonial period.[49] Whatever the magnitude of this sum, it will never make up for the fact that the West is in debt to Africa, as well as to America and Asia, for its industrial rise. The latter, and thus the entry into the Anthropocene, were made possible by ecologically unequal exchange with these regions in the eighteenth and nineteenth centuries.

The world-ecology of the British world-system

The second half of the nineteenth century saw the development of two closely linked phenomena: on the one hand, the infrastructures of economic globalization were established, while on the other hand, massive economic gaps appeared between Europe and North America on one side, and Asia on the other.

The world-system then centred on Great Britain was based on an unequal world-ecology: by dramatically increasing the economic

---

46   John R. McNeill, 'Ecology, Epidemics and Empires: Environmental Change and the Geopolitics of Tropical America, 1600-1825', *Environment and History*, 5:2, 1999: 175–84.

47   Jerome O. Nriagu, 'Mercury Pollution from the Past Mining of Gold and Silver in the Americas', *Science of the Total Environment*, 149, 1994: 167–81.

48   Richards, *The Unending Frontier*, 612; John R. McNeill, *Something New under the Sun: An Environmental History of the Twentieth-Century World*, New York: Norton, 2001, 238.

49   'Trillions Demanded in Slavery Reparations', BBC News, 20 August 1999, bbc.com.

metabolism of the industrial countries, coal correspondingly amplified the demand for organic materials from the tropical world. Besides, in the last third of the nineteenth century, the industrialized countries embarked on a new cycle of capital accumulation bound up with the second industrial revolution: organic chemistry, electricity, then the automobile. If they were self-sufficient in energy and in iron,[50] the technologies that lay at the root of their prosperity depended on certain key products drawn from the peripheral countries: ores such as tin from Malaysia for the processed-food industry, as well as mineral oil; copper from the Andes and the Congo for electrification; gutta-percha for the telegraph network; rubber for mechanical industries (transmission belts, sealants for steam engines, etc.) and then for automobiles.[51]

In the same way, maintaining soil fertility in Europe and America depended on the extraction of guano from Peru, Bolivia and Chile[52] (where reserves were exhausted in a few decades), as well as phosphates from Tunisia, Morocco and Algeria. Before the First World War, the rich countries already imported 41 per cent of their phosphate consumption, or 2.9 million tonnes per year.[53] Despite these contributions, agricultural productivity in the United Kingdom stagnated in the first two-thirds of the nineteenth century, and to feed its population at low cost the country was importing more than 60 per cent of its foodstuffs in 1900, as against 15 per cent in 1850.[54] The ghost hectares that fed the British population were as large as the country's agricultural surface.[55]

---

50   Paul Bairoch, *Mythes et paradoxes de l'histoire économique*, Paris: La Découverte, 1999.

51   John Tully, 'A Victorian Ecological Disaster: Imperialism, the Telegraph, and Gutta-Percha', *Journal of World History*, 20:4, 2009: 559–79.

52   John Bellamy Foster and Brett Clark, 'Ecological Imperialism and the Global Metabolic Rift: Unequal Exchange and the Guano/Nitrates Trade', *International Journal of Comparative Sociology*, 50, 2009: 311–34.

53   Bairoch, *Mythes et paradoxes*, 99.

54   Heinz Schandl and Fridolin Krausmann, 'The Great Transformation: A Socio-Metabolic Reading of the Industrialization of the United Kingdom', in Marina Fischer-Kowalski and Helmut Haberl, *Socioecological Transitions and Global Change: Trajectories of Social Metabolism and Land Use*, London: Edward Elgar, 2007, 83–115, especially 110.

55   Ibid., 91 and 110–11.

If Great Britain exported coal and industrial goods, it was an importer of mineral ore between 1850 and 1939 (the deficit being 12 million tonnes on the eve of the First World War), and above all, of biomass (the deficit rising from 5 million tonnes in 1855 to more than 30 million by the late 1930s).[56] No other industrial country has had a development model so dependent on biomass from the rest of the world.

These elements substantially qualify the thesis of Paul Bairoch, according to whom the industrialized countries scarcely needed products from the peripheral countries before 1940. This unequal world-ecology was bound up with a very outward-turned capitalism. The economy was financialized and globalized in the context of a stable international monetary system based on the pound sterling (and thus on the gold standard). Limited liability (the Companies Act of 1862, the reform of *sociétés anonymes* in France in 1867, the German law of 1892 establishing GmbH) made shareholding less risky,[57] particularly for firms operating outside the national territory. The generalization of stock-exchange quotation further oiled the cogs of finance capitalism. This legal stabilization of capital led to a massive shift from the state to private companies. In 1860s, British Treasury bills made up half of London capitalization, but the figure fell to less than 5 per cent by 1914.

European finance capital turned massively towards overseas investment. In 1913, equities made up 40 per cent of French national wealth, with nearly half of this total invested abroad.[58] Between 1870 and 1913, Great Britain invested 4.5 per cent of its GDP abroad each year. In 1913, these stocks (£3.8 billion) represented 40 per cent of the nation's wealth,[59] and half of all direct investment abroad. Capital of this kind played a key role in

---

56   Heinz Schandl and Niels Schulz, 'Changes in the United Kingdom's Natural Relations in Terms of Society's Metabolism and Land-Use from 1850 to the Present Day', *Ecological Economics*, 41:2, 2002: 203–21.

57   Timothy W. Guinnane et al., 'Pouvoir et propriété dans l'entreprise. Pour une histoire internationale des sociétés à responsabilité limitée', *Annales. Histoire, sciences sociales*, 63:1, 2008: 73–110.

58   Suzanne Berger, *Notre première mondialisation. Leçons d'un échec oublié*, Paris: Le Seuil, 2003, 26.

59   A. K. Cairncross, *Home and Foreign Investment 1870–1913*, Cambridge: Cambridge University Press, 1953, 104.

the Anthropocene: Great Britain projected fossil capitalism onto the whole world.[60] In 1913, railways represented 40 per cent of British foreign direct investment, followed by mines (more than a thousand mining companies were quoted on the London Stock Exchange in 1898), gas lighting, water supply and tropical plantations.[61] These foreign investments were both highly profitable and self-generating: between 1870 and 1914 the revenue they yielded (5.3 per cent of GDP) was greater than the value of capital exported (4.5 per cent of GDP).[62] In this way, Great Britain could compensate for a balance of trade that was heavily in the red, attract the raw materials it needed and maintain the pound sterling as the pillar of the international monetary system.[63]

This financial capitalism was embodied in technologies that were high emitters of CO_2, reorganizing flows of matter, energy and goods on a world scale. Trans-continental canals, railways, steam ships, docks, grain silos and telegraph lines constructed a second nature of planetary dimensions, penetrating to the interior of the peripheral countries and mooring them to the world-economy. These networks reduced the cost of coordination and strengthened the power of the giant firms that managed them.

Whereas in the eighteenth century it had taken six months to travel from London to Calcutta, it took only two weeks by the end of the nineteenth century. The cost of sea transport fell steeply. The world merchant fleet rose from 9 to 35 million tonnes between 1850 and 1900, 60 per cent of it being under the British flag. This hegemony was favoured by the massive export of coal (25 per cent of British production): British ships were then alone in being able to carry full cargos on both legs of their voyage.

---

60   Only 6 per cent of this investment was made in Europe, with 45 per cent in the English-speaking world, 20 per cent in Latin America, 16 per cent in Asia and 13 per cent in Africa.

61   Darwin, *The Empire Project*, 112–20.

62   Niall Ferguson, *Empire: How Britain Made the Modern World*, London: Penguin, 2003, 245.

63   Even if the age of the 'gold standard' was also based on the exploitation of the subsoil: the 'gold rushes' in California and South Africa enabled the central banks of the great powers to restock their reserves.

The world telegraph network was likewise established in the main by British firms. It facilitated the governing of empires and improved the speed and reliability of commercial information, which in turn made the trade in bulky cargo more profitable, as a marginal difference in price here could play a major role. In the 1860s, the practice of 'tramping' was established: cargos were dispatched without an advance destination and travelled from one port to another as a function of commodity prices.[64] Correlative with this, the last third of the nineteenth century saw the creation of a world market. Prices converged: in 1870 wheat was sold 57 per cent higher in Liverpool than in Chicago, but the difference fell to 15 per cent by 1914.[65] This was due to a general process of marketization and the integration of local economies into world trade.

The world railway network, which grew from 100,000 to 1 million kilometres between 1860 and 1920,[66] was chiefly financed by private capital, very often British. In 1860, for example, the engineering firm Peto, Brassey and Betts employed 100,000 workers on five continents, building lines in Russia and South America, Algeria and Canada.[67] By the late nineteenth century, foreign direct investment was galvanized by mineral and agricultural resources. In Africa, South America and Asia, railways were systematically associated with mineral extraction or the transport of agricultural cargos for the international market: the draining of copper and guano from Peru and Chile, of cotton from India, coffee from Brazil, meat from Argentina, bananas from Central American monoculture, peanuts from Senegal, etc. The countries of the periphery provided not only raw materials but also cheap labour: workers 'engaged' by mines and plantations in a state of semi-slavery, in particular Chinese coolies fleeing the civil wars caused by the Opium War and the Taiping Rebellion, were exploited on railway construction across the whole world.[68]

---

64   Daniel Headrick, *The Tentacles of Progress: Technology Transfer in the Age of Imperialism, 1850–1940*, Oxford: Oxford University Press, 1988, 18–45.

65   Berger, *Notre première mondialisation*, 18.

66   Darwin, *The Empire Project*, 115.

67   Marc Linder, *Projecting Capitalism: A History of the Internationalization of the Construction Industry*, Westport: Greenwood Press, 1994, 35–42.

68   Ibid., and Arnold J. Meagher, *The Coolie Trade: The Traffic in Chinese Laborers to Latin America 1847–1874*, Philadelphia: Xlibris, 2008.

This infrastructure placed the countries of the Third World in a situation of outward orientation, specialization and economic dependence. Whole countries could now be strangled by the cutting of credit, preparing their economic or political subjugation. As Tim Mitchell has shown for the case of oil, the hierarchy of the world-system depends on a carefully chosen distribution of technological mechanisms: for example, drilling wells without building storage and refining facilities ensures the dependence of the producing countries. Capitalism's second nature precipitated the integration of the peripheral regions into the world-system, as well as the disintegration of pre-capitalist economies now transformed into a de-industrialized periphery. The post-colonial states of the twentieth century inherited this infrastructure, making a more harmonious development of their economies a difficult task.

In the course of this establishment of a world market, a great reversal took place between 1850 and 1900: famine definitively disappeared from Western Europe but spread with devastating effects in the colonial world. Two series of famines between 1876 and 1898, linked to an El Niño climate episode, caused between 30 and 50 million deaths across the world, principally in China and India. Neither of these countries had previously known a disaster such as this. Similar droughts in eighteenth-century China had been satisfactorily managed by the Qing dynasty, thanks to the system of imperial granaries, long-distance transport by the Grand Canal linking north and south China, and emergency grain distribution.

To understand the human impact of this climate episode, therefore, we need to look beyond natural causes: the vulnerability of both Indian and Chinese societies was due to the dislocation of systems of resilience and assistance. China was emerging from the two Opium Wars and the terrible Taiping Civil War (due largely to the weakening of the Middle Kingdom under the hammer blows of European colonialism). As for India, the aim of British policy was to increase its agricultural exports despite famine. This great disaster must therefore be understood as the combination of a regular and quite commonplace climate phenomenon with the construction of the world cereals market centred on London and Chicago (Indian harvests being already purchased on a futures market), and finally, the dismantling of Asian societies by colonialism.[69] Thus, in the midst of the famine, an ever-greater share of India's agricultural products was destined for export: jute, cotton and indigo, but also wheat and rice for the world market. Rice exports in particular grew from less than 700,000 tonnes to over 1.5 million tonnes in the course of the last third of the nineteenth century.[70]

The ecological consequences of the second industrial revolution in the peripheral countries were equally dramatic. The gutta-percha tree disappeared from Singapore in 1856, then from several Malaysian islands.[71] At the end of the nineteenth century, the stampede for rubber took hold of Amazonia, causing deforestation and massacres of Indians. In the early twentieth century, rubber production moved from Brazil to Malaysia, Sri Lanka, Sumatra and then Liberia, where British and American companies (Hoppum, Goodyear, Firestone) established immense plantations. These destroyed millions of hectares of indigenous forest, causing the exhaustion of the soil and introducing malaria.[72] In the Congo in the 1920s, the development of rubber plantations, mining exploitation and railways caused the first regional spread of HIV.[73]

It was in this way, in the last third of the nineteenth century, that 'underdevelopment' was born. The massive economic gap between Europe and North America on the one hand, and Asia on the other, dates from this time. Between 1800 and 1913, European per capita income rose by 222 per cent, that of Africa by 9 per cent and that of Asia by only 1 per cent.[74] The last third of the nineteenth century, and

---

69   Mike Davis, *Late Victorian Holocausts: El Niño Famines and the Making of the Third World*, London: Verso, 2002.

70   Brian Mitchell, *International historical statistics 1750–2005: Europe*, London: Palgrave Macmillan, 2007, Table C17.

71   John Tully, 'A Victorian Ecological Disaster'.

72   Richard Tucker, *Insatiable Appetite: The United States and the Ecological Degradation of the Tropical World*, Berkeley: University of California Press, 2000.

73   N. R. Faria et al., 'The Hidden History of HIV-1: Establishment and Early Spread of the AIDS Pandemic', *Science*, 346, 2014: 56–61.

74   Paul Bairoch, 'The Main Trends in National Economic Disparities since the Industrial Revolution', in Paul Bairoch and Maurice Levy-Leboyer (eds),

the beginning of the twentieth, finally saw the emergence of rival powers that undermined British hegemony. The United States first of all, but also Germany, France and then Japan. The rise of competition accelerated imperial projects: in 1800 the European powers controlled 35 per cent of the Earth's surface politically, 67 per cent in 1878 and no less than 85 per cent in 1914.[75] Empire played a key role in world economic development, keeping the British world system afloat. India in particular constituted an immense captive market, becoming the leading importer of British products. Without Asia, which generated 73 per cent of British commercial credit in 1910, this country would have been forced to abandon free trade with its commercial partners (the United States, the white dominions, Germany and France), which would have then experienced a loss of outlets and a slow-down in economic growth. The world economy would have fragmented into autarchic trading blocs, similar to what happened in the wake of the 1929 economic crisis.[76]

The unequal world-ecology of the Great Acceleration

After two world wars and a great economic depression, the world entered a period of historically exceptional growth after 1945, marking the 'Great Acceleration' of the Anthropocene. Whereas in the first half of the twentieth century, an annual increase of 1.7 per cent in the use of fossil fuel was required for an economic growth rate of 2.13 per cent, between 1945 and 1973 an annual rise of 4.48 per cent in fossil fuels (not to mention uranium) corresponded to an economic growth rate of 4.18 per cent. Between 1950 and 1970, the world population grew by 46 per cent, world GDP by 2.6 times, the consumption of minerals and mining products for industry by 3.08 times, and that of construction materials 2.94 times.[77] By substituting mineral resources for biomass in

---

Disparities in Economic Development since the Industrial Revolution, London: Macmillan, 1985, 7–14.

75   Arrighi, *The Long Twentieth Century*, 54.

76   Ibid., 271; Davis, *Late Victorian Holocausts*, 324–6.

77   For GDP and population, see the Maddison Project, ggdc.net/maddison; for consumption of materials and energy, see the Institut für Soziale Ökologie,

construction, petroleum products for animal energy and fertilization in agriculture, and synthetic products for vegetable dyes and agriculture fibres for clothing, it was only the consumption of biomass that grew more slowly than economic growth, a sign of the globalization of a switch from an organic economy to a fossil one. The number of humans who moved from the metabolism of an agricultural society (annual energy consumption per capita of about 65 gigajoules) to an industrial metabolism based on fossil energies (223 gigajoules per capita) grew from 30 per cent of the world population in 1950 to 50 per cent by 2000.[78]

The Great Acceleration was thus not a uniform phenomenon of accelerated growth, but a qualitative change in lifestyle and metabolism, tying strong world growth to an even stronger growth in fossil fuels (especially oil, which dethroned coal) and mineral resources, and so representing a loss of matter and energy efficiency on the part of the world economy. This process was also unequal geographically and socially, shaped by the dynamic of a world-system that was now dominated by the United States in the context of the Cold War. Emerging from the Second World War, American power was at its apogee. While the European economy was ruined, the GDP of the United States had more than quadrupled since 1939, and the country possessed immense currency reserves. At the end of the 1940s, the US made up 60 per cent of world industrial production, produced nearly 60 per cent of world oil (and consumed as much) and made up a third of world GDP, whereas Great Britain at its apogee in 1870 had only a 9 per cent share.[79]

In the immediate post-war years, the US government was concerned to create conditions favourable to the expansion of its economy, and to

---

'Growth in Global Materials Use, GDP and Population during the 20th Century: Online Global Materials Extraction 1900–2009 (Update 2011)', uni-klu.ac.at/socec.

78   Marina Fischer-Kowalski, Fridolin Krausmann and Irene Pallua, 'A Sociometabolic Reading of the Anthropocene: Modes of Subsistence, Population Size and Human Impact on Earth', *Anthropocene Review*, 1:1, 2014: 8–33.

79   Christopher Chase-Dunn et al., 'The Trajectory of the United States in the World-System: A Quantitative Reflection', *Sociological Perspectives*, 48:2, 2005: 233–54.

the growth of the Western camp in general. It was in this context that a new international economic order was established, based on free trade and growth: the Bretton Woods Agreements of 1944 established the dollar as world currency, the General Agreement on Tariffs and Trade (GATT) liberalized trade in 1947, coupled with the Marshall Plan and the fourth point of the Truman Doctrine on development aid. This world order made it possible to find outlets for the United States's gigantic industrial and agribusiness production and ensured full employment and social pacification after the great strikes of 1946. It also aimed to stabilize the Western camp socially by drawing it into growth. The Fordist and consumerist social compromise was then viewed as the best rampart against Communism.[80] It was also the goal to 'develop' the Third World so as to avoid its turn to Communism, while ensuring cheap raw materials for the United States and its industrialized allies. In the 1950s and '60s, a gigantic exploitation of natural and human resources enabled the Eastern bloc to put up a good show in the arms race, in space, in production and even in consumption, which was by no means the least important terrain of Cold War confrontation (see Chapter 7). To outrun the Communist camp, the OECD (heir to the Marshall Plan) constituted the strategic arm of the Western camp's growth policies.

The creation of abundance in Europe and Japan, and the Pax Americana, depended on a key product, oil, to which 10 per cent of Marshall Plan funds were devoted. This oil aid greatly enriched the US oil majors (Standard Oil, Caltex, Socony-Vacuum Oil, etc.) from whom three-quarters of the oil financed by the Marshall Plan was bought, at higher-than-world-market price.[81] But oil was also a major geopolitical weapon, by disempowering left-wing European workers' movements tied to coal (Chapter 5) and stimulating the growth of the Western allies.

The Soviet Union, for its part, could not provide its allies with fossil

---

80   Björn-Ola Linnér, *The Return of Malthus: Environmentalism and Post-war Population–Resource Crises*, Isle of Harris: White Horse Press, 2003.

81   David Painter, 'Oil and the Marshall Plan', *Business History Review*, 58:3, 1984: 359–83, especially 362–3.

fuels but instead drew on the resources of Eastern Europe. Oil also transformed European agriculture, which adopted tractors, chemical fertilizer and pesticides. This 'petro-farming' proved highly costly in terms of energy: the rate of energy return from agriculture (number of calories obtained in food per calorie used in its production) fell in Britain from 12.6 in 1826 to 2.1 in 1981, in France from 3 in 1929 to 0.7 in 1970, and to 0.64 in the United States and Denmark by 2005.[82]

Whereas in the age of empires Western Europe had to import grain, meat and oilseeds, a new world 'food regime' set in after 1945. Stimulated by cheap oil and supported by state policy and export aid (the US Public Law 480 of 1954), the agriculture of the industrial countries (including continental Western Europe) became an exporter of agricultural products to the Third World, cereals in particular. This transformation promoted a rural exodus and a low labour cost in the countries of the South seeking a path of industrialization, while the agribusiness multinationals conquered the world and shifted eating habits.

The geopolitical and economic success of this growth-oriented Pax Americana was equalled only by the enormity of its ecological imprint, weighing on the entire planet. The indicator of global human ecological imprint[83] rose from 63 per cent of the planet's bioproductive capacity in 1961 to 97 per cent in 1975,[84] reaching today a level of 150 per cent, or a consumption of 1.5 planets per year. Imports of materials, measured in tonnes and aggregating all products together (minerals, energy carriers, biomass, construction materials and manufactured goods) rose by 7.59 per cent per year between 1950 and 1970 in the Western industrial

---

82   Gilles Allaire and Benoit Daviron, 'Agriculture et industrialisme', in *Transformations et transitions dans l'agriculture et l'agro-alimentaire*, Versailles: Quae, forthcoming.

83   This indicator is based on an estimate of the area of land or sea needed to produce the resources consumed by a given population and absorb its waste (particularly including greenhouse gases). This area is measured in 'bioproductive hectares', calculated by taking account of the functioning of different environments across the globe. See footprintnetwork.org.

84   Global Footprint Network, 'National Ecological Footprint and Biocapacity for 2007: Results from the National Footprint Accounts 2010 Edition', footprintnetwork.org.

countries – North America, Western Europe, Australia, New Zealand and Japan.[85] Almost self-sufficient in iron, copper and bauxite during the first half of the twentieth century, by 1970 the Western industrial countries presented a negative balance of 85 million tonnes of iron, 2.9 million tonnes of copper and 4.1 million tonnes of bauxite.[86] In total, measured in tonnes, the imports of these countries rose from 299 million tonnes in 1950 to 1,282 million tonnes in 1970.[87]

If we consider the evolution of the balance of trade in materials (Figure 14) between the different parts of the world, it seems that the basic ecological difference between the Communist and the capitalist systems lay in the fact that the Communist camp, for its development, exploited and degraded its own environment above all, whereas the Western countries built their own growth on a gigantic draining of mineral and renewable resources from the rest of the non-Communist world, emptying this of its high-quality energy and materials.

This colossal extraction of material from the peripheral regions of the world-system was the object of a deliberate strategic attention on the part of the US political leaders. In May 1945, Secretary of the Interior Harold Ickes wrote to President Roosevelt: 'It is essential . . . that we fulfill the Atlantic Charter declaration of providing access, on equal terms, by all [Western] nations to the raw materials of the world'.[88] Continuing the supply logic of wartime, access to such crucial resources as uranium, rubber and aluminium (as the key ingredient for modern aircraft) now became a matter of state, with policies implemented to secure energy and access to resources, from Venezuelan and Middle Eastern oil to Indian manganese and Congolese uranium. Whereas its rise in economic power between 1870 and 1940 was largely based on the intensive use of its own domestic resources (wood, coal, oil, iron, copper, water, etc.), after the war the United States moved from the position of net exporter of raw materials and energy to one of

---

85   Anke Schaffartzik et al., 'The Global Metabolic Transition: Regional Patterns and Trends of Global Material Flows, 1950–2010', *Global Environmental Change*, 26, 2014: 87–97.

86   Bairoch, *Mythes et paradoxes*, 97 and 102–3.

87   Schaffartzik et al., 'The global metabolic transition'.

88   Quoted by Linnér, *The Return of Malthus*, 29.

Physical Trade Balance

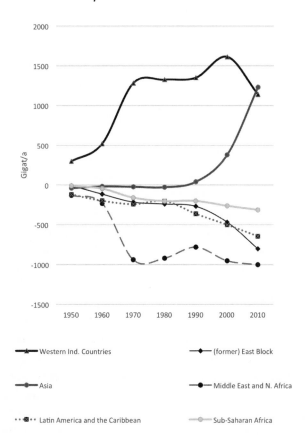

Figure 14: *Material balance of six major groups of countries since 1950*

net importer: Congressional reports and commissions (the Paley Commission of 1951–52), backed up by private think-tanks (Resources for the Future), now proposed the mobilization of world resources to secure the West while preserving American resources for the future.

The United States supported the movement of decolonization as a means for securing its supplies by direct access to resources without the mediation of the European colonial powers. It initiated the 'UN Scientific Conference on the Conservation and Utilization of Natural

Resources' (UNSCCUR, 1949). Representatives of forty-nine countries called for the inventory and 'rational use' of the planet's natural resources that were as yet unexplored or underutilized for lack of adequate technologies, or (in rare cases) deemed overexploited for want of scientific knowledge. The United States and the UN's Western experts thus set themselves up as masters of world resources and guardians of their 'right use'.[89]

US corporations also played a predominant role in the reorganization of world metabolism. With the advantage of more advanced know-how (particularly in connection with oil, atom and chemical technologies, but also in marketing techniques) and solid networks in the Pax Americana, the globalization of US corporations was fostered by the Second World War and ensuing Cold War. During the Second World War, the US Army was deployed on every continent, bringing with it the great supply corporations. The construction of military bases was alone worth $2.5 billion in contracts, to the profit of Morrison-Knudsen, Bechtel, Brown & Root, and the like. Added to this were the enormous needs in food and oil supply, logistics, etc. These companies developed the capacity to project themselves across the world and produce on a large scale, as well as the connections with military and political decision-makers that would transform them after the war into great multinationals. They established military bases, oil installations, pipelines, dams, refineries or petrochemical installations, nuclear power stations and mines, as well as factories for cement, fertilizers, pesticides and food products.[90] Between 1945 and 1965, US corporations were responsible for as much as 85 per cent of the world's new foreign direct investment.[91]

---

89   Thomas Robertson, "'This Is the American Earth'": American Empire, the Cold War, and American Environmentalism', *Diplomatic History*, 32:4, 2008: 561–84; Yannick Mahrane and Christophe Bonneuil, 'Gouverner la biosphere. De l'environnement de la guerre froide à l'environnement néoliberal', in Dominique Pestre (ed.), *Le Gouvernement des technosciences. Gouverner le progrès et ses dégâts depuis 1945*, Paris: La Découverte, 2014, 133–69.

90   Linder, *Projecting Capitalism*, 126.

91   Geoffrey Jones, 'Multinationals from the 1930s to the 1980s', in Alfred D. Chandler Jr. and Bruce Mazlich, *Leviathans: Multinational Corporations and the New Global History*, Cambridge: Cambridge University Press, 2005, 81–103, especially 88.

The control gained in this way permitted access to world resources in highly favourable conditions. While according to Paul Bairoch, the terms of trade improved for the Third World between the end of the nineteenth century and 1939, the striking phenomenon of the post-war years is the clear deterioration for those 'developing' countries that were exporters of primary products to the industrial countries and importers of manufactured goods from these: a deterioration of nearly 20 per cent between 1950 and 1972. For the oil producers, this phase came to an end with the oil shock of 1973, but it continued until the 1990s for the countries exporting mining products or renewable raw materials.[92] Economic growth and the social model of the Western industrial countries would have been impossible without this unequal exchange. Economists have recently shown that two-thirds of the growth of the Western industrial countries has been due simply to an increasing use of fossil fuel, with only one-third resulting from sociotechnical progress.[93] The incomes of states and their ability to finance investment and social redistribution were also based on oil. In 1971, when the oil majors agreed with OPEC to raise the price per barrel from $2 to $3, the refined product was being sold in Europe at $13, 60 per cent of which went in tax to the consuming country. That means that on each barrel of oil sold the European states received three times more than the OPEC producers.

This economically unequal exchange was also ecologically unequal. Among the three great countries rich in resources, the USSR reached 100 per cent of its biocapacity in 1973, and China reached this level in 1970 (and has continued to grow since, arriving at 256 per cent in 2009), whereas the US footprint was already 126 per cent of its territory's biocapacity in 1961 and reached 176 per cent in 1973.[94] Comparable

---

92   Bairoch, *Mythes et paradoxes*, 161.

93   Gaël Giraud and Zeynep Kahraman, 'How Dependent Is Growth from Primary Energy? Output Energy Elasticity in 50 Countries (1970–2011)', parisschoolofeconomics.eu.

94   The statistical series for different countries' footprints are taken from Global Footprint Network, *National Footprint Accounts 1961–2010* (2012 edition), available online at footprintnetwork.org. (It should be noted that the revised data from the Global Footprint Network differ slightly from those from another source: storymaps.esri.com/globalfootprint.)

figures for 1973 are 377 per cent for Great Britain, 141 per cent for France, 292 per cent for West Germany and 576 per cent for Japan, while many Asian, African and Latin American countries had a ratio below 50 per cent at that time, showing that the driving phenomenon of the Great Acceleration embarked on in 1945–73 was the tremendous ecological indebtedness of the Western industrial countries. These literally emptied the rest of the world of its materials and high-quality energy, a phenomenon that is the key to the Cold War (Figure 14). With access to these cheap resources, they embarked on an unsustainable model of development, with their massive emissions of pollutants and greenhouse gases dependent on the restorative capacities of the rest of the world's ecosystemic functioning.

The Great Acceleration thus corresponds to a capture by the Western industrial countries of the ecological surpluses of the Third World. It then appears as the construction of an ecological gap between national economies that generated a great deal of wealth without subjecting their own territories to excessive impacts, and the countries of the rest of the world whose economies were burdened by a heavy footprint on their territory. Figure 15 gives a striking representation of this.[95]

This map illustrates the unequal relations of ecological credit and debt that set in with the Great Acceleration. A team from the University of California at Berkeley has measured both the unequal ecological footprints of nations and the regions that these footprints especially burdened. It showed that the poorest countries have a small footprint, with very little effect on the spaces of the rich countries, whereas the rich countries have a large footprint with a heavy burden on the spaces of the poorest countries.[96] For one dollar of GDP today, Mali and

---

95   This map represents an ecological balance in bioproductive hectares, but it is also possible to estimate this unequal ecological exchange in dollars. This has not yet been done for 1973, but a map of this kind can be found for the year 2000, a kind of balance of unsettled ecological payments. Paul C. Sutton et al., 'The Real Wealth of Nations: Mapping and Monetizing the Human Ecological Footprint', *Ecological Indicators*, 16, 2012: 11–22.

96   U. T. Srinivasan et al., 'The Debt of Nations and the Distribution of Ecological Impacts from Human Activities', *Proceedings of the National Academy of Sciences of the USA*, 105:5, 5 February 2008: 1,768–73.

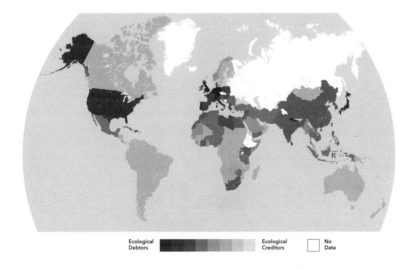

Figure 15: *Creditor and debtor countries in terms of ecological footprint in 1973*

Bolivia, for example, have to extract twenty times more material from their territory than does the United States, and India and China ten times more.[97]

Take for example the situation of the forests during the Great Acceleration. Since the last glaciation, 10 million square kilometres of the world's forest cover have been lost (forty-three times the area of Great Britain), half of this in the twentieth century alone, reducing the planet's capacity for capturing carbon dioxide and increasing the risk of major climatic disturbance, as well as transforming the soil equilibrium and rainfall of the regions affected.[98] But whereas the seventeenth and eighteenth centuries saw a major deforestation in Western Europe

---

97   'Visualizing Global Material Flows', materialflows.net.
98   McNeill, *Something New under the Sun*, 213; Michael Williams, 'A New Look at Global Forest Histories of Land Clearing', *Annual Review of Environment and Resources*, 33, 2008: 345–67, 354.

(continuing until 1920 in the United States), in the twentieth century, and especially since 1945, there has been an increase in forest cover in Western Europe and a quasi-stabilization in the United States – meaning that the 5 million hectares of forest lost in the twentieth century has been all in the economically poorest countries,[99] generating forest and agricultural products consumed largely in Europe and the United States, which in this same period have improved the ecological quality of their own territories.

In conclusion, there would be many heuristic and explanatory advantages in speaking of a 'Capitalocene' rather than an Anthropocene. This particularly means that the rich countries would neither have succeeded in industrializing nor attained the post-war affluent society without the possibility of unequal ecological exchange with the rest of the world, and that unequal ecological exchange is indeed a major explanatory factor for the combined genesis of the asymmetries of wealth characteristic of the historical dynamic of capitalism, and the rise of human impacts that caused the geological derailment of the planet in the Anthropocene. A rematerialized and ecologized history of capitalism appears as the indispensable partner of the Earth system sciences in order to understand our new epoch.[100]

---

99   Tucker, *Insatiable Appetite*; Michael Williams, *Deforesting the Earth: From Prehistory to Global Crisis*, Chicago: University of Chicago Press, 2002; Williams, 'A New Look at Global Forest Histories of Land Clearing'.

100   A history of this kind should go on to analyse the transformations of the world-system since the 1970s, after the oil shocks and the age of cheap petrol, in the age of the financialization of capitalism, the neoliberal and neoconservative revolution as an attempt to maintain US hegemony, the problematic 'uncoupling' of the Western industrial economies, the rise of China as potential centre of a new world-system in still embryonic competition with the United States, the enormous flows of toxic and electronic waste to the poor countries, and the increased geopolitical tensions over resources and atmosphere. Some elements of this can be found in Harvey, *The New Imperialism*; Moore, *Capitalism in the Web of Life*; Andrew K. Jorgenson and Brett Clark, 'Are the Economy and the Environment Decoupling? A Comparative International Study, 1960–2005', *American Journal of Sociology*, 118:1, 2012: 1–44; Andrew K. Jorgenson, 'The Sociology of Ecologically Unequal Exchange and Carbon Dioxide Emissions, 1960–2005', *Social Science Research*, 41:2, 2012: 242–52.

CHAPTER 11

Polemocene: Resisting the Deterioration of the Earth since 1750

Once the long history of environmental reflexivity and environmental inequalities resurfaces in our understanding of the last two hundred years, the centrality of conflict in the history of the Anthropocene becomes self-evident. It would be clearly anachronistic to speak of an 'ecological movement', when the very word did not exist until 1866, but a patronizing history that failed to rescue the socio-environmental resistances to industrialism from what E. P. Thompson called 'the enormous condescension of posterity', a history that would neglect to give voice to the defeated or to marginalized alternatives (technical, social, environmental), would be no less anachronistic.[1] This chapter explores the existence, since the eighteenth century, of an 'environmentalism of the poor' fighting for social justice and environmental decency, active both in core countries and in the periphery.[2]

---

1   E. P. Thompson, *The Making of the English Working Class* (1963), London: Penguin, 1980, 12; François Jarrige, *Face au monstre mécanique. Une histoire des résistances à la technique*, Paris: IMMHO, 2009, and *Technocritiques. Du refus des machines à la contestation des technosciences*, Paris: La Découverte, 2014.

2   Ramachandra Guha, *Environmentalism: A Global History*, New York: Longman, 2000; Joachim Radkau, *The Age of Ecology*, Cambridge: Polity, 2014; Joan Martínez Alier, *The Environmentalism of the Poor: A Study of Ecological Conflicts and Valuation*, Cheltenham: Edward Elgar, 2002.

Challenging the 'material deterioration of the planet' at the dawn of industrialization

Anthropocenic undertakings that massively disturbed moral and natural economies did not proceed without criticism, challenge and struggle. Colonial expansion and monoculture; liberal laissez-faire; the reinforcement of property rights and private initiative to the detriment of customary or collective rights; the runaway growth of wood and coal burning for forges, heating and machinery; pollution from the nascent large-scale chemical industry; the transformation of rural landscapes by urbanization, agricultural specialization, railways – all these great changes that expanded the ecological footprint of Western Europe provoked innumerable conflicts right across the planet. All kinds of social and ethnic groups, communities and professions found their values, resources and ways of life affected or overturned by the process of industrial 'modernization': uprooted and over-exploited slaves in the Americas, colonized peoples whose use of nature was radically redefined by the colonists, villagers deprived of commons by enclosures, then of access to woodland by the new forest codes, urban and rural workers in trades threatened by machinery, owners of land adjacent to polluting industries, common people losing a precious source of subsistence with the pollution of rivers or the destruction of forests, the landed nobility losing its social ascendancy over the industrial bourgeoisie, as well as a fringe of artists and scientists hostile to the rise of utilitarian and mercantile logic, etc.

If these groups were not aligned, either in their battles over the political regime or in the class struggle, they nevertheless sketched out an arc of resistance, and we shall establish some connections between them around three major questions of that time: forests and climate, machinery, and pollution.

Defending the forest, its rights of usage and the planet

In an organic economy marked by energy scarcity, the needs of the navy, the proliferation of forges, glass-works, lime-kilns, brickyards and tile-works increased the pressure on forest resources in Western Europe from the late seventeenth century on.[3] Private landowners and royal foresters sought to 'rationalize' the management of forests so as to make them profitable in both the long and short term. What was already called 'regulated' or 'sustainable' management of forests (this term is found in a German forestry treatise of 1713, and even in medieval texts) functioned according to the principle of rotation (clear-cutting followed by homogeneous plantation). This management implied in practice that the usage rights of villagers were reduced or abolished altogether, such as the right to pasture animals and collect dead wood, which created very intense social conflicts from the mid eighteenth to the mid nineteenth century.

In the French royal forest of Chaux in the Jura Mountains, a 'War of the Demoiselles' flared up in 1765. Where the royal forest managers congratulated themselves on a rational and sustainable production along German lines, the villagers and small artisans saw an appropriation that deprived them of cheap wood. They harassed the guards and helped themselves to wood, leading the authorities to send cavalry and grenadiers.[4] Everywhere in France, the books of grievances of 1789 attest to countless complaints against industrial activities, forges and salt-works in particular, which were accused of causing deforestation and increasing the price of wood.[5]

The French Revolution and the Empire, however, saw a great expansion of forest exploitation, made possible by the sale of national property and the law of 29 September 1791, of liberal inspiration, which strengthened the rights of landowners and abolished the control of royal forestry agents over the management of private lands.[6] The forest code of 1827 abolished certain customary rights of village collection in the forests. In the sub-prefecture of Saint-Girons

---

3   Martine Chalvet, *Une histoire de la forêt*, Paris: Seuil, 2011.

4   François Vion-Delphin, 'La révolte des demoiselles en forêt de Chaux – 1765', in Andrée Corvol (ed.), *Violences et environnement. XVIe–XXe siècles*, Cahier d'études, CNRS, 1991, 44–8.

5   Arlette Brosselin, Andrée Corvol and François Vion-Delphin, 'Les doléances contre l'industrie', in Denis Woronoff (ed.), *Forges et forêts. Recherches sur la consommation proto-industrielle de bois*, Paris: EHESS, 1990, 11–28.

6   Chalvet, *Une histoire de la forêt*, 167.

the number of hearings for forest crimes rose from 192 in 1825 to 2,300 in 1840. In Tarbes, an old man was condemned to a heavy fine of 11.60 francs for having 'stolen' a quarter of a litre of acorns in the forest! This assault on collective usage rights opened a half century of violent or latent conflicts in the French forests. In July 1830, while the people of Paris were overthrowing Charles X, the Pyrenean peasants were fighting another 'War of the Demoiselles' in the Pyrenees, against the forge-masters and charcoal burners. The newly established Louis-Philippe had to send thirteen infantry companies in an effort to regain control of this territory.[7]

In the German states, the 'sustainable' management of forests, which transformed the woodland areas into timber factories, aroused similar tensions. In Bavaria in the 1840s, forest infractions, punished by fines or even prison terms, counted in the hundred thousands.[8] In Prussia in the 1840s, five-sixths of legal prosecutions were bound up with thefts of wood. The young Karl Marx discovered the class struggle not in the English industrial cities but by way of this great question of political ecology, the privatization of forests and the exclusion of communal uses.[9]

These popular mobilizations were combined, between 1780 and 1830, with a denunciation of the retreat of European forests and their recent excessive felling for industrial uses. The forest question was at the same time an environmental alert and a critique of liberal capitalism. The climatic and hydrological effects of deforestation, in fact, showed the lack of fit between the individual interests of the forest proprietors, the interest of the nation and even – already – that of the 'planet'. In France, in the first half of the nineteenth century, this was a central political and scientific debate that resurged with every climate aberration and major flood.[10]

---

7   Peter Sahlins, *Forest Rites: The War of the Demoiselles in Nineteenth-Century France*, Cambridge, MA: Harvard University Press, 1994, 11.

8   Richard Hölzl, 'Historicizing Sustainability: German Scientific Forestry in the Eighteenth and Nineteenth Centuries', *Science as Culture*, 19:4, 2010: 431–60.

9   John Bellamy Foster, *Marx's Ecology: Materialism and Nature*, New York: Monthly Review Press, 2000, 67.

10   Jean-Baptiste Fressoz and Fabien Locher, *Le climat fragile de la modernité*, Paris: Seuil, 2016.

It was in this context that Charles Fourier wrote an extraordinary text with the title *De la détérioration matérielle de la planète* (1821).[11] This early socialist thinker opposed Saint-Simon's industrialism, accusing him of spreading a false religion, a 'false progress', and not placing the 'association of workers before that of the masters'.[12] Fourier gave his critique of 'civilized industry' (i.e., industrial capitalism) an ecological dimension. Starting from the observation of a disturbance in the climate, he diagnosed a 'decline in the health of the globe'. The underlying source of the evil was social: it was individualism that led to deforestation and the exhaustion of natural resources: 'These climatic disorders are a vice inherent to civilized culture; it overturns everything . . . by the struggle of individual interest against collective interest.'[13]

Any attempt to manage the planet without an exit from the 'civilization' of the mercantile and individualist stage and an advance to the higher stage of 'association' was condemned to failure:

> It is thus completely ridiculous to stop at making decrees [on the forests] that enjoin civilization to be no longer itself, to change its devastating nature, to stifle its rapacious spirit . . . One might as well decree that tigers should become docile and turn away from blood.[14]

For many thinkers of that time, testimonies of climate disturbances and social conflicts over wood, the restoration of forests and climate necessarily involved a reform that would deeply challenge the dominant industrialism and laissez-faire. The German historian Joachim Radkau imagined the possibility of a different outcome to the forest

---

11   Charles Fourier, 'Détérioration matérielle de la planète', in René Schérer, *L'Écosophie de Charles Fourier. Deux textes inédits*, Paris: Economica, 2001, 31–125, 79. These were preparatory notes from 1820–21 for Fourier's *Traité de l'association domestique agricole*, later titled *Théorie de l'unité universelle* (1822), finally published in *La Phalange* in 1847.

12   Charles Fourier, *Pièges et charlatanisme des deux sectes. Saint-Simon et Owen*, Paris: Bossange, 1831, 10.

13   Fourier, 'Détérioration matérielle de la planète', 67.

14   Ibid., 117.

and climate question at the turn of the nineteenth century. Why should a 'broad Green alliance',[15] bringing together anti–laissez-faire foresters, scientists fearful of climate change, romantic or revolutionary utopian intellectuals and the people of the villages defending the commons, not prevail over mercantile and industrialist doctrine?

The question may seem an idle one, inasmuch as this 'alliance' appeared heterogeneous and unlikely. But it offers the advantage of forcing us to a more open and political reading of environmental history. What if the entry into the Anthropocene, rather than an unconscious slippage or even the simple result of technical innovation (the steam engine), was the result of a political defeat in the face of the forces of free-market economics? The socio-environmental tension around the forests was only settled in Western Europe at the cost of many illusions and pseudo-solutions typical of the Anthropocene: first, a massive use of coal, explicitly promoted as a solution to preserve European forests (see Chapter 9); second, an increased import of wood from the Baltic and the colonial periphery; and finally the normalization of the foresters' environmental critique by placing them at the head of large forest administrations disciplining the relations between the poor and nature, and promising a sustainable management of the globe by science, a model that would soon be called 'conservationism'.

Questioning machines and mass production

A conflict just as central for European societies at the dawn of the Anthropocene concerned the mechanization of production. A wide movement of challenging and breaking machines swept the whole of Western Europe from the late eighteenth century to the middle of the nineteenth. In the 1780s, machine breaking represented a tenth of all labour conflicts in Great Britain,[16] coming to a head in the English textile triangle in 1811–12. In Normandy, where large-scale textile industry developed very early, more than half of *Cahiers de doléances* (list of

---

15   Radkau, *The Age of Ecology*, 17.
16   Jarrige, *Face au monstre mécanique*.

grievances) demanded the suppression of mechanical looms.[17] In the town of Falaise, in November 1788, two thousand workers armed with sticks destroyed a spinning machine, and in Rouen on 14 July 1789 hundreds of workers invaded a cotton mill and broke thirty mechanical looms. At the time of the revolution of July 1830, seven hundred Paris typographers destroyed the mechanical presses of the Imprimerie Royale. There were hundreds of such actions in Europe between 1780 and 1830.

The machine-breaking movement was made up of urban artisans (typographers, textile workers) and rural labourers (peasants who spun, wove and knitted by hand, seasonal cereal threshers, etc.). They expressed their refusal to see themselves dispossessed of their skills, their livelihood and a way of life that combined agriculture with manufacture. They rejected poor-quality industrial products and championed the idea of a fair price for their labour against the machines that were the cause of imbalance and inequality.[18] This 'moral economy' opposed to the increasingly triumphant laissez-faire political economy was shared by many small masters and local elites (French mayors often defended machine breakers).

A challenge to machines also came from elements of the Romantic movement. In France, in the wake of the July 1830 revolution, there was a noticeable circulation between artisan and worker milieus and the young students and clerks marked by Romantic literature, such as the movement of the '*boussingots*' in the wake of Hugo's *Hernani*.[19] In England, Byron famously spoke out against capital punishment for Luddites in 1812. The Luddites were supported by the English middle classes worried by a deterioration in the quality of products and the

17 François Jarrige, *Au temps des 'tueuses de bras'. Les bris de machines à l'aube de l'ère industrielle, 1780–1860*, Rennes: Presses universitaires de Rennes, 2009, 23–51.

18 Thompson, *The Making of the English Working Class*; Adrian Randall, *Before the Luddites: Custom, Community and Machinery in the English Woollen Industry, 1776–1809*, Cambridge: Cambridge University Press, 1991, Chapter 7.

19 Michael Löwy and Robert Sayre, *Esprits de feu. Figures du romantisme anti-capitaliste*, Paris: Éditions du Sandre, 1999, 60–102. On the other hand, John Tresh shows the fascination that the machine exerted on certain of the Romantics: John Tresch, *The Romantic Machine: Utopian Science and Technology after Napoleon*, Chicago: University of Chicago Press, 2012.

misery caused by the machines. In 1811, for example, the *Nottingham Review* wrote:

> The machines . . . are not being broken for being upon any new construction . . . but in consequence of goods being wrought upon them which are of little worth, are deceptive to the eye, are disreputable to the trade, and therefore pregnant with the seeds of its destruction.[20]

The Luddite critique thus targeted a fundamental bifurcation that set in with the entry into the Anthropocene: the profitability of costly machines led capitalists to prioritize the quantity of products over their quality or durability. In the phalansteries imagined by Fourier (the harmonious societies designed in response to embryonic industrial capitalism), however, there are only a limited number of machines, as the objects produced are of such quality that they do not need frequent replacement.[21] The denunciation of machinery also lay at the heart of the British Chartist movement, whose press in the 1840s was full of workers' poems denouncing the loss of the countryside of their childhood, the 'old woods' and clear streams, for the profit of the morbid world of manufacture where 'the noonday was darker than night'.[22]

Opposition to innovations

In fact, machine breaking constituted only the historically visible part of a quite general opposition to mechanization. Historians have shown that what was formerly classified as 'resistance to technology' or 'inertia' represented rather an alternative mode of production, no less innovative but turned more towards flexible and specialized production, allowing a better adaptation to the market and towards quality products.[23] Different technical and social pathways were conceivable

---

20   Quoted by Thompson in *The Making of the English Working Class*, 518.

21   Jarrige, *Technocritiques*.

22   Ernest Jones, 'The Better Hope', *Northern Star*, 5 September 1846.

23   Charles Sabel and Jonathan Zetlin, 'Historical Alternatives to Mass Production: Politics, Markets and Technology in Nineteenth-Century Industrialization', *Past and Present*, 108, 1985: 133–76.

within an industrial context, as well as different ways of organizing labour. The historiography of the 'industrial revolution' that dominated the decades after 1945 and depicted mechanization and mass production as inexorable – and thus the struggles of Luddites and artisans as retrograde – deprived us of the possibility of conceiving the technological and industrial bifurcations of the Anthropocene in a more open manner. This resistance was never against technology as such, but against a particular technology and its ability to crush others, and we need to unfold the spectrum of alternatives that existed at each moment: canals instead of railways; improved oil lamps instead of gas lighting; flexible and quality production instead of mass production; and an artisanal chemistry with expertise in qualities and sources rather than industrial chemistry, etc.

In the case of gas lighting, for example, the problems raised by its opponents in the 1820s and '30s emphasized not only the danger of explosions at gasworks located in built-up areas, but also the unhealthy nature of the process of gas manufacture from coal and its poor yield in a context of finite coal resources. We should note in passing that history generally confirmed the fears of these opponents: gasometers frequently exploded, and the by-products of coal distillation proved to be highly carcinogenic, polluting the soil for a long time ahead.[24]

In the same way, the standard reading of resistance to the steam train highlights the cultural rejection of the Romantics (though in reality, against a few verses by Alfred de Musset, far more Romantic authors hymned praise to steam and rail) and medical fears that were subsequently judged irrational. But an analysis of studies of public utility conducted prior to railway construction constitutes a source of prime importance for a more realistic history of opposition to the railway. The arguments mobilized reveal a great variety of good reasons for opposing the new means of transport: unprofitable lines, competition with canals, which if slower were far less costly, the disappearance of horses for transport and thus a shortfall of fertilizer for agriculture,

---

24   Jean-Baptiste Fressoz, 'The Gas Lighting Controversy: Technological Risk, Expertise, and Regulation in Nineteenth-Century Paris and London', *Journal of Urban History*, 33:5, 2007, 729–55.

and in general, the concentration of wealth in large transport companies to the detriment of small ones.[25]

Opposition to pollution and nuisance

> Your world is proud, your man is perfect!
> The hills are levelled, the plain lit up;
> You have cleverly trimmed the tree of life;
> All is swept clean on your iron rails;
> All is great, all is fine, but we die in your air.
>
> —Alfred de Musset, 'Rolla', 1833

This well-known verse of Alfred de Musset not only expresses the
strength of Romantic critique but also echoes the many warnings
there already were about the dangers of industrial pollution. In the
context of the environmental aetiologies of the neo-Hippocratic
medicine of the early nineteenth century, industrialization and its
unprecedented train of diverse pollutions appeared extraordinarily
threatening. Historians have discovered thousands of petitions from
the first half of the nineteenth century in which local residents refer
to current medical doctrines to accuse industrialists of increasing
mortality or causing epidemics.

Around Marseille in the 1820s, for example, opposition to the wide-
spread damage caused by chemical factories united a large part of
Provençal society: from rich landowners and peers of the realm,
through mayors, doctors and judges, down to small farmers who saw
their fields devastated. The judiciary, moreover, played a very promi-
nent role in the struggle against factories: in the 1820s, nearly 10 per
cent of legal cases in the rural districts around Marseille concerned
pollution, and it was thanks to the damages awarded by the courts that
industrialists were compelled to install condensers on their chimneys
to limit the effects of pollution.[26]

---

25   A summary of this is given in Jarrige, *Technocritiques*.
26   Jean-Baptiste Fressoz, *L'Apocalypse joyeuse. Une histoire du risque
technologique*, Paris: Seuil, 2012, 149–94.

Manchester, the home of the textile industry, a city of steam engines and laissez-faire economics, swallowed up the surrounding countryside and absorbed millions of tonnes of coal and American cotton to fuel its mechanical looms. Gigantic chimneys, 500 of them by 1843, belched out a dark and highly toxic smoke that blended with that from domestic emissions.[27] This 'Cottonopolis', responsible for 40 per cent of British exports in the early part of the nineteenth century,[28] was then one of the most polluted and wretched cities in the world, as Tocqueville observed:

> A sort of black smoke covers the city. The sun seen through it is a disc without rays. Under this half daylight 300,000 human beings are ceaselessly at work . . . From this foul drain the greatest stream of human industry flows out to fertilize the whole world.[29]

Manchester had Britain's highest rates of mortality from both respiratory diseases and rickets (for want of light and proper nourishment). In 1899, the majority of Mancunians who volunteered for the second Boer War were rejected on account of their defective constitution.[30] The first public parks, established in 1846, soon saw their trees die from 'acid rain' (the term dates from 1872), which also transformed the region's flora and acidified lakes. The denunciations and complaints of contemporaries multiplied, emphasizing a loss of sunlight in the city of close to 50 per cent, the deterioration of goods and buildings, the destruction of vegetation, the loss of birds and the epidemics of respiratory diseases. As far back as 1819, a committee of inquiry was disturbed by the scale of toxic waste from steam engines, and in 1842 the Association for the Prevention of Smoke was established, soon followed by other similar bodies. But industrial interests

27 Stephen Mosley, *The Chimney of the World: A History of Smoke Pollution in Victorian and Edwardian Manchester*, Isle of Harris: White Horse Press, 2001.

28 Stephen Mosley, *The Environment in World History*, New York: Routledge, 2010, 104.

29 Alexis de Tocqueville, *Journeys to England and Ireland*, Rutgers, NJ: Transaction, 1987, 105.

30 Mosley, *The Environment in World History*, 106–7.

were too strong for this problem to be really tackled politically before the twentieth century.

Challenging the damages of progress in the age of empires and the second industrial revolution

In the mid nineteenth century, John Stuart Mill put forward a critique of economic growth that was very detailed and combined with a politically progressive and redistributive standpoint (as opposed to the conservatism of Malthus). In his *Principles of Political Economy*, in fact, Mill declared himself in favour of a halt to growth in the near future and 'a stationary state of capital and wealth', rather than the pursuit of a constant economic struggle. He argued for a better distribution of wealth by the combined effect of 'prudence and frugality':

> If the earth must lose that great portion of its pleasantness which it owes to things that the unlimited increase of wealth and population would extirpate from it, for the mere purpose of enabling it to support a larger, but not a better or a happier population, I sincerely hope for the sake of posterity that they will be content to be stationary, long before necessity compels them to it.[31]

If this programme seems to anticipate that of the stationary state and degrowth economists of the late twentieth century, Mill was not so much a precursor as one of the last classical economists whose thought remained bound to the processes of life and their finite character.

In the second half of the century, however, the wind changed. Classical economists and the idea of a stationary state gave way to a largely dematerialized marginalist paradigm (see Chapter 9); environmental medicine was displaced by new public-health doctrines and eventually Pasteurism, which downplayed the health effects of

---

31   John Stuart Mill, *Principles of Political Economy*, Oxford: Oxford University Press, 1999, 128 and 129.

pollution. The question of anthropogenic climate change also lost importance, with the emergence of the theory of glaciations that saw humanity caught up in great climatic cycles over which it had no control; and Luddism dwindled away.

After the revolutionary defeats of 1848, the majority of the workers' movement rallied to the industrial world and machinery, both in the trade unions and among the socialists. The challenge to machinery was dismissed as archaic and doomed to defeat by Marx and his successors, opening the way to the socialist productivism that the USSR embodied in the twentieth century.

It was in the second half of the nineteenth century, in fact, that 'progress' imposed itself as the central ideology of the industrial West. This movement is indissociable from the rise of European nationalisms that saw science and industry as indispensable vectors of power. Progress, the veil of modesty clothing the damages of industrial capitalism, was originally an ideology of consolation and struggle. It magnified the grandeur of goals the better to exorcize disasters and combat opponents. The promises of progress justified the fate of its victims. The ideology of progress was also built upon a contrast between the technological West and the barbarous rest. As explored in Jules Verne's novels such as *Five Weeks in a Balloon* or *Around the World in Eighty Days*, the great Western fantasy of the time was to penetrate into dangerous and barbarous extra-European places in a safe and technological European bubble: balloons flying over Africa or trains crossing India. The ideology of progress bore within it a devalorization of the rest of the world. Its triumph coincided with the second industrial revolution and economic globalization; it justified the growing gulf between rich and poor nations, and in return used this widening discrepancy in wealth and power to discredit opponents of industrialism in the West.

The shift of forest damage and conflict to the South

It was in this context of a stabilization of the industrial order in the North and the incorporation of the economies of the South into the world economy that criticism and opposition arose again in new forms.

If in Europe, for example, recourse to fossil fuel made it possible to attenuate both social tensions and ecological degradations around forestry, this was at the cost of an accelerated deforestation in the tropical zones after 1850, or else their transformation into monoculture plantations of eucalyptus (for paper), hevea (for rubber) or oil palm.[32] In the second half of the twentieth century, the model of 'regulated forestry' (born in Germany, then spread by the École Forestière of Nancy) was universalized. The creation of the Indian Forest Service in 1860, then the establishment of similar administrations in Canada, Australia, New Zealand and the colonial territories of Africa, meant that by the end of the nineteenth century British foresters managed an area some ten times that of Great Britain. Led in the early twentieth century by Gifford Pinchot, a former student of the École de Nancy and a leading figure of 'conservationism', the public forest domain in the United States was just as gigantic: together with that of Canada, it covered 15 per cent of the land surface of the North American continent. With the backing of nation-states and empires that gave a growing place to scientific expertise, the 'sustainable' management of forests made it possible to redefine these immense spaces as national or imperial property and to organize their 'managed' exploitation. It also facilitated control of local populations in their relationship with nature.[33]

In the Indian case, the forest administration came into conflict with almost every social group: communities of hunter-gatherers, those practising slash-and-burn agriculture or extensive stock-raising, village communities who found themselves deprived of usage rights, and traders who dealt in precious woods. From the 1870s on, serious disturbances over forest restrictions broke out across the country: the revolts of Gudem and Rampa in 1879 and Chotanagpur in 1893. The formation of forest reserves invariably led to the destruction of many villages and the eviction of their inhabitants. At the time of the Madhya

32   John R. McNeill and Erin Stewart Mauldin (eds), *A Companion to Global Environmental History*, London: Wiley-Blackwell, 2012, 274.

33   Gregory A. Barton, *Empire Forestry and the Origin of Environmentalism*, Cambridge: Cambridge University Press, 2002.

Pradesh troubles of 1910, the Indian government had to send in the troops. Hunger strikes, telegraph wires cut, railways sabotaged, police stations burned: more than 900 rebels were captured.[34] In 1915, in the foothills of the Himalayas, immense pine forests designed for commercial use were burned down by the local people.[35] These popular revolts were linked to the Indian national movement. In January 1930, after the Purna Swaraj (declaration of independence), the nationalist movement led by Gandhi argued for civil disobedience in regard to forest laws and for a democratic management of the forests that would involve local populations in a conservation policy.

As in Europe around 1800, forest conflict in India was a major social struggle between an 'optimized' nature connected to the market for the purpose of serving the needs of distant consumers and an 'environmentalism of the poor', of village communities deprived of usage rights and common management. The historian Ramachandra Guha draws an overall negative environmental balance-sheet for this technocratic forestry, emphasizing that the forests of India today are in a 'far worse condition' than in 1860. While the forest service still manages 22 per cent of India's surface area, less than half of this amount is actually wooded.[36]

Questioning industrialism

Machine breaking began to decline in Western Europe after the 1830s. Across the whole continent, moreover, 1848 dealt a blow to revolutionary ardour, followed by 1871 in France. The Third Republic, from this point of view, not only 'ended the revolution', but also, thanks to the authority bestowed by science, stabilized the bourgeois and industrial social order – moderated by an agrarian protectionism that kept the

---

34 Madhav Gadgil and Ramachandra Guha, *This Fissured Land: An Ecological History of India*, Berkeley: University of California Press, 1993, 156.

35 Ramachandra Guha, *The Unquiet Woods: Ecological Change and Peasant Resistance in the Himalaya*, Berkeley: University of California Press, 1990.

36 Ramachandra Guha, *Environmentalism: A Global History*, New York: Longman, 2000, 41.

peasants as a counterweight to industrial workers.[37] The social reforms of the late nineteenth century supported the Marxist thesis that industrial capitalism was a necessary stage towards socialism. In the early twentieth century, a large part of the European socialist movement, and even of its anarchist counterpart, rallied to industrialism. The ideology of progress and the valorization of the future (François Hartog's 'futurist historicity') even won over oppositional and anti-capitalist movements. A new 'politics of the past' weakened the rhetoric of loss which had been so present with the first socialists in their utopia of rebuilding a just and harmonious society on the basis of an 'untamed' or pre-industrial past.[38]

It would however be wrong to believe that the integration of the anti-industrial popular movement into the progressive, pedagogic and industrial vision of the world, that of the parliamentary, liberal and bourgeois left (of which socialism would not form part until the late nineteenth century), simply left the critique of anthropocenic activity to socially conservative voices. The late nineteenth and early twentieth century actually saw a renewal of the critique of anthropocenic activity structured around three distinct poles.

The first pole, that of 'conservationism', pertains to the 'industrial polity' analysed by Boltanski and Thévenot.[39] It appealed to efficiency and science, and promised to improve industrial domination over nature by an increase of industrial logic itself: valorizing nature, optimizing flows, limiting losses, adjusting harvests, standardizing for a better long-term management, etc. We can include here 'scientific forestry', the movement for industrial recycling (promoted by Peter Lund Simmonds in Britain, for instance), the sanitarian movement or the policies of President Theodore Roosevelt.

Conservationists denounced the merely extractive logic as unsustainable. The question of the finitude of the planet was also clearly

37   Guillaume Carnino, *L'Invention de la science. La nouvelle religion de l'âge industrielle*, Paris: Seuil, 2015.

38   Alastair Bonnett, *Left in the Past: Radicalism and the Politics of Nostalgia*, New York and London: Continuum, 2010.

39   Luc Boltanski and Laurent Thévenot, *On Justification: The Economies of Worth*, trans. Catherine Porter, Princeton, NJ: Princeton University Press, 2006, 118ff.

posed, in the context of the 'end of the frontier' decreed in the United States by Frederick Jackson Turner (1893) and the completion of a process of four centuries of European expansion. We have reached the 'limits of our cage', wrote the geographer Jean Brunhes in 1909, shortly after Roald Amundsen's conquest of the South Pole. Around the same time, Max Weber introduced another 'cage' metaphor, noting that the growing concern for material goods was becoming an 'iron cage' that came into conflict with the exhaustion of resources:

> The modern economic order ... bound up with technological and economic conditions of mechanical and machine production determines with an irresistible force the style of life of all individuals. Perhaps it will so determine them until the last ton of fossilized coal is burnt.[40]

In the columns of *La Nature*, the main periodical of scientific popularization in France, a mining engineer and member of the Académie des Sciences extended the calculations of Jevons and envisaged distant exhaustion of 'the world's combustible resources'. In particular, he concluded his essay by evoking another danger:

> In order to produce some 8,000 million [tonnes] of mineral combustibles, how much has been needed in the way of vegetable matter accumulated and very accidentally preserved from combustion over a geological timescale? The day that this carbonic acid will have been restored to the lower layers of air by our factory chimneys, what changes (of which we already have the first signs in the large industrial cities) will not be realized bit by bit in our climates?[41]

At the same time in Germany, the notion of *Raubwirtschaft* (pillage economy), originally introduced by Liebig to describe the metabolic rift, made its way into geography. Friedrich Ratzel, one of the founders

---

40 Max Weber, *The Protestant Ethic and the Spirit of Capitalism* (1904–05), London: Routledge, 2001, 123.
41 Louis de Launay, 'Les ressources en combustibles du monde', *La Nature*, 1914, 238, cited by Jarrige, *Technocritiques*, 175.

of geopolitics (and of the ill-fated concept of *lebensraum*) utilized it in a classic manner to refer to the practices of exploitation of nature of 'primitive' or 'barbaric' peoples. But his colleague Ernst Friedrich applied the notion of *Raubwirtschaft* to show the unsustainability of Western development by continuous territorial expansion, the extraction of non-renewable resources at the periphery, and the ejection of pollution and waste.[42] However, Brunhes and Friedrich remained confident in the ability of the white man to improve his 'cage'; enlightened by conservation-oriented science, he would necessarily become conscious of his mistakes and decide to organize a more rational and sustainable management of the globe.

A second pole, 'preservationism', defended nature on non-utilitarian grounds. Whether for aesthetic, scientific, recreational or spiritual reasons, they argued for protecting nature from any utilitarian interference. This current was represented by the Sierra Club in the United States, by various leagues for the protection of nature in Europe and by renowned naturalists (such as Edmond Perrier in France and Paul Sarasin in Switzerland). Preservationism was institutionalized in the establishment of national parks and gained international standing at the beginning of the twentieth century. In 1913 the first International Conference for the Protection of Nature was held in Bern, and in 1934 the notion of 'integral natural reserve' was adopted internationally.[43] In 1913, Perrier, the director of the Muséum National d'Histoire Naturelle in Paris, delivered an address denouncing the destruction of biodiversity and natural milieus in the colonial peripheries of the European empires:

> Do we have the right to monopolize the Earth for ourselves alone, and
> to destroy for our profit, and to the detriment of future generations,

---

42   Ernst Friedrich, 'Wesen und Geographische Verbreitung der "Raubwirtschaft"', *Petermanns Geographische Mitteilungen*, 50, 1904: 68–79 and 92–5.

43   Yannick Mahrane, Frédéric Thomas and Christophe Bonneuil, 'Mettre en valeur, préserver ou conserver? Genèse et déclin du préservationnisme dans l'empire colonial français (1870–1960)', in Charles-François Mathis and Jean-François Mouhout (eds), *Une protection de la nature et de l'environnement à la française? (XIXe–XXe siècles)*, Paris: Champ Vallon, 2013, 62–80.

everything it has produced that is finest and most powerful in the course of more than 50 million years' development?[44]

If this current represented a quite radical anti-utilitarian critique of the Western project of exploiting the globe economically, it also participated in the expulsion of indigenous populations from their territories, in the name of their protection and a touristic consumption of nature by world elites.[45]

A third pole, which some historians have called 'back-to-nature socialism', corresponded to a more global critique of industrial capitalism, mixing environmental and health observations, social demands and cultural criticism. We can include in this the English 'sentimental' socialists, the German *Lebensreform* movement and some French anarchist currents known as '*naturiens*'. While the new 'politics of the past' of the post-1945 modernist left (and most professional historians) had edged out these diverse forms of eco-socialisms, they are now the object of rediscovery.

In Great Britain, for example, in the second half of the nineteenth century, a utopian anti-industrial current known as 'sentimental socialism' developed around John Ruskin, William Morris, Robert Blatchford and Edward Carpenter. This inherited the Romanticism of Wordsworth and Carlyle: the desire to preserve communitarian social relations in the face of individualism, to protect the countryside against the aggression of the modern world, and to maintain artisan and artistic skills in the face of industrial standardization. To this conservative Romanticism it added a revolutionary aspect in the form of a rejection of capitalism and parliamentary reformism and commitment to socialism (Morris was one of the founders of the Socialist League in 1884, together with Engels).[46] Its protagonists

---

44   Edmond Perrier, 'Discours du président de la Société nationale d'acclimatation de France', *Bulletin de la Société nationale d'acclimatation*, 60, 1913: 210.

45   John MacKenzie, *The Empire of Nature: Hunting, Conservation and British Imperialism*, Manchester: Manchester University Press, 1997; Mahrane and Bonneuil, 'Mettre en valeur, préserver ou conserver?'

46   Peter C. Gould, *Early Green Politics: Back to Nature, Back to the Land, and Socialism in Britain, 1880–1900*, Brighton: Harvester Press, 1988.

promoted socialism as a politics of beauty and conviviality in harmony with nature. A novel that expresses this current, Samuel Butler's *Erewhon* (1872) depicts a civil war between the champions and opponents of mass industrialism. The victory of the latter opens the way to a new harmonious society, socially just and close to nature. In *Merrie England*, published in 1894, Robert Blatchford, publisher of the *Clarion*, the most widely read socialist newspaper of that decade, led a frontal attack on the 'industrial system', denounced in four points, the first two of which were 'because it is ugly, unpleasant and mechanical' and 'because it is harmful to health'.[47] To ensure a good life for all in the beauty of nature, Blatchford called for the nationalization of the means of production. Montagu Blatchford, his brother, likewise denounced a system that 'dirties the sky, poisons rivers and poisons the atmosphere'.[48] Walking and cycling clubs were established around the *Clarion*, a kind of socialist scout movement, with some 8,000 members in 1913.

A parallel current developed in Wilhelmine Germany, with the large-scale *Lebensreform* movement: the struggle against the corset and urban pollution, with pedagogic arguments, urban health and garden cities, protection of nature, naturopathy, sun-bathing and naturist culture, vegetarianism.[49] The Wandervögel movement, launched in 1896, included both conservative and socialist youth groups seeking in nature emancipation from imperial, authoritarian and industrial society. Emancipation took the form of camping, hiking and living in the countryside. Close to these movements, the philosopher Ludwig Klages drew up a violent charge-sheet in 1914 against a 'progress' that destroyed animal and vegetable species, made the countryside 'sinisterly silent' and crammed 'hordes' of humans into cities with 'chimneys vomiting soot': 'like a fire that devours everything on its passage, "progress" turns the

---

47   Quoted by Charles-François Mathis, *'In Nature We Trust': Les paysages anglais à l'ère industrielle*, Paris: Presses de l'université Paris-Sorbonne, 2010, 484.

48   Montagu Blatchford, 1896, quoted in ibid., 488.

49   Ulrich Linse, *Ökopax und Anarchie: Eine Geschichte der ökologischen Bewegungen in Deutschland*, Munich: Deutsche Taschenbuch Verlag, 1986; Frank Uekötter, *The Greenest Nation? A New History of German Environmentalism*, Cambridge, MA: MIT Press, 2014.

whole Earth upside down'.[50] He denounced the extermination of hundreds of millions of birds across the world for the demands of the fashion industry, as well as the elimination of non-Western cultures. The anti-industrialist critique included Marxism in its targets. For instance, the libertarian socialist Gustav Landauer rejected any progressive and mechanical view of history and saw Marxism as the 'child of the steam engine'. Against the prediction of the automatic advent of socialism on the basis of a certain level of development of the productive forces, Landauer stood for a non-centralized socialism, to be brought about not by an evolutionist law of history but 'when a sufficient number of men wish it'.[51]

In France, the radical critique of industrialism and 'progress' is to be found from the pens of a number of writers, as well as in the context of 'individualist' anarchism, whose social base was made up of artisans and occasional or migrant workers, resisting factory discipline.

Within this fringe there developed vegetarian practices and a 'naturien' current around publications such as *L'Humanité nouvelle*, *L'État naturel* and *La Vie naturelle*, whose authors also wrote in more influential anarchist organs such as *Le Libertaire*.[52] Here are two voices of its protagonists at the dawn of the twentieth century:

> We are deeply tired, disheartened, fed up with the Artificial Life . . . and we want a rapid return to a better regime, anti-civilization, to the natural state . . . We are, above all, revolutionaries . . . we have vowed hatred against everything that makes for human suffering, everything that takes from Man a fragment of his liberty: army, police, judiciary, clergy, family, country, government . . . and we add Science, Progress, the new religion.[53]

---

50   Ludwig Klages, *Mensch und Erde* (1913), Berlin: Matthes & Seitz, 2013.

51   Gustav Landauer, *Aufruf zum Sozialismus*, Frankfurt: EVA, 1967, 97–8 and 108.

52   Jean Maitron, *Le Mouvement anarchiste en France*, vol. 1, Paris: Gallimard, 1992, 379–408. On naturism, see Arnaud Baubérot, *Histoire du naturisme. Le mythe du retour à la nature*, Rennes: Presses universitaires de Rennes, 2004.

53   Henri Beylie, *La Conception libertaire naturienne*, 1901 pamphlet, reproduced in *Invariance*, supplement to 4:9, 1993: 75–83, 76.

Figure 16: Le Sauvage satirique, *Journal de Gravelle, 'naturien' anarchist paper, 1898*
The Cities – hells on earth and burning centres of Hatred – will be abandoned!

A Humanity aware of the causes of Evil will tear down the Tree of supposed
science! By the triumph of Nature over the Artificial, the Earth will regain its green
adornment! And men will rediscover the Joy of living!

The smoke from the factories, the gunshots fired at ceremonies and in
war, the continuing deforestation and the poisoned air, abused by the
sickly smells arising from the factories – these are the causes of atmospheric disturbance . . . What use are the telegraph, telephone, air travel
and electricity? Just a life of hot air! The civilized are people in a great
hurry, living always at a rush! . . . How our poor mother Earth has been
damaged! . . . now the land largely only produces with the help of
chemical fertilizers: . . . a moment will come when a person walking on
foot will be regarded as a phenomenon . . . and we know that organs
that get no exercise inevitably end up atrophying . . . Return to the

Figure 17: L'En dehors (The outsider)
Postcard from a woodcut by Louis Moreau, 1922

natural state is not a turning back; it is no turning back to want to be happy with natural means alone.[54]

These sandal-wearing, anti-industrial currents combined speech and action. Continuing the experiments of the Owenite, Fourierist and other utopian communities, the experiments of return to the land in egalitarian, socialist or anarchist communities proliferated in the United States (New Harmony, 1826; Fruitlands, 1843), Great Britain (Millthorpe, founded by Edward Carpenter in 1884), France (Vaux, Bascons, and some fifteen 'free milieus' before 1914), Brazil (La Cecilia) and Switzerland (Monte Verità, 1900–25, on the shores of Lago Maggiore, where both Herman Hesse and Isadora Duncan stayed).[55]

The thought of the young Gandhi was formed under the influence of this radically anti-industrial socialism or anarchism. A reader of Carpenter, Ruskin, Tolstoy and Thoreau during his studies in London,

---

54 Henri Zisly, 'Réflexions sur le naturel et l'artificiel', August 1901, reproduced in ibid., 91–2.

55 Kaj Noschis, *Monte Verità. Ascona et le génie du lieu*, Geneva: PPUR, 2011.

Gandhi published his first articles in the Tolstoyan journal of the Vegetarian Society. His first book, *Hind Swaraj* (1909), rejected industrialization as a possible path for an independent India.

Citing Edward Carpenter, Gandhi denounced a 'civilization' in which

> thousands of men for the sake of maintenance work in factories or mines. Their condition is worse than that of beasts. They are obliged to work, at the risk of their lives, at most dangerous occupations, for the sake of millionaires.[56]

His thought proceeded from a critique of Western modernity in all its forms, but it distanced itself both from traditionalist currents that hymned the ancient Hindu civilization and from modernizing nationalists like Nehru who sought to catch up with the West. For Gandhi, environmental questioning was bound up with the future of the colonized countries once emancipated by non-violence. In an analysis that linked British industrialism, imperialism and the degradation of the planet, Gandhi maintained the fundamentally inegalitarian nature, not generalizable to the whole planet, of the British model of industrial development:

> The economic imperialism of a single tiny island kingdom (England) is today keeping the world in chains. If an entire nation of 300 millions took to similar economic exploitation, it would strip the world bare like locusts.[57]

It is important to stress that resistance to industrialism was not the monopoly of a far-sighted elite or radical intellectuals. On the contrary, as a result of their impact on the environment, and because they deeply altered ways of living, the major technologies of the Anthropocene have aroused opposition both general and sporadic. Historians have begun to uncover from archives the hundreds of struggles that

---

56   M. K. Gandhi, 'Civilization' (Chapter 6), in *Hind Swaraj or Indian Home Rule*, 1909.

57   *The Oxford India Gandhi: Essential Writings*, New Delhi: Oxford University Press, 2008, 276.

surrounded the various health and environmental problems of 'progress'.

For example, in England civil society mobilized strongly against urban industrial pollution, with the National Smoke Abatement Institution (1882), the Coal Smoke Abatement Society (1898) and the Smoke Abatement League of Great Britain (1909); legislation was obtained in 1866 and 1891, even if this did not actually reduce emissions. The pollution of rivers and dams mobilized fishermen across Europe.

Struggles against industrial pollution, though often arbitrated by law, sometimes took a tragic turn. Thus in 1888, the Rio Tinto copper mine in Spain was the stage of a revolt in which workers, peasants and local dignitaries all took part. The British mining company that exploited it paid starvation wages and used a technology of open-air calcination of gigantic quantities of ore, 200-tonne *teleras*. On 4 February of that year, at the call of an anarchist trade-union leader and local leaders of the Anti-Smoke League, 1,500 persons demonstrated in the village to demand an end to the calcination of *teleras* and a reduction of the working day from twelve to nine hours. But soldiers dispersed the demonstration in blood, leaving several dozen dead.[58] A few years later, a similar drama was played out in Japan, likewise against a copper mine. A Japanese-European consortium that exploited the Ashio mine north of Tokyo massively contaminated agricultural land downstream. In 1901, the local notable Tanaka Shôzô resigned his seat as deputy to protest against parliamentary indifference to this contamination. By direct action and at the risk of his life, he enjoined the emperor to 'put an end to a poisonous mining industry'.[59]

Far more than the train had done in a previous period, the motor car, in all probability the single technology with the greatest share of responsibility for the present climate crisis, was far from arousing unanimous approval. Switzerland gives a good sign of this, on account of its tradition of referendum by popular initiative. In the early 1900s, after a series of accidents, the communes of the canton of Graubünden passed decrees

58   Martínez Alier, *The Environmentalism of the Poor*, 155–7.
59   Dominique Bourg and Augustin Fragnière, *La pensée écologique. Une Anthologie*, Paris: PUF, 2014, 111.

prohibiting automobile traffic. No less than ten referendums between 1900 and 1925 confirmed the ban on individual motorcars on cantonal roads (ambulances and fire engines remained authorized). The arguments against the individual car at the time were chiefly economic: cars increased considerably the cost of maintaining the roads, and above all came into competition with the public rail network, which would sooner or later have to be subsidized out of taxation.[60]

Beyond Switzerland, the monopolization of the public space by motorists aroused very lively opposition everywhere. During its first decades, moreover, motoring only benefited a narrow fringe of bourgeois keen on strong sensations and meant an immense pollution for the majority of the population. The car imposed a new urban discipline and made many other uses of the street impossible, in particular children's games. Children were perhaps the greatest losers from motorization: in 1910, in New York, they made up 195 out of 376 victims of fatal traffic accidents.[61] Would the car have been accepted in a genuine democracy?

Challenging the Great Acceleration

The historical sequence that runs from the First World War to the atomic bomb, with its unprecedented unleashing of violence, opened a new phase of questioning of Western industrial modernity and its human, social, ecological and spiritual disasters. The Great Depression and the mass unemployment incriminated mechanical overproduction for the social disorders of the time. On the other hand, industrial wars and the patriotic dimension it granted to productivism, the rise of the consumer society and the establishment of the Fordist model, the confrontation between East and West, the developmentalist dream of a 'catching up' on the part of the countries of the South, the dismissal of dissidents of 'progress', or again the management of the 'secondary' effects of progress by expert authorities, operated as so

60   Wolfgang Sachs, *For Love of the Automobile: Looking Back into the History of Our Desires*, Berkeley: University of California Press, 1992, 18–27.

61   Clay McShane, *Down the Asphalt Path: The Automobile and the American City*, New York: Columbia University Press, 176.

many strategies of legitimization, marginalizing or ridiculing political critiques and scientific warnings that pointed out global ecological imbalances. As early as 1916, Léon Jouhaux, general secretary of the French Confédération Générale du Travail trade-union federation, rallied to productivism and the scientific organization of labour for a 'maximum yield',[62] and after the Second World War, American trade unions likewise accepted the Cold War Keynesian compromise (see Chapter 7). Dissidents of progress were dismissed either as irrevocably superseded nostalgists or even as internal enemies linked to the opposing camp (capitalist, Communist or fascist). We shall trace here some elements of this dialectic of criticisms, challenges and their control.

In the aftermath of the First World War, the writings of Oswald Spengler, Martin Heidegger, Georges Duhamel, Paul Valéry, the emerging personalist movement, or again the solid body of work of the American Lewis Mumford, *Technics and Civilization* (1934), illustrate the rise of an ambivalence on the part of intellectual elites. Henri Bergson summed this up in a formula: 'Mankind lies groaning, half crushed beneath the weight of its own progress.'[63] An outdated historiography was able to see these critiques of the ravages of 'progress' as a temptation to 'return to the soil' that prepared the way culturally for fascism, Nazism and the ideology of the Vichy regime. In actual fact, if these regimes did sometimes appeal to the past and the 'soil', they were in no way traditionalist but rather 'reactionary modernist', profoundly technocratic and pervaded by a posture of domination of nature.[64] In

---

62   Jarrige, *Technocritiques*.

63   Henri Bergson, *The Two Sources of Morality and Religion*, University of Notre Dame Press, 1991, 317.

64   Jeffrey Herf, *Reactionary Modernism: Technology, Culture and Politics in Weimar and the Third Reich*, Cambridge: Cambridge University Press, 1984; Johann Chapoutot, 'Les Nazis et la "nature": protection ou prédation', *Vingtième siècle*, 113, 2012: 29–39; Eric Dorn Brose, 'Generic Fascism Revisited: Attitudes toward Technology in Germany and Italy, 1919–1945', *German Studies Review*, 10, 1987: 273–97; Eric Hobsbawm, *The Age of Extremes: A History of the World 1914–1991*, New York: Vintage, 1996, 262; Robert Kuisel, *Capitalism and the State in Modern France: Renovation and Economic Management in the Twentieth Century*, New York: Cambridge University Press, 1981; Chris Pearson, 'La politique environnemental de Vichy', *Vingtième siècle*, 113, 2012: 41–50.

the inter-war period, in both Europe and the United States, the leading elites of the right rallied generally to technology (as against one Céline, how many Henry Fords, Ernst Jüngers, SS technocrats and fascist futurists?), whereas the critique of technology was more associated with an egalitarian and emancipatory thought (Mumford, the Surrealists, Orwell, Gandhi, etc.) or represented by a youth described as 'nonconformist' and with varied political trajectories.[65]

In France, Jacques Ellul and Bernard Charbonneau illustrate the emergence within the personalist movement (around the journal *Esprit*) of a critique of industrial modernity that was at the same time social, environmental and moral. In their 'project for a personalist manifesto' of 1935, they rejected capitalism, fascism and Communism alike. All three regimes were deemed equally dangerous for the primacy that they gave to technology and for their proletarianization of man in all dimensions of life: economic, but also political and spiritual.[66] They proposed to replace progress understood as power by progress understood as autonomy (reduction of working time, importance of art and culture, guaranteed minimum income) while accepting a certain simplicity in living standard. This idea of a technological totalitarianism, characteristic of Communist and fascist regimes and liberal democracies alike, is found in the works of such writers as George Orwell,[67] Georges Bernanos and Aldous Huxley, as well as the former Trotskyists Cornelius Castoriadis and Claude Lefort. It was popularized by the success of Herbert Marcuse's *One-Dimensional Man* (1964), followed by Ivan Illich's *Tools for Conviviality* (1973).

After 1945, Ellul and Charbonneau broke away from the dominant orientation of personalism represented by Emmanuel Mounier

<hr />

65   Jean-Louis Loubet del Bayle, *Les Non-conformistes de années 30. Une tentative de renouvellement de la pensée politique française*, Paris: Seuil, 2001.

66   Jacques Ellul and Bernard Charbonneau, 'Directives pour un manifeste personnaliste' (1935), in B. Charbonneau and J. Ellul, *Nous sommes des révolutionnaires malgré nous. Textes pionniers de l'écologie politique*, Paris: Seuil, 2014, 47–62.

67   George Orwell, *The Road to Wigan Pier* (1937), London: Penguin, 2001, Chapter 12.

and *Esprit*, which embraced the modernization slogan along with the Christian-Democrat movement as a whole.[68] In 1954, Ellul theorized the autonomy of technological systems in *La Technique ou l'enjeu du siècle*. This critique of the neutrality of technology found echoes in the philosophy and social theory of former students of Heidegger (Günther Anders, Hannah Arendt), as well as in representatives of the Frankfurt School (Adorno, Horkheimer, Marcuse). These German theorists, who had known Nazism and escaped to the United States, strongly resented the loss of a part of their identity in an American society that they considered technocratic, industrialist and consumerist. For them, Auschwitz, Hiroshima and the post-war consumerism all participated in the same supremacy of technology and instrumental reason over the natural, social and moral world.[69] Hannah Arendt pursued this line of reflection in *The Human Condition* (1958), seeing the posture of domination of nature as 'an instrumentalization of the world and the earth' and a 'limitless devaluation of everything given': 'Our whole economy has become a waste economy, in which things must be almost as quickly devoured and discarded as they have appeared in the world, if the process itself is not to come to a sudden catastrophic end.'[70] What was threatened by this mobilization of nature was not simply the environment, but the very possibility of human freedom.

In the time of the Great Acceleration of the Anthropocene, these philosophical and cultural critiques of a technological civilization echoed with the environmental warnings formulated by leading

---

68   Christian Roy, 'Charbonneau et Ellul, dissidents du "progrès". Critiquer la technique face à un milieu chrétien gagné à la modernité', in Céline Pessis, Sezin Topçu and Christophe Bonneuil (eds), *Une autre histoire des 'Trente Glorieuses'. Modernisation, contestations et pollutions dans la France d'après-guerre*, Paris: La Découverte, 2013, 283–301.

69   Theodor W. Adorno and Max Horkheimer, *The Dialectic of Enlightenment* (1944), Stanford: Stanford Unversity Press, 2007; Hannah Arendt, *The Human Condition* (1958), Chicago: University of Chicago Press, 1998; Günther Anders, *Die Antiquiertheit des Menschen. Über die Seele im Zeitalter der zweiten industriellen Revolution*, München: C.H. Beck, 196; Herbert Marcuse, *One-Dimensional Man* (1964), Boston: Beacon Press, 1991.

70   Hannah Arendt, *The Human Condition*, 185.

scientists. These already depicted man as a 'geological force' by virtue of his reproductive, technical and industrial activity.[71] Henry Fairfield Osborn, in *Our Plundered Planet*, shared with Bernanos, Anders and Huxley the refusal to see the ideological confrontation between East and West as the most fundamental tension affecting humanity, and warned against

> the other war, the silent war, eventually the most deadly war, was one in which man has indulged for a long time, blindly and unknowingly. This other world-wide war, still continuing, is bringing more widespread distress to the human race than any that has resulted from armed conflict. It contains potentialities of ultimate disaster greater than would follow the misuse of atomic power. This other war is man's conflict with nature.[72]

'Man against Nature' was also the title of an exhibition in 1955 at the Muséum National d'Histoire Naturelle in Paris. Its director Roger Heim, one of the founders of the International Union for Protection (later changed to Conservation) of Nature along with Osborn, wrote a preface to the French translation of Rachel Carson's *Silent Spring* (1962), which denounced the effects on environment and health of the biocides used on a massive scale after the war. In this text, Heim presented a charge-sheet against 'blind industrialization' and the 'pollution, chemical as well as radioactive, that darkens the atmosphere and acidifies the water', as being 'often conducted by strict financial concern and not by collective interest'.[73]

Alongside these intellectual critiques, the inter-war period and the decades after 1945 saw frequent controversies and mobilizations against the various dangers and disturbances of the time. No more than the nuisances of industrialization in the early nineteenth century did the Great Acceleration of the Anthropocene pass without scientific warnings, popular resistance and challenge by the

---

71   Henry Fairfield Osborn Jr., *Our Plundered Planet*, London: Faber and Faber, 1948, 38.

72   Ibid., 9.

73   Roger Heim, preface to Rachel Carson, *Printemps silencieux*, Paris: Plon, 1963, 12.

social groups affected. We can take the case of France in the years 1945–68, traditionally viewed as a period rich in ideological and social confrontations but consensual in terms of support for a 'necessary modernization'. The history of the ecological movement is usually written as starting only after 1968. Were the French politically anaesthetized by the growth of the so-called '*Trente Glorieuses*'? In no way. Well before the images of Earth seen from the moon, the atom bomb appeared as the event that unified the human condition and the planet. As Bernard Charbonneau put it, 'an event analogous to the discovery of America, the bomb closes the world' instead of opening it, since 'under the threat of the final explosion, the Earth forms a whole';[74] and Georges Bernanos wrote in 1945 that 'the planet is being transformed into a gigantic laboratory'.[75] In France as elsewhere, the environment was already discussed as a global problem in the years immediately after the war, with warnings from writers and such leading scientists as Roger Heim, Théodore Monod and Jean Rostand.

On the ground, many opponents confronted the steam-roller of modernization: the construction of dams that condemned villages to disappear; the modernization of agriculture that counted on young 'advanced' farmers and dismissed elderly small peasants; the decline of handicrafts and small-scale trade in the face of industry and large-scale distribution; modern town planning. Each time, a genuine cultural war was waged between modernizers and populations perceived as backward – Jacques Tati's film *Mon Oncle* (1958) is a comic illustration of this. In Tignes, in the early 1950s, as many riot police as villagers were needed to protect the construction site of a new dam from sabotage. The pollution of rivers mobilized thousands of fishermen and many associations were formed. Inhabitants of the towns organized campaigns against pollution. The writer René

74   Bernard Charbonneau, 'An deux mille' (1945), in Bernard Charbonneau and Jacques Ellul, *Nous sommes des révolutionnaires malgré nous. Textes pionniers de l'écologie politique*, Paris: Seuil, 2014, 193–215, 198.

75   Georges Bernanos, 'L'homme menacé de faillite' (15 November 1945), in Michel Estève (ed.), *Essais et écrits de combat II*, Paris: Gallimard, 1995, 1103–10, 1104.

Barjavel, author of the anti-industrial novel *Ravage*, wrote in the press in the following vehement terms in 1962:

> If your generation does not immediately become aware of the dangers, everything is lost . . . The air will rot. Green spaces will rapidly dwindle. Oxygen will be less and less renewed, while combustion of every kind, doubled or tripled in twenty years, will tend to replace it increasingly quickly by carbon dioxide and all kinds of aggressive waste products. If you are content to tell yourself 'it'll sort itself out, nature will see to it', you will bleed for a long time in the flesh of your children. 'Nature' will not see to it, and 'it' won't sort itself out.[76]

Nuclear energy and atom bomb tests were widely opposed in France in the 1950s, not only by the French Communist Party but also by such 'non-aligned' forces as the Gandhian Catholic community of l'Arche founded in 1948 by Lanza del Vasto, who also sided with anti-colonial struggles in Algeria. L'Arche went on to play a central role in the Larzac resistance starting in 1972 against the establishment of a large military camp. And many French contemporary ecologists (such as the non-violent alter-globalist leader José Bové) began their activist careers in this struggle. Bee-keepers mobilized (in vain) against the chemicals that threatened bees right from the appearance of the first synthetic pesticides in the late 1940s.[77]

In 'developing countries', the post-war decades similarly saw major socioecological movements: the Sarawak communities' struggle in Malaysia against the deforestation of their territory; the Chipko movement in defence of forests and collective rights in India, in the wake of colonial struggles; the AGAPAN movement and the opposition of Amazonian gatherers in Brazil, led by Chico Mendes, to the advance of the tree-fellers and latifundist rancheros; civil disobedience against the eucalyptus plantations in Thailand; the Narmada movement in

---

76   René Barjavel, 'Vénus et les enfants des hommes', *Les Nouvelles littéraires*, 13 December 1962.

77   All these and other oppositions are tackled by the various authors of the recent collective work: Pessis, Topçu and Bonneuil, *Une autre histoire des 'Trente Glorieuses'*.

central India against a gigantic dam project, etc. On every occasion, this 'environmentalism of the poor' was faced with developmentalist governments and the associated economic interests.

Nor did the ecological disturbances heralded by the Great Acceleration pass unperceived in the world of science. Books such as *Road to Survival* by William Vogt and *Our Plundered Planet* by Osborn, both published in 1948, sold millions of copies across the world, and there was a proliferation of international conferences on various environmental questions under the aegis of the UN Food and Agriculture Organization and UNESCO. The post-war years saw an assertion of the claims of the environment in multilateral international arenas. In part the scientific discourse warning about the degradation of the planet already under way or impending went together with a preservationist project that aimed to establish parks in the colonial territories, then on the path of emancipation. It also supported a new conservationist project of scientifically organizing the exploitation of the whole planet under United States leadership, with a view to securing and sustaining the Fordist model of the 'free world' (Western Europe, North America and Japan), as well as promoting 'development' in the non-Communist South (the 'green revolutions' in Latin America, India, the Philippines, etc.; see Chapter 10).

Other scientific warnings, however, represented in particular by Rachel Carson and Barry Commoner in the United States, René Dumont in France, contributed to the building of the ecological movement, linked in the United States to the struggle for civil rights and the opposition to the Vietnam War. This current, and its counterparts in other industrialized countries, helped to put the environment on the world agenda with the UN Conference on the Human Environment in Stockholm in 1972, soon followed by dozens of international environmental conventions and stricter controls on pollution in the North. The high point of this ecological movement was between 1968 and 1978. It was however gradually institutionalized (particularly with the expansion and professionalization of NGOs in the conservation sector),[78] and a part of its strongest critiques (against capitalism and

---

78   Kenneth I. MacDonald, 'The Devil Is in the (Bio)diversity: Private Sector

imperialism, against unequal exchange and ecology, against the ideology of growth) was stifled. In the context of neo-liberal globalization promoted by the WTO agreements and the financializing of the economy, the environmental norms of the rich countries led rather to a delocalizing of polluting activities to the poor countries than to a global improvement.[79]

In the face of the Club of Rome's *Limits to Growth* and the works of the first degrowth economists, a section of the planet's economic and political leaders in the 1970s dismissed any idea of a limit to growth, arguing that technological innovation would readily find solutions to these problems (see Chapter 9).

The last fifteen years have witnessed a return of the radicalization of ecological warnings and mobilizations. On the one hand, the data coming from the life and Earth sciences tend to confirm the unprecedented character of planetary ecological disturbance, whether in the 2007 and 2013 reports of the IPCC (International Panel on Climate Change) or with the broad adoption of the notion of the Anthropocene. On the other hand, criticizing the modest achievements of pragmatic 'green' politicians in national governments and international arenas (the failure of the Copenhagen Climate Change Conference in 2009, then that of Rio+20 in 2012), this decade saw a proliferation of new forms of mobilization and commitment: anti-extractivist struggles in Latin America (around the concept of '*buen vivir*'), the international movement of 'transition towns' initiated in England, and the movement of objectors to growth (a concrete echo of economists' reflections on prosperity without growth) as well as 'Blockadia' movements, as Naomi Klein call them, reclaiming a place for nature and for alternative ways of living and fighting against 'large dangerous and useless projects' such as pipelines, tar sands exploitations, airports and highways.

As we see, the environmental warnings, socioecological challenges and critique of the 'damages of progress' did not await the scientific

---

"Engagement" and the Restructuring of Biodiversity Conservation', *Antipode*, 42, 2010: 513–50.

79   Rob Nixon, *Slow Violence and the Environmentalism of the Poor*, Cambridge, MA: Harvard University Press, 2011.

thesis of the Anthropocene and its embodiment in scientific literature after 2002. When we consider the multifarious and general character of these oppositions and the intensity of environmental reflexivity through time, the major historical problem seems to be not that of explaining the emergence of a new 'environmental awareness', but rather to understand how these struggles and warnings could have been kept to the margins by industrialist and 'progressive' elites, before being largely forgotten (a second death in which the human and social sciences participated), so that it can be claimed that the discovery that we are living in the Anthropocene is only very recent. These two centuries of scientific warnings and continuous challenges likewise suggest that the attribution of a name to a new geological era is not sufficient to inflect a trajectory of two centuries of assaults to planet Earth. We need to guard against the scientistic illusion that ecological awareness and 'salvation' can only come from scientists and not also from the struggles and initiatives of other Earthlings and citizens of the planet.

Surviving and Living the Anthropocene

Thinking the Anthropocene means taking on board the data and models of the Earth system sciences that tell us in increasingly certain terms of a disturbance on the geological timescale that will radically overturn the conditions of human existence (Chapter 1). It means taking the measure of the telluric force of industrialization and commodification, which has derailed the Earth beyond the stable parameters of the Holocene, and of the need to give our freedom different material foundations; it means mobilizing new environmental humanities and new political radicalisms (movements of *buen vivir*, common goods, transition, degrowth, eco-socialism and many more) in order to escape the blind alleys of industrial modernity (chapters 2 and 11).

Thinking the Anthropocene also means challenging its unifying grand narrative of the errant human species and its redemption by science alone (chapters 3 and 4). It means meticulously listening to scientists and putting their results and conclusions into public and democratic discussions, rather than sinking into a geocracy of technological and market-based 'solutions' to 'manage' the entire Earth. The less that the science of the Anthropocene pretends to stand above the world, the more solid and fruitful it will be, and the less the seductive concept of the Anthropocene will risk serving as a legitimizing philosophy for an oligarchic geopower.

Thinking the Anthropocene, finally, means abandoning the hope of emerging from a temporary 'environmental crisis'. The irreversible break is behind us, in that brief and exceptional moment of two centuries of industrial growth. The Anthropocene is here. It is our new condition. We have therefore to learn to survive, that is, to leave the Earth habitable and resilient, limiting the frequency of catastrophes and sources of human misery. But surviving is not enough. To continue to thrive as communities, individuals and citizens, we all must strive for change. We have to strive for a decent life for everyone, in a diversity of cultures and an equality of rights and conditions, in relations that liberate human and non-human alterities, in an infinity of aspirations, a sobriety of consumption and a humility of interventions.

'What words must we sow, for the gardens of the world to be fertile again?' asked the poet Jeanine Salesse. What histories must we write to learn to inhabit the Anthropocene?

First of all, we must make sense of what has happened to us, producing multiple, debatable and polemical narratives rather than a single hegemonic narrative that is supposedly apolitical. Rather than a universal history of the 'human species' distorting the 'Earth system', we have proposed seven historical workshops, seven possible narratives.[1] First of all, we have shown the technological contingencies (other choices would have been possible) and political dimensions of our new geological epoch. The entry into the Anthropocene was intrinsically bound up with capitalism, with the commercial nation-state and the genesis of the British Empire, which dominated the world in the nineteenth century and forced other societies to serve its model or seek to follow it. Similarly, the Great Acceleration cannot be understood without the Second World War, the Cold War in which two blocs rivalled one another in the mobilization of the globe, and – since it emerged victorious – without American imperialism (Chapter 5). The history of capitalist world-economies lies at the heart of the change in the Earth's geological regime (Chapter 10), with their Soviet and Chinese avatars being simply a part of this. Secondly, military

---

1   Many other historical narratives remain to be written, in particular a global and non-teleological history of technology, which the Anthropocene calls on us to rethink (see: David Edgerton, *The Shock of the Old: Technology in Global History since 1900*, Oxford: Oxford University Press, 2011), or again accounts of the Anthropocene starting from the experience of its subalterns and victims.

apparatuses, war and the logic of power, with the unsustainable technological choices subsequently imposed on the civilian world, bear a heavy responsibility in the disturbance of local environments and the whole Earth system (Chapter 6). Thirdly, the history of the Anthropocene is also one of the unfurling of a capitalist world-economy, a world of increasing commodification; a history of the genesis of a new system of material needs and consumerist subjectivities that today are globalized (Chapter 7). Finally, it is impossible without fundamental self-deception to represent the last 250 years as the progressive emergence from an initial unawareness of environmental damage, from a model of industrial development at the end of which we are supposedly now better equipped with the skills for inflecting our trajectory (Chapter 8), nor as the gradual rise of an environmental movement that was initially embryonic and gradually matured (Chapter 9).

The contemporary moment is not one of a new awareness, nor one of a moral leap leading us towards a better humanity and a nice planet governed by sustainable geo-management, nor one of a reconciliation with Gaia. We have not suddenly passed from unawareness to awareness, we have not recently emerged from a modernist frenzy to enter an age of precaution. One of the determining aspects in the history of the Anthropocene is that of disinhibitions that normalize the intolerable: public-health policies that rejected the environmental medicine of the eighteenth century; the technological norm that undermined challenges and formed the ontology of dealing with environmental nuisances; the proliferation of objects that constructed the free-floating anthropological subject; GDP and the notion of an 'economy', which naturalized the absurd idea of limitless growth; technoscientific 'solutions' that claimed at every point to manage nature for a maximal sustainable yield; and many others more.

By envisaging the Anthropocene as a geohistorical event, we have avoided the gesture of the clean slate, of grandiose and impotent narratives about modernity. The multiplicity and variety of the processes of disinhibition reminds us that modernity is not this majestic, inexorable and spiritual movement that philosophers speak of. On the contrary, it can be conceived as a series of successive small coups, of imposed situations, of normalized exceptions. Rather than incriminating certain familiar *monstres sacrés* that are too enormous to be inflected (the biological gift of intelligence made to *Homo sapiens* but poorly used; demographic fate; the Judeo-Christian stance of domination of nature; blind 'modernity', separating and dominating), we should rather learn much from the various tactics and mechanisms of disinhibition that have made it possible for two and a half centuries to ignore successive environmental knowledges and warnings, and defeat those challenges and alternatives that opposed themselves to industrial and consumerist action.

The history we have proposed may seem depressing, i.e., that our ancestors destabilized the Earth and its ecosystems despite knowing what they were doing. Since there was not a transition from unawareness to awareness, since the present financialized capitalism has its own new forms of disinhibition, everything leads us to fear that things will continue as they have up till now.

But to abandon the official narrative of an awakening permits a more lucid and fruitful dialogue with the warnings of the Earth system scientists. We also have in hand several histories of the Anthropocene that invite us to conceive in political terms the metabolisms of energy and matter commanded by those mechanisms – of production, exchange and consumption – that were invented and imposed by quite particular groups, imaginaries and institutions, and in specific circumstances. These histories invite us to take a political grip on the institutions and oligarchies, the powerful symbolic and material systems, that led us into the Anthropocene: military apparatuses, the system of consumerist desire and its infrastructure, the gaps of income and wealth, the energy majors and the financial interests of globalization, the technoscientific apparatuses when these work in commodity logics or silence criticisms and alternatives.

To strive for decent lives in the Anthropocene therefore means freeing ourselves from repressive institutions, from alienating dominations and imaginaries. It can be an extraordinary emancipatory experience.

Illustration Credits

Figure 1: Trends from 1750 to 2010 in (a) globally aggregated indicators for socio-economic development; (b) indicators for the structure and functioning of the Earth System

1*a*. Data from igbp.net; Will Steffen, ed., *Global Change and the Earth System: A Planet Under Pressure*, New York: Springer, 2005, 132–3.

1*b*. From Will Steffen, Wendy Broadgate, Lisa Deutsch, Owen. Gaffney and Cornelia Ludwig, 'The Trajectory of the Anthropocene: The Great Acceleration', *The Anthropocene Review,* January 2015: 1–18.

Figure 2: Temperature and human history over 100,000 years

Climate data from GRIP Ice Core Data, Greenland; archaeological data from Tim Appenzeller, 'Human Migrations: Eastern Odyssey', *Nature*, 485:3, May 2012: 24–6.

Figure 3: Standard representations of human activities in relation to the Earth system

3*a*. The famous 'Bretherton Diagram' (1986). From *Earth System Science Overview: A Program for Global Change* (NASA science advisory committee, 1986, 19).

3*b*. After Berkes, Folke and Colding (2003).

3*c*. After Benett, Peterson and Gordon (2009).

Figure 4: CO_2 emissions, 1750–2009 and 1750–1913

Data from Carbon Dioxide Information Analysis Center, cdiac .ornl.gov.

Figure 5: The Earth seen from midway to the Moon, Apollo 17, 7 December 1972
NASA/Apollo 17 crew

Figure 6: Annual energy consumption per capita in England and Italy (in megajoules)
Graph from Tony Wrigley, *Energy in the Industrial Revolution*, Cambridge: Cambridge University Press, 2011, 95; on the basis of data from Paul Warde, *Energy Consumption in England and Wales*, Naples: CNR-ISS, 2007, 115–36.

Figure 7: Annual emissions in thousand tonnes of carbon
Data from Carbon Dioxide Information Analysis Center (CDIAC), cdiac.ornl.gov.

Figure 8: UK and USA's share in global cumulative CO_2 emissions
Data from Carbon Dioxide Information Analysis Center (CDIAC), cdiac.ornl.gov.

Figure 9: Defoliant spraying in South Vietnam, 1961–1971

Figure 10: The Japanese seen as lice in a wartime US magazine
From *Leatherneck*, 28 March 1945.

Figure 11: German motorways in 1936

Figure 12: The post-war world as technological consumerist paradise, General Electric advertisement, 1943

Figure 13: Thomas Burnet, 'Ideas of Different Stages in the Formation of the Earth'
Engraving from *Sacred Theory of the Earth*, vol. 1 (1690), London: John Hooke, 1726, 312. (© BNF: French National Library)

Figure 14: Material balance of six major groups of countries since 1950
Graph formed from data presented in Anke Schaffartzik, A. Mayer, S. Gingrich, N. Eisenmenger, C. Loy, F. Krausmann, 'The Global Metabolic Transition: Regional Patterns and Trends of Global Material Flows, 1950–2010', *Global Environmental Change* 26, 2014: 87–97. We thank the authors for offering their raw data.

Figure 15: Creditor and debtor countries in terms of ecological footprint in 1973
From Global Footprint Network, storymaps.esri.com/global footprint.

Figure 16: *Le Sauvage satirique*

Journal of Gravelle, 'naturien' anarchist paper, 1898

Figure 17: L'En dehors (The outsider)

Postcard from a woodcut by Louis Moreau, 1922

Index